PRAISE FOR *MY JOB: MORE PEOPLE AT WORK AROUND THE WORLD*

"I was really drawn into the stories from all over the world of people trying to make a living and make a difference in the lives of others. This book could be a useful tool for helping college students thinking about vocation and how to approach work with a sense of meaning and purpose. There are many lessons, but they are shared via stories rather than through didactic 'telling.'"

—MARK ELSDON, Executive Director and Pastor, Pres House, University of Wisconsin-Madison

"A must-read. The book brings to life actual work experiences across the world, showing that we have a lot in common. It illustrates that we're not alone."

—CRAIG NEWMARK, Founder, Craig's List

"The stories in *My Job* reveal the universal human spirit through the common, quotidian aspirations to create, thrive and leave something better behind—and the myriad hardships and joys that are inherent in this struggle."

—DAVID BORNSTEIN, *New York Times* Columnist; Author, *How To Change the World*

"Skees has done a great job unearthing touching personal stories, meaningful insights and inspirations, and diverse perspectives on the world we all share."

—DARIAN RODRIGUEZ HEYMAN, Author, *Nonprofit Management 101* and *Nonprofit Fundraising 101*

"*My Job* is very well researched. In what seems to be an increasingly 'us and them' world, this book helped me feel a connection with each of the diverse set of interviewees."

—VIVEK ULLAL NAYAK, Cofounder, TerraClear Inc.

"There's a mythic quality in these stories; they cross national borders and income brackets to explore how people make a living and make a life through their work. *My Job* is not only an enjoyable and meaningful read; it's a demonstration of the principle that we grow together through stories."

—PAUL VANDECARR, Author, *Working Narratives*

"I loved the global perspective presented by this book. It opened my mind to consider how much we have in common across cultures and geographic distance. The distinct voice of each narrator drew me in and held me spellbound. Pain and trauma mark many of the stories, but resilience predominates."

—PEG CONWAY, Author of *Embodying the Sacred: A Spiritual Preparation for Birth*

"No matter your station in life, you'll find a piece of yourself in these stories. *My Job* bridges the divide of geo-political barriers and reveals the universal human desire to make the world better. It sheds light on the powerful impact a job can have, not only in terms of the product produced or service delivered, but on the person doing the job. One need not have riches to make difference. One only needs passion, desire and willingness"

—HENRY BERMAN, Ed.D, CEO, Exponent Philanthropy

"A celebration and a true gift to people everywhere who work hard to make our world a better place.

—CRISTI HEGRANES, CEO, *Global Press Journal*

"Satisfies the voyeur in me who is always wondering what it would be like to live in someone else's shoes."

—EDEN ROCK, Operations Director, Placer Land Trust

"Despite our diverse cultures and life experiences, we transform our trauma and dreams into the work that gives meaning to our lives. We meet on common ground in the pages of this book, as human beings striving daily to make the world a little better place. With what brief time we have on this planet . . . That's the best we can do, and it is a lot."

—SHERI SOBRATO BRISSON, Philanthropist; Author, *Digging Deep: A Journal for Young People Facing Health Challenges*

"A tapestry of rich storytelling, inspiring you to discover your own authentic hustle and providing a brilliant peephole into the makeshift destiny that so often accompanies everyday work and employment. *My Job* explores themes of meaning, craft, grit, hustle, and exposes the often-invisible humanity at the core of our economy."

—ALEXA CLAY, Author, *The Misfit Economy*

"This is not as much of a book about jobs as it is a book about lives. Each individual's distinct voice comes through. The stories illustrate that there is not just one way to have a 'good' job or a 'good' life, but also that poverty, hunger, traumatic experiences, and loss of freedom can make any life a struggle. The interviews also address the question of women's changing place in the work world. Perhaps through reading this book in groups and initiating discussions, readers can build greater understanding of how they want to create their work in the world."

—AMANDA C. PETERS, Associate Director, Career Coach, Office of Career Advancement, John F. Kennedy School of Government, Harvard University

"Each first-person account stands on its own, and they can be read in any order. Skees nimbly maintains a consistent narrative flow, resulting in highly personal, often poignant, sometimes gritty, portraits that will inspire readers."

—*KIRKUS REVIEWS*

MY JOB

More People at Work
Around the World

SUZANNE SKEES

GREENLEAF
BOOK GROUP PRESS

Published by Greenleaf Book Group Press
Austin, Texas
www.gbgpress.com

Distributed by Greenleaf Book Group

For ordering information or special discounts for bulk purchases, please contact Greenleaf Book Group at PO Box 91869, Austin, TX 78709, 512.891.6100.

Design and composition by Greenleaf Book Group
Cover design by Greenleaf Book Group
Cover image of ox and cart, ©iStockphoto.com/brytta.

Publisher's Cataloging-in-Publication data is available.

Print ISBN: 978-1-62634-586-7

eBook ISBN: 978-1-62634-587-4

Part of the Tree Neutral® program, which offsets the number of trees consumed in the production and printing of this book by taking proactive steps, such as planting trees in direct proportion to the number of trees used: www.treeneutral.com

Printed in the United States of America on acid-free paper

18 19 20 21 22 23   10 9 8 7 6 5 4 3 2 1

First Edition

To my cherished son, Isaac—a multitalented Renaissance man whose work spans from visual art and musical composition to philosophical and media research to graphic design and web development. With beautiful grace and tenacious determination, you always have and always will accomplish your dreams.

CONTENTS

Health and Recovery

Education and Finance

Agribusiness and Food Processing

Arts and Culture

Activism and Diplomacy

THE FUTURE OF WORK

The future of jobs is no jobs.

New technologies—robots, software, artificial intelligence—have already destroyed millions of U.S. jobs, and in the next decade they will eliminate millions more. A third of all American workers are at risk of permanent unemployment. And this time, the jobs will not come back.

A job crisis is underway—we have to work together to stop it, or risk losing the heart of our country. The stakes have never been higher.

In my thirties, I ran Manhattan Prep, a national education company that grew to become number one in the country. I also met my wife, Evelyn, and got married. When Manhattan Prep was acquired in 2009, I dedicated my efforts to fixing what I considered to be the biggest problem facing our country: a lack of economic activity and available jobs. As a response, I founded Venture for America to help recent graduates with an interest in entrepreneurship create jobs in cities like Baltimore, Detroit, Pittsburgh, and Cleveland.

For years I believed new business formation was the answer: If we could train a new generation of entrepreneurs and create the right jobs in the right places, we could stop the downward spiral of growing income inequality, poverty, unemployment, and hopelessness. VFA created jobs by the thousands and continues to do amazing work across the country. But along the way, it became clear to me that job creation would not outpace the massive impending job loss due to automation.

Here are the facts. Since 2000, we've automated away four million manufacturing jobs. Eighty percent of the manufacturing jobs lost in the

Midwest were due to automation, *not* globalization. And we've already started to see the consequences of this: an opioid crisis, declines in labor force participation, and Donald Trump.

And things are going to get much worse. Silicon Valley is working to solve the business problems of our time. But their solutions won't improve your lives. They are working on things that will make most people's jobs irrelevant to the modern economy.

This may seem far-fetched to some, but look around you. Have you noticed stores closing in your area? Online retailers are driving out local businesses while automating away the jobs of their warehouse workers. Truck driving is the number one profession in twenty-nine states; those jobs are at risk once self-driving vehicles are viable. By most estimates, those trucks are 98 percent of the way to being ready to roll out. There are thousands of call center workers across the U.S.; Google recently demonstrated software that will replace them. McDonald's is rolling out self-serve kiosks in every store. And if you think it's only low-wage jobs that are at risk, just look at the advances in bookkeeping and research AI. Accountants and lawyers, among others, aren't immune to the automation trend.

We are going through the greatest economic and technological shift in human history. Some say, "We must educate and retrain Americans for the jobs of the future." This is a great talking point, but the reality of these programs is that they don't work. Only a few of those who have already lost their jobs have qualified for retraining programs, and the job replacement rate for them was under 20 percent. The truth is about half of all manufacturing workers left the workforce and haven't come back; nearly a quarter of those folks went on disability. It is simply a fact that it is beyond the capacity of our government to magically retrain hundreds of thousands of workers.

Instead, we need to fundamentally change the way we view jobs and value in this country so that we can talk about viable solutions to fundamentally new challenges.

In my book, *The War on Normal People: The Truth About America's Disappearing Jobs and Why Universal Basic Income Is Our Future*, I address in greater length these problems, but also the solutions to these challenges.

First, we must implement the Freedom Dividend, a form of Universal Basic Income (UBI),* which would put $1,000 in the hands of every adult in the country every month, free and clear. This would be paid for with a value-added tax on the companies benefiting most from automation.

The Freedom Dividend will permanently grow the economy by 12.56 to 13.10 percent—or about $2.5 trillion by 2025—and will increase the labor force by 4.5 to 4.7 million people. Instead of giving money to corporations for stock buybacks, investing in people would allow them to pay their bills, educate themselves, start businesses, be more creative, stay healthy, relocate for work, spend time with their children, take care of loved ones, and have a real stake in the future.

Can we afford it? Of course. Our economy has grown to $19 trillion, up $4 trillion in the last ten years alone. We are the richest and most advanced society in the history of the world. We can afford to invest $1,000 per adult per month. What we can't afford is the future we face, should we *fail* to act.

If the prospect of UBI seems far-fetched to you, consider that a nearly identical measure passed the House of Representatives in 1971; it had received a legacy of support from an ideologically diverse group consisting of both Richard Nixon and Martin Luther King, Jr. One thousand economists signed a letter saying it would be great for our economy and society.

And, in fact, one state already has a similar dividend. For nearly four decades, Alaska has provided every resident with between $1,000–2,000 each year, which has improved child nutrition and created thousands of jobs. It's no surprise it's wildly popular. What is surprising is that it passed in a deeply *conservative* state under a Republican governor.

---

* Friends of Andrew Yang, "What is UBI?," 2018. Web. www.yang2020.com/what-is-ubi.

It is paramount that the nation as a whole begins to invest in our people; to build a new trickle-*up* economy that starts with our families and in our communities.

At the same time, we must also change how value is measured in our economy. I believe this is the second, and equally crucial, step for shaping a better future.

Consider this: My wife spends her days raising our two sons, aged 5 and 2—one of whom has special needs—and yet our current economic metrics place her work's value at zero. This, of course, is nonsense. To suggest that her work is less valuable to society than that done by a hedge fund investor or a software programmer reflects a fundamental misprioritization in our economy today.

Take another example: Unemployment is currently at 3.9 percent. However, anyone living in a struggling community knows that this ignores those who are on disability, are underemployed, or have given up looking for work. A former manager at a manufacturing plant who is currently driving for Uber an hour per week counts towards employment. Our labor force participation rate is under 63 percent. Even those who can find employment are struggling, with 59 percent unable to pay an unexpected $500 bill.

We're measuring and incentivizing the wrong behaviors, and it's preventing us from creating viable solutions.

Right now, our life expectancy has declined for two straight years. Eight Americans die from a drug overdose every day. These devastating numbers reflect the reality faced by most Americans, while the headline economic news mostly reflects a stock market that largely benefits only the top 10 percent of Americans.

These examples illuminate the fundamental mismatch between our markers of economic success and our lived realities. We need new ways to measure and improve what actually matters to us—things like childhood success rates, mental health, freedom from substance abuse, median income, environmental quality, and the proportion of our elderly receiving quality care.

These are the problems of our time, and *this* is where our energy should be going.

UBI, in conjunction with a new, more human-centered approach to capitalism, would have the power to course-correct us off our current, dangerous path. Let's build a more durable, human-centered future, where people are free from working many jobs just to struggle, and instead can focus on working towards a better future.

—Andrew Yang

OUR JOB = OUR SELF: IS THAT TRUE?

How much of your identity, health, and wellbeing stem from what you "do"?

Even if your work is grossly underpaid or underappreciated, cobbled together with a combination of gigs, or completely overlooked by society (e.g., caring for family members), your job may be what compels you to get out of bed every morning. For better and for worse, your job may provide you with purpose and connection.

Our jobs are our lifeline to the salary that feeds and sustains our families. We spend the majority of our life, second only to sleep, on the clock. More than five billion people currently work jobs too varied to count (once source cites twelve thousand different types of jobs[1]). It takes each of us fulfilling those roles to keep the machine of society functioning.

And in an era of isolation and instability, when so many aspects of who we are—race, nationality, gender, religion, politics, and socioeconomics—divide us, *jobs* unite us in a shared human experience of work. Everyone has or had a job, wants a job, or wants to be free from a job.

Those unemployed for more than six months suffer three times higher rates[2] of depression, as well as increased insomnia, anxiety, and physical illness.[3] The converse also proves out: People with stable, well-paying jobs enjoy greater access to healthcare, safe neighborhoods, and nutritious foods—and they live longer.[4]

The vast majority of the world's workers have never had a shot at stable, well-paying jobs. Meanwhile, the workplace itself rapidly continues to shift from career to contract work, salary to gig, and job stability to unreliable income.

Long gone are the days when my own father (first in his rural Kentucky family to graduate college—who then earned a master's in chemical engineering while co-parenting seven children) retained employment with the same paper-printing company for decades and retired with a gold watch and pension. The work-world now lacks stability on both sides: Today, those lucky enough to choose a career change jobs an average of twelve times,[5] while two-thirds[6] of the global workforce gets by with gig jobs in the informal economy, without benefits, social support, or job security.

Perhaps, the future of jobs is fewer jobs for humans, as robots take over the world. Conversely, automation may allow for improved virtual workplaces, where shared-economy workers can access reliable income, benefits, and even forge a sense of community—imagine videoconference standups and virtual agents replacing the cubicles and managers of the twentieth century.

Having written about people in their jobs for the past fifteen years and edited two books in the *My Job* series, what I know for sure is that the stories of our jobs become the stories of our lives. They have the power to connect us, narrator to reader and readers to each other. We all know what it's like to work until midnight while our family sleeps, like Sena in Chapter 8; to strive to bring humor into stressful situations, like Mike in Chapter 1; and to fuel ourselves with coffee as our daily schedule swells, like Tania in Chapter 11.

If you've picked up this book on paper or online, you're about to travel from the Appalachian Mountains of West Virginia, where Junior fights to heal both people and planet . . . to the rural villages of Guatemala, where Sandra strives to provide a healthy birth to every child . . . to a beach in Israel, where Mickey describes how to have a frank conversation with a terrorist.

The courageous narrators of *My Job: More People at Work Around the World* delve deep into what it really takes to conduct their work, pay their bills, and eke out a sense of hope for the future. These fifteen true stories, told in first-person by individuals as diverse as the readers of this book, prove that humans have the capacity for immense creativity and invention, tenacity, and compassion. Their strength will transcend any changes in automation and scarcity of work that the future of jobs might bring. And they just might transpose the equation with which I commenced this preface, by sculpting their job to fit the parameters of their particular talents and needs: *My job = the expression of my self.*

—Suzanne Skees, San Francisco, California, 2019

ACKNOWLEDGMENTS

Andrea Atkinson of One Square World, my friend and collaborator on *My Job* Book 1, who introduced me to the ultimate "Mountain Man," Appalachian environmental activist Junior Walk, who narrates Chapter 13.

Brienne Nicole Skees, my stellar niece and Skees Family Foundation coworker, who hosted my visit to South Korea and facilitated the interview with English teacher Kelly Kang, narrator of Chapter 5. Brienne also expertly fact-checked *My Job* Book 1 and Book 2.

Christopher Hest of Metrics for Management for recommending our friend **Karl Grobl**'s entrepreneurial wife, Srey Pouv Kai, to narrate Chapter 7. And **Jill Cohen** of the Granola Group for her friendship and cheerleading during that interview and throughout the book process.

Deirdre Hegarty of Stanford University, who connected me with the Telos Group, through which I interviewed Christina Ganim the online lingerie entrepreneur (*My Job* Book 1, Chapter 3), Greg Khalil the Mideast peace diplomat (Chapter 14), and Mickey Bergman, who boldly practices work he terms "fringe diplomacy" (Chapter 15).

Elizebeth Tucker of Grameen Foundation, my "African daughter" from Nashville who toured three countries with me—Ghana, Uganda, and Zambia—tirelessly championing the *My Job* cause from Sena Ahiabor's tomato sauce factory (Chapter 8) to Mary Gibutaye's banana farm (Chapter 9) to Misozi Mkandawire's mobile-banking kiosk (Chapter 6).

Gary Tabasinske of the Association for Leadership of Guatemala for nourishing leadership among dedicated social sector professionals in Latin America and for introducing me to Chapter 3's narrator, Sandra López.

Karen and John Godt of Hope 4 Honduran Children (H4HC) for their tenacious faith in the "forgotten children" of Honduras (see Chapter 2 by Kevin Zazo), and my big-hearted brother **Tony Skees** of Charlotte, NC for connecting me to H4HC.

Sammie Rayner of HandUp (formerly of Lumana Credit), who invested in social enterprises in Africa and connected me with Sena Ahiabor, narrator of Chapter 8.

Sharon Peregrin, my California neighbor friend who inspired her daughter, Michele Peregrin (Chapter 12 narrator), to pursue her dream of being a U.S. diplomat and me to keep writing through the hills and valleys of human life.

Sister Donna Liette and **Father Dave Kelly** of "The Center" (pbmr.org) for restorative justice in Chicago, who connected me to Alberto Alaniz, who recounts in Chapter 10 his path from gang life and prison to art and family, and who proudly cites fatherhood as his most important job.

The Philanthropy Workshop (TPW) board, staff, and worldwide network of high-impact philanthropists humble enough to spend years studying effective ways to make the world a better place. It was with TPW that I traveled to Rwanda and met college admissions recruiter Nadine, narrator of Chapter 4.

Tom Ferguson of Imagine H2O for introducing me to Chapter 1's narrator, Mike Kenward—the funniest addiction-recovery counselor you'll ever meet.

Health
and
Recovery

MIKE

GAMBLING RECOVERY COUNSELOR

London, England

Editor's note: We're in a different London than many tourists ever see. You take the Tube far from the Thames River with its iconic interlacing of bridges, away from the West End with its museums and abbeys and palaces. In an hour, you get to South London, Clapham Junction, where, according to Mike Kenward,[1] drinking and gambling are just part of the culture of poverty.

Mike grew up dreaming of being a comedian. He studied social anthropology and then decided to work in a casino. There, he could rub elbows with the wealthy and observe how they interact with money. It would be a sort of petri dish of humanity, a place to earn coin at night while writing brilliant stand-up monologues and comedic playscripts all day. He went to work at a big casino, Grosvenor (G Casino), on Piccadilly.

It didn't surprise me to hear that Mike's plan went awry. Although he didn't succumb to the addiction of gambling (he cites studies that, while 75 percent of Brits gamble, only 1 percent of that group ends up with a gambling problem), he ended up not writing, not earning much, never sleeping, and just despising the pecking order of bullying within the casino ranks, from dealers down to pit bosses.

So, he went to the other side, working for a gambling-addiction recovery nonprofit called GamCare. Eventually, he ended up running their business development.

Mike is now preparing to dive into a dry nonprofit-management master's program, and he's about to "run off" to marry his emergency-room doctor fiancée, Fran.

When I visit him at the cusp of these two major life changes, he shakes my hand and leads me into what looks like a broom closet. He leans back and smiles, comfortable in this stifling, tiny room used for one-on-one counseling. The pressing August heat and close quarters have me feeling a little trapped . . . and then he proceeds to fill the small room with his big, disarming, entertaining personality.

At the end of our interview, he admits that he had trepidations about how much to share. "I was going to just throw some pat answers at you and then say I had to get back to work," he admits, what he dubs his "peanut-butter-and-jam belly" bouncing as he laughs.

We're all better off that he chose, instead, to open up both his life-story and self.

He's *plucky*, I say. He asks me what that means. "That means you're a little bit of a troublemaker," I say, "and a really funny one, too."

I Wanted to Be a Comedian, but I Ended Up in *This* Unfunny Job

My name is Michael Christopher Kenward. I'm thirty-one years old. I'm a business development manager at GamCare in London.

GamCare is a charity that supports people who are affected by gambling problems. I attempt to improve the way that GamCare works with people with gambling problems, people who are affected by someone else who's gambling, and the gambling industry. I've worked here for eight years.

Growing Up, I Wanted to Be a Comedian

When I was a little kid, it wasn't exactly my dream to be a gambling addiction counselor! I wanted to do lots of different things.

I wanted to be creative. I wanted to write comedy and drama. I love kitchen-sink British drama. Do you know what I mean by "kitchen sink"?

It's just a generic British term for a deep sort of natural realism, where everyone's miserable. [Laughs.] It's fairly gritty working-class dramas about just the pain of being a person, going to work every day, coming home to a relationship that has its flaws, bringing up children that are a pain in the ass, and trying to balance all the misery of this world with occasional glimmers of joy.

I find that hugely heartening. It used to really touch me as a child. I wanted to make films and make people laugh. My dream was to be a comedian, to do stand-up or writing of some kind.

My childhood was full of laughter. I was an only child living with a single-parent mother. My relationship with her was very closed and very close as well, for a long time. But my mum was one of five, and my aunties and my uncles were all nearby, and their kids were like my brothers and sisters. So, I grew up with that sort of extended family.

It was a very funny family, very sort of—I don't want to use the word "acerbic"—but very cutting and sarcastic, also extremely loving and warm. The way that they deliver love and affection, as I do now as an adult, is through endless putdowns. Does that make sense? You know that the love is there, so you can push the boundaries with the things you say and the ways you behave.

My Dad Left When I Was Five

My dad basically saw me only occasionally until I was five. Then, he met his current wife, who is from Connecticut, and he decided to move to the States. I didn't know my dad at all during my childhood.

Then, about the age of twenty, I started corresponding with my father on email, and I met him in person at age twenty-two in Los Angeles International Airport [LAX].

You know those travelators [moving walkways]? It's like an escalator. I love them.

I remember standing on one in a pair of jean shorts without a button to hold them together at the waist, sort of slumped in a pair of sandals and a shirt. Those of you who are reading this will not be able to see, but I'm quite overweight, and I didn't look a great state when I was going along on that travelator.

I remember it so strikingly. At the end of the corridor, there were these two glass panels that opened to reveal this extremely slick-looking, smart businessman. I hadn't seen a picture of him. He'd sent me an email about a week prior and said, "You should send me a picture of you so I can recognize you in the airport." I sent him a picture of a transvestite and said, "You're just going to have to try and find me."

I thought, the first time you meet your father, you shouldn't have to send a picture of what you look like. They should be able to instinctively find out who you are. But if there had been anyone else there, I think I'd have struggled.

It was just him and me on this travelator, moving towards this glass door opening, in one of those sort of touch-point moments that you come back to for the rest of your life and think, "Shit. *That's* how that happened."

I remember him smelling the same as he did when he left when I was five. There is something quite bizarre about that, I think, the idea that you can give someone a hug and all of a sudden be transported back to being a child.

Choosing NOT to Be a Successful Businessman Like My Father

My father is an extremely successful businessman, and he's extremely wealthy, which is not something that I grew up with. There is something about that juxtaposition that feels quite movie-like and also quite bizarre. I grew up with a very happy family, in a very loving environment, and I didn't want for anything, even though I knew we were poor. But to see this other life as so at odds with everything I'd ever known was strange.

He's a good man. He was very young, twenty-one, when he had me. I think he had a lot of hopes and dreams for his own life that, by having a kid with somebody that you had a very short relationship with, would have been off-putting.

I don't condone him having left without having any more contact. But in terms of the way I would live my life, I don't judge him in the way that he lives his life now.

It's difficult, because he lives in California. I've only seen him nine times, maybe once a year. So, it's a long and slow-burning process to get to know this man. And he is, unfortunately, still just a man in my life. It's so hard to get to know him when you live that far away.

He will come to my wedding in two weeks. He's a nice guy. He's a funny, intelligent, charming man, but you don't necessarily want those things, I don't think, from a father. You want consistency and stability and unequivocal, unconditional love, the things I got from my mom and other members of my family.

Workaholics Are Similar to Gambling Addicts

When I was growing up, I had a general kind of awareness that I couldn't have things. I was never deprived, but I was definitely told outright, "You can't have that. We can't afford it."

But I think that's extremely healthy, and I would never, even if I had a huge amount of wealth, just provide endless things for my children. It does a lot of damage, actually.

I consider relationships with people to be about going through hardships together and forging a sort of dependency and resilience. My dad feels extremely confident in his realm at work, but at home, I think he feels terrified. I don't think he knows how to build those relationships and keep them.

Maybe I'm wrong. If he ever reads this, he can correct me, but like with gambling, there are environments where we feel confident in who we are, and we know the boundaries and the limitations. We can become a *role*. Work provides that for many people. It provides a safe environment. Their home lives are a chaotic mess, and so they find themselves migrating more and more into work.

And feeling successful because you're earning a fortune and you've got a big house, and you've achieved huge amounts in those sort of physical terms . . . that would allow you to push down the thoughts of failure you've got about yourself, the same way that gambling allows people to push down thoughts of failure by letting them feel like they're winners on a slot machine.

I Went to a Dodgy School in a Not-Very-Nice Area of London

When I was a kid, I went to a quite rough, quite dodgy primary school not far from here. It was actually just a normal primary school, but it was in a not-very-nice area of London. But it wasn't as if I got jumped on the way to school. I was only bloody four.

My teachers put me forward to do an entrance exam for a private school called Dulwich College Prep School. They pushed me to do this exam, and I did it, and I got into that school, and that was a good thing, because it got me out of that primary school and into a better one.

So, I went there, and then, I left by age eleven and went to a grammar school in Kent in a place called Gravesend. After which, I went to the University of Edinburgh, and I studied social anthropology.

Working in a Casino to Gain Insight into Wealthy People

After Edinburgh, I left Scotland [to return to London], and I went to work in a casino. I'd only gone into it because I thought it would be an interesting kind of platform from which to write, because I wanted to write comedy and theatre.

It was an odd choice to work there—but anthropology is obviously all about understanding people and the way that they interact and class systems and all of that.

You could say my first [anthropological] study was at my first job, at my uncle's flower store, every weekend from age twelve. I felt I was very entrenched in the working-class environment there. I knew and understood how poor people lived and interacted with money and interacted with each other, and I loved it.

I thought, "I know what I'll do when I leave Edinburgh. I'll work in an environment where everybody's rich, to try to get an insight into the way that wealthy people exist and how they live."

I've Got a Great Chip on My Shoulder about Rich People

I treated them with complete contempt, and I still do. I've got a great chip on my shoulder about very wealthy people. Even with my fiancée,

Fran—I've got a chip on my shoulder about her wealth as well. Her background is more affluent than mine. So, I'm aware of those things.

This is a very English thing, class awareness. Wealth awareness. *Huge*.

Again, we propagate it. We love it. I love working-class culture. I always have, but I like it in opposition to middle class and aristocratic culture. At the University of Edinburgh, I spent all my time with a bunch of extremely wealthy people with noble or dignified backgrounds. And a part of me loves the sort of charade I was playing by being their friend. It's like, "Look, they're taking the time to spend time with a poor urchin from the street."

Casino People Are Poor, Desperate, and Alone

Anyway, so I went to work in a casino to see how wealthy people interacted with money, and then, I rapidly realized the casinos are full of extremely *poor* people, not wealthy—extremely poor people who are very desperate and alone. [Laughs.]

But it wasn't some kind of great crusade that made me think I needed to get out of the casino and help people—not at all. It was because it was an unhealthy lifestyle, and I was unhappy and not challenged. Horrendous hours: I was getting up at 5:00 in the afternoon to go to work at 8:00 at night and get home at 6:00 in the morning.

All the people I lived with, who were the people I had just left university with, were starting their roles as researchers or building careers. I just felt like I was treading water.

I was planning to write comedy, but I wasn't writing. That was the point of it all, but I wasn't writing anything. I wasn't creating characters, developing great ideas, or even gaining any insight into anybody's culture. I was just there, and I was unhappy there.

Also, I was being bullied. Can you believe that? I was being bullied as a grown man. It does happen. It's extraordinary.

I hadn't experienced that since I was on a bus in school. I went into this professional working environment and was treated badly, basically by people who were higher up the chain than me.

I worked as a *croupier*, a dealer. That's a French word for blackjack, roulette, poker, whatever you like. In French, it means you're a jockey, the person who keeps the thing moving, because the ball never stops spinning. You've got to be good at numbers. You've got to be hypervigilant and very manually dexterous. So, you've got to have a certain level of skill, but it's not massive. It's not like you have to be smart.

When you start off and you're not very good, you're slow. There's a hierarchy, a chain that you climb. You start as a trainee dealer, and then, you become a dealer. You become an inspector, then a top inspector, then a pit boss, then a manager, and so on. And the only way to become a manager is to start at the bottom, and that (like military) is an environment of bullying. People exist in their role because they've had to fight to get there. So, you're going to bloody well fight to get there. It's just completely offensive.

When you've spent four years studying at university and becoming an autonomous and educated person, you think you're reasonably smart; then, you're being told that you're shit, because you can't do the seventeen-times table, and you can't hand out 250 chips to someone, and you feel like, "What's the point?"

I understand it in a way, because you have to be sharp to deal correctly, and you don't want to overpay someone by two grand, because then you'd screw over the casino. Those things are important, but the way in which it was carried out was unpleasant. It ended up taking its toll on me, and I thought, I can't do this anymore. So, then I left.

Dealing Myself out of Gambling and into Recovery

I then started working at GamCare as a helpline advisor. I did that for about five years.

You're a first-line support for people who are in crisis to deal with things like suicide and debt problems and relationship issues. You sort of absorb the initial pain that someone experiences when they've got a gambling problem, help them accept what's going on, look at why they might be doing it, and help them challenge themselves a little, because often their perceptions are quite skewed about why they do it. They think they're gambling to make money, or that they're greedy, or that they're sick and they can never get better.

At one point when I was doing counseling work on the helpline, I also went to clown school. I thought maybe I could enmesh these two skill sets and create a "clownselor," where you sit there as a clown and the client just metes out all of their anger and frustration on you. I would love it if we used comedy here as a means of helping people recover.

We Use Motivational Interviewing Rather Than the Twelve-Step Program

Do you know Alcoholics Anonymous [AA] or Gamblers Anonymous or Overeaters Anonymous? They're all based on this twelve-step program, which is this constant rigorous vigilance of going through twelve steps every day to manage behavior, to make sure they don't stray or lapse. People will sit in a circle and talk about, "When I was fifteen, I was blah, blah, blah, and then, I started drinking."

That model is based on a "one day at a time" approach. It feels so enormous. It's like, "I've got the rest of my life to live without gambling, where I haven't lived the last six months without gambling for one day. How can I imagine the future without gambling? That's too unbearable. In fact, I'm going to go out and gamble right now."

Here, we use Motivational Interviewing techniques, in a very light-touch sense. Motivational Interviewing (MI) actually comes from America.

We think about it on a smaller scale, that just for *today* I won't bet, so it's easier. It's more manageable. We have to acknowledge that lapses and relapses will happen. They can be extremely painful, but they're also a learning opportunity.

If I lapse in my ambitions to not gamble anymore, maybe I can see that when I have arguments with my partner, it's a trigger for me to go out and gamble. Or when I'm thinking about financial problems, it's a trigger. We help people to try and identify those triggers and recognize, "I'm vulnerable at those times. I need to have someone to talk to. I need to put a network of support in place."

We do a brief intervention, a counseling methodology that will help you to move from a place of ambivalence. Let's say, I don't know if I want to stop drinking. I feel good when I'm drinking, but I feel terrible when I'm drinking, too. This technique works for gambling or taking drugs or whatever it might be. It helps the person to tip the balance towards making a change that's constructive for them.

It's encouraging the individual to reflect on what they actually want. If somebody says, "I'm gambling too much," we might suggest to them that they exclude themselves from betting shops, for example, which is something that you can do in the U.K. You can ban yourself from a betting shop, an online gambling site, etc., etc.

They might say, "No, I don't want to do that, because"—and then give a bunch of reasons. That is an expression of their ambivalence. They want to change. They know that they don't want to carry on gambling in this way, because it's damaging them. It's affecting their relationship or their finances or their mental health. But equally, the pull of the gambling is very strong, because it's giving them something. It's giving them escape, a place to go and release their stress and their anxiety, that kind of thing.

The Five-Stage Interview Takes You from Ambivalence to Action

So, we might work with their lack of readiness, if you like, to take action. Motivational Interviewing is based on something called the *wheel* or *cycle* of change, which involves five stages:

1. **Pre-contemplation**. That's when we're quite happily sailing along with our bad behavior, not doing anything about it.

2. **Contemplation**, which is where we start to think, "Actually, maybe it's not helpful for me to be watching TV all day long or buying stuff or gambling, whatever it might be. It's not helping me in the long run."

3. **Planning**, where you start to think, "Okay, this is how I'm going to tackle the problem. This is how I'm going to stop. I'm going to self-exclude myself from the betting shops, or give my debit cards and my credit cards to my wife, or make sure I walk a different route to work every day so I don't go past that place where I go and gamble all the day long. That's my plan."

4. And then, **action**. I put the plan into action. I do all of those things.

5. Then, **maintenance**. If it's going well, we maintain it, and we're not getting into trouble anymore. You'll have lapses and relapses, very common features in the cycle of change. So, "Yeah, I did all that. I was doing really, really well, and then, all of a sudden, bang. Some trigger hit me, like I had an argument with my wife, or my mum died, or I lost my job, and that trigger made me revert right back into that cycle of behavior, that unhelpful behavior again."

That's it. I think recovery feels huge for a lot of people.

Here in the U.K., Everyone Gambles

In the U.K., 75 percent[2] of British people gamble. It's a big part of the culture. That includes the national lottery, which was introduced around 1994. I remember when it first launched. I was only ten. It was exciting because it was like a weekly thing that everybody did. Now, I think it's slightly diluted, because there are runs every day.

Bizarrely, GamCare's helpline number is on the back of every single national lottery ticket in the country and scratch cards as well, in case someone's got a problem with those products. I've received calls from people who've won massive amounts on scratch cards. They say, "I don't know where to go and collect it," and you say, "Well, I'm afraid the helpline is to help with gambling problems. I'm not the person to tell you."

In terms of the amount of clients we see every year, I think we get about forty thousand calls a year on the helpline, so something like 150 calls a day. And for counseling, we would see somewhere in the region of five or six thousand face-to-face clients a year.

We work with a big partner network across the U.K., delivering face-to-face counseling, twelve sessions of one-to-one therapy where we talk about why you gamble, what the underlying causes are. There are partner networks and agencies that provide drug and alcohol services, but we've trained them to work specifically with gamblers as well.

The Profile of a Problem Gambler: Eighteen- to Thirty-Four-Year-Old Males

Here, less than 1 percent of the people who gamble have a problem, and about 7 percent of people who gamble are at risk of developing a gambling problem, according to scoring tools like the DSM [*Diagnostic and Statistical Manual for Mental Disorders*]. We use the DSM-IV and also the PGSI, which is the Problem Gambling Severity Index.

Gambling addiction is predominantly a male problem. About 80 percent of people who contact us on our helpline are men. Twenty percent are women. Of that 20 percent, 50 percent of them (so 10 percent in total), are calling about their husband or their brother or their whatever. So, it's mostly men.

Eighteen- to thirty-four-year-olds are the predominant contact for our helpline services. They contact us because the impact of the gambling is starting to really hit home. So, you might have people who have gambled problematically from the age of about fourteen or younger. In the U.K., there's no age restriction on our children playing slot machines of a certain level, which is unique in the world, as far as I know. A lot of people don't like that.

Usually, people contact us when they have financial issues as a result of their gambling problems. Your mortgage isn't getting paid, you're in debt, and you can't afford to buy food—whatever it might be. Or it could be relationship issues. Your wife just said to you, "If you don't stop this gambling, you'll get thrown out of this house," or whatever.

We also do get contacts from people ranging up to about sixty years old. After that, we tail off a lot, because by that time, if someone's been gambling forty years, they're not ready to make a change.

The Link between Gambling and Mental Health

We sometimes do see a correlation between mental health issues and gambling. We're not psychiatrists. So, someone might come through who might have borderline personality disorder, or they might have depression or be bipolar, and they might flag that with us, but we wouldn't be able to do anything with it. We would provide them with face-to-face counseling.

We might signpost them on to speak to their psychiatrist and say, "Look, you mentioned this is not working, because you're looking for outlets to cope with your life because your depression is still entrenched and you're not feeling any better from that. That's having an impact, but you can also do these things to stop."

I Don't Know If I Believe in an "Addiction Gene"

I don't know about gambling and the addict gene.[3] I'm slightly indoctri-nated by the heavily psychodynamic/psychoanalytic approach to recovery that we deliver here.

We don't diagnose or classify people as being addicted. We say, "You're struggling with your gambling. You've got problems with your gambling, and you'd like to change your gambling behavior." I think it's cliché to say it, but we don't like to work with labels, partially because we're not quali-fied to. We're not psychiatrists who can run you through the mental health kind of stuff, and we don't give you medication for it.

We see gambling as an expression of other problems in life. So, we look at early abuse or neglect or bereavement, stress, mental health, and other things where the gambling is a way of coping with that difficulty. If you look at it through that lens, if you work on and hopefully solve the underlying problem, the gambling should disappear and not be replaced by something else.

We often get people on the fence, "I know I've got an addictive per-sonality, because my mum used to be a bad drinker." In my head, I think, "Well, the reason you might be gambling problematically is because your mum was an alcoholic who mistreated you, neglected you, and abused you, and, therefore, you're now looking for emotional nourishment from a fruit machine or a game of roulette that makes you feel valued and better about yourself when you win."

I don't think it's endemic in your genes or your bloodline, that you're just destined, and your children are destined, to have problems.

People talk about this stuff, but also that's a fantastic escape route for somebody who doesn't want to make any changes. If they say, "Yeah, I have an addictive personality," and you say, "Okay," where does the conversation go from there?

"Okay, fine. Well, in that case, go upstairs and hang yourself." So, I can't advocate that to anybody on our helpline. [Laughs.]

We Get Our Funding from Gambling (!)

GamCare is not government supported. It's not part of NHS [National Health Service]. There is some NHS provision for problem gambling, but the lion's share of it is funded by an independent trust called the Responsible Gambling Trust. Actually, it's quite an interesting setup in the U.K. I don't know how it is elsewhere.

There's a government levy here that requires the drinks industry to pay money for the treatment for alcohol problems. There's not the same for gambling.

It obviously has impacts on us as a charity and the Responsible Gambling Trust, because, as organizations, we are to some extent beholden to the industry that we are here to deliver services to support. It's difficult to say, "All of your products are causing damage," when those products are also the way that you get paid. It's a philosophical thing. I can't speak on behalf of GamCare, but I like the notion that an industry cleans up its own mess. I like the notion that the drinks industry pays for alcoholics to get through recovery.

Strangely, I like gambling. I don't have a problem with it at all, and I don't gamble that much.

Before the 1960s, gambling was illegal here. It was all just done completely underhand, you know, dodgy odds, dodgy bookmakers, dodgy gambling rackets run by gangsters. What good's that? You want something that's freely available, legal, regulated, and taxed. Then, you put that tax into things like public services, and you eventually hopefully get some support for those who are affected by the problem, which is a minuscule number of people in comparison with the people that actually do it.

I think if people want to do it, it's going to get done. It's the same as drugs. If people want to use them, then legalize them, tax them, take the money in, provide services for people who develop problems with them, and educate people in how to use them better.

That's what this charity does as well: educate people on how to gamble, myths around gambling such as thinking that if you're holding your lucky rabbit, red's going to come in or whatever—because there's sort of the sense that you think people are and have the capacity to be responsible individuals.

Gambling Sells the Illusion of a Better Life

Gambling sells the illusion that "I'm going to win big, and then, I'm going to suddenly have wealth, and I'll have the life of ease and the life that I want."

It's unfortunate. It tends to attract poorly educated and unemployed[4] people from lower incomes, less education, more deprived basically, where gambling is part of their culture. It's not just fun. An element of it is actually necessity. It's like, "I would quite like to have an extra fifty quid, so I could afford to do this, this, and this." The dream of winning big is much more easy to sell to somebody who doesn't have any money.

If you have a pound to buy a ticket and there's a massive dream payoff, you can invest yourself in that dream for that short amount of time.

What My Uncle Spent on the Lottery

I used to work at my Uncle Chris's flower stall at Elephant & Castle. (It's one of the more strangely named underground stations in London.) That's where my whole family is from. We would drive home on Saturday after a long day of working in the flower stall, and he would talk about, if he won the lottery, what he would like to do with it.

He wanted to do simple things such as going on holiday, paying off his mortgage, getting tiling done in the bathroom, or buying himself a new car—all those things that you want to be able to do when you haven't got money.

I only really started thinking about it after I started working here, how invested he was in that dream. It's a bit sad, because there's a man who's constantly measuring his life up against a dream that would never be bestowed upon him.

But, on the other hand, he's a hardworking man who's got a good job, works hard to bring in money, and indulges himself once a week in a dream. I think he spent seven pounds a week on the national lottery. He had seven lines on the lottery.

It was a very controlled budget. I remember once trying to tot up the years that he'd been doing it. I calculated it all to be something like ten, twelve grand [$14,000–17,000 USD] that he would have spent, and I said that to him, and I don't think that he regretted it.

I don't think he felt like, "All of that time, I could have had ten grand in my pocket," because it's not ten grand in your pocket. It's the dream you're paying for every week, and you enjoy and indulge in it. I don't see a great deal of harm in that.

People refer to the lottery as a tax on idiots, but actually it performs a function for people. It gives them something to hold on to. There's nothing wrong with that.

We All Have Means of Escaping Reality: Mine Is Peanut Butter and Jam

Gambling is just one way of escaping. My mother watches probably four or five hours of TV every day. I would say that is supplanting her good relationships; it's a substitution for happiness. It's providing her with a way of quieting down her anxiety levels and her positive relationships (or lack thereof) by giving her something that keeps her calm. It's the same effect people look for with gambling.

We all think we're moving through life and we're better than people who are addicted or that it could never happen to us. Actually, we are all addicted to various things.

Me, for example: The moment I have a stressful conversation with somebody on the helpline, before the phone's gone down, I've made myself a peanut butter and jam sandwich, or I've had a packet of crisps or have eaten something... because for me, it's food. It's a way of just escaping any pain that's happening. It's so unconscious. Yet now, it's conscious! I've had enough therapy that I can see that's what's happening, but I still do it, and I still enjoy it. [Laughs.]

A Medium-Sized Nonprofit with a Culture of Mediocrity

I'm now a manager here. Next, I probably could be the head of education and prevention services and the chief operating officer and then the chief exec. So, yeah, there are a few rungs left above me.

There's such a diverse group, a bunch of skills here. Some people have worked in the gambling industry. My two bosses were both Playboy Bunnies in the Playboy Club, working as croupiers for years. Some are ex-addicts, people who've come through various programs of recovery and got into therapy.

I love my colleagues. They are a mixture of highly passionate, enthusiastic people who love what they do—but there's a skills ceiling, I think. If you come to an organization and work the same way every day, if no one gives you guidance or sends you to training, you can't get better. So, you end up with people in a medium-sized charity like this who are hugely passionate, but they don't know how to move things in a direction.

And the charity hasn't got the money to help educate them. It all ends up being a little bit like kids in a playground. Unless the leadership at the top is very clearly aware that this is an issue, it ends up becoming an endemic culture of mediocrity. I'm concerned by that here.

Nonetheless, I love working with the people, and I think my colleagues respect me and like me. It's nice to feel you're a big fish in an extremely small pond, not to blow my own trumpet. But I do feel like I achieve a lot here and that, if it wasn't for me, things wouldn't happen. I could learn more and write cases for why we should do things differently. I don't know what I'm doing; half the time, I'm googling it.

I'm starting a master's in voluntary sector management at Cass Business School [at the City University London] in a couple weeks' time, so I'm going to learn more about how to deliver at work, which is really good.

Growing Older and Giving Up Childhood Dreams

The future is a puzzling concept, isn't it? I've dreamt for years of being a world-class stand-up comic and never did any work towards it.

As that dream starts to fade and I accept the tangibles of what my life actually looks like and where the future is going, I have a mixture of mourning for that dream but also a happiness that the things I'm trying to achieve are more manageable.

Doing this master's is a sort of tacit acknowledgement that [laughs] the dream is dying. Even the title of the master's is insanely boring: "Voluntary Sector Management."

The several [degree] letters after my name, that's the main ambition. I'm accepting this segment of society that I'm floating into. I'm quite happy to just bobble along and not push any further. That worries me.

At the moment, my creativity is a part of my life that's completely neglected. This is my vulnerability showing: I'm sad that I don't do more comedy. I'm frustrated in myself that I don't write and perform and persevere.

It means so much to me to make people laugh. I've done a number of stand-up gigs around London. I found it exhausting and sometimes completely soul destroying when it didn't go well. You need to be resilient if you're going to cope with that. But, for me, comedy has also been a sort of savior. Making people laugh has been my kind of modus operandi; it's more valuable than anything else.

Taking Calls Here Makes Me Feel Highly Anxious

I've definitely suffered as a result of taking difficult calls with people here. The emotional impacts of having a phone conversation with someone who's in huge amounts of distress can last you for a long, long time, and they can come back to you later on. I still think about callers that I've had, and I can remember their scenarios and what was going on with them that made me feel highly anxious.

After you hang up, you don't know what happens to them. You don't know if they go and jump off the bridge. You don't get to find out.

I find it difficult to deal with mothers of a son who has a problem gambling. The mother wants to take control, stop the kid from gambling, take away his autonomy. Even though he's behaving appallingly, my sympathies ally with him. I, in my frame of reference, identify with the son rather than the overbearing mother.

I think, "Leave him alone. No wonder he's a gambling addict, you horrible, horrible woman," even though all she wants to do is help him. You only come to these things where you've already experienced it, don't you? . . . Because it's never about the other person, really. It's always about you.

If I Didn't Cycle, I'd Be the Size of a House

I cycle here every day, through rain and shine. If I didn't cycle, I'd be the size of a house. I like it. It's one of my favorite parts of the day, getting on my bike and going home. It takes me an hour.

I just let go of everything that's been going on during the day, all of the "I don't know how to do this" or "So-and-So's bitching to me about that," "I'm being micromanaged by him or her," or whatever. By the time I'm at about London Bridge, the traffic starts getting pretty unpleasant, and I've got to focus on whether or not I'm going to get hit by a bus. I've forgotten all about the pain of being in an office all day.

In addition to biking, I do quite enjoy going home and cooking and Fran and I having a nice meal and watching something. I still love Bill Hicks, and I still listen to anything that he has done, ever. He's an American comedian from Texas. He's very, very funny, and I love him to pieces. I also like Paul Merton and Eddie Izzard.

My Worst Day and Best Day Here Were Back-to-Back

My worst day here was when I'd just come back from an eight-week holiday where I cycled to Istanbul with some friends, which was a wonderful and life-affirming thing to have done.

My manager at the time was an incompetent, chaotic pain in the ass. I got back, and I threw myself into a project without any pay or additional sort of recognition. It ultimately resulted in me getting promoted, but [initially] I wasn't getting any recognition, and I was getting challenged left, right, and center by her in her incompetence.

We had a full-on argument about something. She felt that I was trying to take over or treading on her toes somehow.

I remember waking up one morning, and I just suddenly thought, "This is absolutely not worth it. I don't get paid enough. I don't care enough to have to go into an organization where I feel like that."

When I woke up that morning, I genuinely had an inkling of what it must be like for someone who's got real depression, who wakes up and thinks, "I don't want to get out of bed today." I remember thinking, "Shit, this is horrid."

And I came in that day, and her boss took me aside. He said, "I heard about what happened yesterday. We'd like to get you much more involved in the project. Actually, without you, nothing would be happening."

It was a sudden acknowledgment that I was valuable. That was all I needed. So, those were the worst and the best days back-to-back. It was a combination of being completely unappreciated and undervalued and unhappy, juxtaposed with someone saying, "Thanks very much, you're doing a lot of good work, you're not incompetent, and you're not trying to get above your station. In fact, you're trying to do something valuable for the charity." It was a nice feeling.

That really is the fuel of everything, I think, in the work environment, somebody just saying, "Well done. Thank you very much, and it hasn't gone unnoticed."

And the next day, I got promoted.

My Laughing Fits and the Cult Factor of Therapy

Without this work, I would never have had any therapy myself or explored those inner depths of the unconscious that I now consider to be a huge tenor of who I am. I like the vulnerability that's exposed here. I remember working in the casino and having this very bizarre relationship with work, where everybody was hypercritical of the managers, and the managers were hypercritical of the staff, and then, everyone went out in the pub at night and got angry and drunk.

Here, within two weeks, I was in a supervision session where I sat with a bunch of helpline advisors in a therapy room, talking about the pain of coming to work every day. It's an odd thing to sit with your colleagues and open up.

I used to have these horrendous laughing fits, where I'd be asked what I felt about how the call had gone and how my job was going, and I would just piss myself laughing.

And then, after the laughter, I would sob my heart out in the room with six colleagues. It was *mental*. I remember going home and being like, "This is a very strange environment, but there's something about it I like." That might have sounded cultish. Therapy is a cult, I think, when you get into it, because you start to invest yourself into it like people do into religion.

If I Didn't Have to Work, I'd Have a Harem and Walk around Naked

If I didn't have to work another day in my life—bloody hell. I think I'd really struggle. I think work for me is a safe environment to cope with and manage other things that don't fit. The same as I said earlier about my dad, it's the same for me. Here, I feel like, in some respects, I can operate as a successful, intelligent, capable achiever, whereas at home, I might not always feel that way.

I've recently started gardening more, and I might do more of that. I'd probably go in five times a week for psychoanalysis, which would probably not be good for me, but I'd enjoy it so much.

If I had all the money and time in the world, I'd also buy a massive area of land, where I could just walk around without any clothes on, because I'm sick and tired of wearing clothes all the time! It gets me down. And I'd try and have some sort of serial, open relationships with lots and lots of different women and have my wife be accepting of that. It would be a harem like in a *Playboy* environment.

We can definitely share the responsibilities of the kids. She can carry on going to work, and I could just sort of sit at home like Hugh Hefner. The kids can see what a tremendous role model their father is providing for them. [Laughs.]

What's Next for Me: Marriage and Children—and Being an Accepting Dad

In real life, I suspect for the next several years I'll be working for some sort of NGO [non-government organization]. I've grudgingly come to acknowledge that my best means of bringing home some earnings is to consolidate what I've achieved here, climb the ladder a fair amount, and then, go somewhere else and earn more money.

I could probably earn a good enough salary that Fran could reduce her hours, and then, we could have children. I won't have to give up work, and she won't have to give up work fully. We can still lead lives that we want, at the same time as having kids.

I will be marrying Fran in two weeks. I think I would like to have three children, a big family. And, to be honest, that's not something that I anticipated that I would do in my life, but I'm now in a relationship with somebody who really does want that, and, you know, we make decisions based on what we want collectively, right?

As a father, I will try to foster a culture of "anything goes" in terms of what they think and feel. And if what they want to talk or think about is not what other people expect, they'll still be accepted. I would like that to be my lasting legacy of fatherhood: "Dad accepted us for who we were and loved us unconditionally."

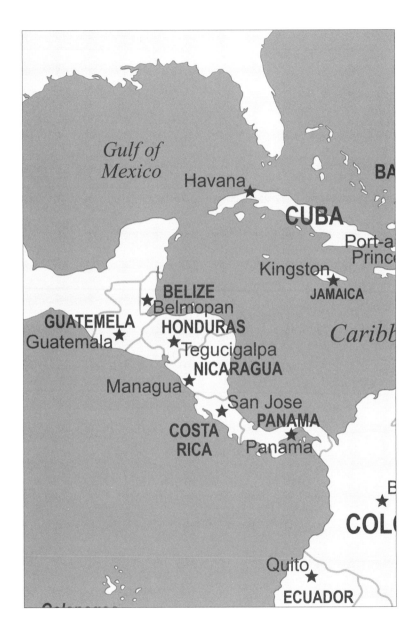

two

KEVIN

NURSING STUDENT

Santa Lucia, Honduras

Editor's note: It seemed like an idyllic, if poor, fishing village where Kevin Zazo grew up on the Caribbean north coast of Honduras. It had neither electricity nor plumbing. There were no streets at all; you had to walk along the beach to find your way home. Kevin and his little sister, Senaida, lived with their grandparents, had family all around, and clung closely to their mom when she had to leave for days at a time, riding buses faraway to sell used clothing.

And then in an instant, when Kevin was five, everything changed forever. His father murdered his mother and then ran off, never to be seen again.

When she died, Kevin's mother was the same age he is now.

Maybe it takes a lifetime to recover from witnessing your mother's murder and learning to live without both parents. But I stare at Kevin and try to figure out what makes him seem so old. Is it his deep, sonorous voice or the serious face behind the glint of his eyeglasses? He looks twenty years older than twenty-three. I wonder if the trauma he witnessed as a child also robbed him of any semblance of youth.

Kevin says, "I was a kid. I didn't know what to feel," and so he felt nothing until he turned thirteen in an orphanage and spiraled into depression.

A group of Midwestern Americans[1] decided he was worth fighting for. They got Kevin into school and stayed by his side for ten years—through Kevin's defiance in adolescence to finding his passion in nursing school.

Kevin revels in taking care of others. No messes, bodily fluids, or human illnesses deter him at all: "I love taking care of people," he exclaims. In the process, he's learned to laugh and to love. He takes the 4:30 a.m. bus into the city and studies until 1 a.m. each night, and he feels lucky to do it. "It's all about opportunity," he says.

Growing Up Garifuna, in a Village with No Future

My name is Kevin Zazo. I'm twenty-three years old. I'm a nursing student at the Universidad Nacional Autonoma de Honduras (UNAH) in the capital city of Tegucigalpa. I live in a home for boys called "Casa Noble" in Santa Lucia, on the outskirts of the city.

I was born in northwest Honduras in Puerto Cortés, the principal port of Honduras and Central America. My father was Guatemalan, my mother Honduran.

My family from my mother's side are from the Garifuna tribe,[2] the black people. They came after the colonization as slaves from San Vicente, Belize. My family speaks Garifuna. They speak Spanish, too. I speak a little bit of Garifuna. I used to speak [it] a lot when I was a kid. But since I moved here, I've lost it to some extent.

I grew up in the town of Sonaguera, on the coast. There are not so many opportunities there. You graduate from sixth grade, and then, the rest of your life is fishing or taking care of cows. That's it. You don't have a future there.

My grandfather was a fisherman, but now he's blind. He's almost eighty-two. And my grandma makes coconut-milk bread and sells it. She still does that. That's how she takes care of the family.

My Earliest Memories: Fighting and Murder

My earliest memory from childhood is getting into a fight over my sister, Senaida. She's one and a half years younger than me. I have taken care of her since I was a kid. She's my everything. I fought with a classmate, because he was bullying her, and that's why I have a scar over here. [Points.] He knocked me down and cracked my head open.

And then, I have other memories of my mother from that time. Since I was like three years old, my mother, Sara, used to travel a lot from Honduras to Guatemala. She would buy clothing in Honduras and then go to Guatemala to sell it there. She would sometimes be gone for more than a week.

We used to stay with my grandma. Every time my mother left, we cried so hard. We would flop down in the sand and just pound our hands and feet and cry. My grandma used to throw water on us so that we would quiet down. I remember my sister used to get so red and cry so hard, and that was the only way to make her calm down.

When I was five years old and my sister was three, my father killed my mom.

My father was a very jealous person. He always thought that my mother was cheating on him with another man. One night, after he came home from Guatemala, I remember he came in and showed us this knife. Then, later that night, he killed my mom.

In our house, my father would sleep in the bed with my sister, and I slept with my mother. I was very close to my mother. When I slept with her, I always hugged her. But at 3:00 that morning, when I woke up, she wasn't there. I started screaming, "Mom! Mom! Mom!" My uncle was there with us, too. He woke up. My mother was outside.

My uncle threw open the door, and my mother was running in circles. She said, "Son, your father, Carlos, just made a disaster," something like that. I ran to my mother. She had a knife wound in her throat and another one close to her heart.

She put her hand in my hand, and she fell and died.

My father ran away. We never saw him again. I heard that he went to Belize and then back to Guatemala. And since then, we stayed with our grandma.

My Grandma Sent Us to an Orphanage "To Have Something in Life"

We lived between two rivers. We didn't have electricity, public service, anything. We didn't have streets. You had to walk on the beach to get to your home. We were about seventy-five seconds from our house to the sea. It's still just like that now.

When I went to school, there were only twenty students there. As a kid, I didn't pay attention too much to what had happened to me. It didn't affect me. But then, when I started growing up, it did so very badly; it had a serious impact on my life.

My grandma heard about an orphanage where they helped kids to study, to finish school and everything. She said, "This is a big opportunity.

I've got to send you there. That's the only way for you to have something in life." But when we arrived, we discovered that my grandmother had misunderstood the situation. She had sent us to a place that was an orphanage only for boys.

Starting Over in One Orphanage after Another

So, they sent us to a different place, a mixed orphanage for boys and girls. I was in fourth grade, and my sister was the same grade, too. We started school together. I had started first grade before her, but I had missed a year of school: Because of what happened with my mom, I had to stop school because of the shock. So, we were now in the same grade.

School there was kind of hard. It was hard to adapt. I had to get used to a new place and to get along with the other kids.

We used to hide behind a tree when groups came. I wasn't that confident with myself, and my sister felt that way too. She was always with me. I never used to laugh.

But then a year later, we met Karen [from Hope for Honduran Children or H4HC], and she always used to make faces so that we'd laugh. She changed my life. I didn't realize it then, but I had been so sad because of my mom. During this time, I lost all communication with my family from Guatemala, with my father. I never heard from them.

I was in that place for two years. Then, I started growing up, so I had to leave. They took me to a place for older kids. I was twelve years old and separated from my sister for the first time. That was one of the hardest moments in my life. My sister wasn't that applied in her classes. Because we were in the same grade, I used to do all her homework. So, the first thing I thought was, "Oh no, my sister's going to fail!" We always kept in touch, always, even though, in that time, I only used to see her twice in a year.

Depression Came Crashing Down on Me

I turned thirteen, and then, all of these problems came all at once. I started complaining. I didn't want to study. I felt I had no reason to study. I was going to die anyways. I had nobody, and this and that. I was depressed. I didn't talk to anybody, and I hated God. I was like, "God doesn't exist. Why has he done this to me?" I didn't believe in anything at all. I was clinically depressed.

That year, I became the worst kid. I fought with the other guys for any reason. I didn't follow too many orders from the people that took care of us.

I used to be good in math, but one time, in a test, I started thinking about all of this stuff and how much I hated the teacher for no reason. So, I erased all of the answers on the exam, crumpled it up, and then put it on the teacher's desk and left the room angry. That was the first year that I failed a class.

I had to leave the school. I almost got kicked out, and the only way I could get back in was with a lot of conditions. My grandma had to come and sign for me, and she had to come and live onsite. It was not embarrassing to me, though, because really I didn't care too much about anything at the time.

Deciding to Become a Good Example, for Once

There was this one boy, Moises, who became an example for me. He was older than me. He was a very polite guy, a good kid. He hadn't been through bad things. He always studied. He'd learned English by himself. So, it was like, "Moises this, and Moises that." He's from a town that is close to mine in Puerto Cortés. So, I used to get along with him.

I started realizing that I wanted to change, to be like him. I wanted to see how it feels being on the other side. I wanted to be a good example, you know? I was used as a bad example for too many years.

The principal told one of the guys there, "Don't be like Kevin. He's losing so many opportunities because of how he acts." And I realized that I was doing all these bad things just to call their attention to me, because I wanted them to say *something* about me, and I didn't care if it was in a bad way. I was far away from my sister and far away from home. I felt that I didn't have anybody.

My First Step Was to Conquer the English Language

I wanted to improve my English. So, I started learning by myself. I told Moises, "I don't want to be like you; I just want to be better than I am." I still try to do that every day.

Moises graduated in computer systems at the university, and he's working on the north coast. He works as an English teacher and in an NGO [non-government organization] that provides school supplies to schools. And I keep in touch with him. The last time I talked to him, we talked for more than an hour, all in English! [Laughs.]

That year, I knew only a few words in English. My first phrase was, "How do you say that in English?" I said that so many times, like maybe more than a hundred times, and I might only learn two words. But I read *English for Dummies* and *English for Latinos*. I also started listening to music in English. I used to listen to classic rock, because they sing English very slowly in those songs.

Now, I speak pretty well, and I listen to the music I like—mostly reggae. That's what we listen to in my town. I like *punta*, which is Caribbean music. I like bachata, merengue, everything that has to do with the north coast. I dance to all of that, too.

My Sponsor Is My American Mom

My sponsors have helped to change everything in my life. There's Gina: She's been with me all this time. And when something new happens in my life, Susie is the first person that I want to call. We do FaceTime. I talk to her at least three times in a week. If I see a pretty girl at school, I'm going to tell her, "I saw this girl. She's so pretty."

But if I tell her, for example, "Susie, I want to get a tattoo," she's going to be like, "No, a tattoo doesn't give you a good presentation, especially if you're a nurse." And, trust me, I'll take her advice. She has been with me through all my ups and downs. I think I was eleven years old when she started sponsoring me. That's twelve years now.

Taking Charge of My Future— and Then Flunking Out

When I was almost sixteen, my main sponsor, Mama Karen, came to visit. We sat together and talked about my future. Then, I called a meeting. I talked to my sponsors, and they agreed they would support my wish and send me to a private school, a famous English-language school in Tegucigalpa called Elvel School. The president's daughter went there—people like that, the high society of Honduras.

On the first day of classes, my science teacher said, "Hey, we're going to read. Each person has to read a paragraph."

At that time, I could have a conversation in English, but I couldn't read or write in that language. So, I was wondering, "Should I pretend to be a stutterer, or should I try my best?" When it was my turn, I got so nervous. "Oh my God, what am I going to do?"

And I did try, but it didn't work out. Everybody saw that I couldn't read English. They said, "This kid is not going to pass the first year."

Only my sponsors, Karen and John, believed in me. I said to Karen, "Oh my God, these kids are so rich, and I don't even own the clothes on my own back. They're donations from America."

I passed my first year. Even though I had to go to summer school, I did it. When I got the results and I found out that I had passed all my classes, I was so happy that I didn't even take the bus from the school. I walked back to the house. It was like five miles away, but I was so happy in the street. Oh my God, I wanted to shout my news to all these people around me!

I did well in eighth grade and ninth grade. But during all this time, it was hard for me to adapt to the school. I was two years older than my classmates, so they called me Grandpa.

They were all these rich kids, boys and girls, talking about their new cellphones, and going out on the weekends, and what alcohol they were going to have. I was like, "No, I can't go." They'd be talking about their driver and the new car their parents just bought. I was thinking, I have to take a taxi if I want to go, and I can't afford even that.

When I started tenth grade, everything was new for me—new vocabulary, new classes. Even though I was learning more English, they were talking about chemistry, and there was all this new vocabulary. I got some good grades, but they weren't enough to pass. So I failed the tenth grade.

Going Back to Being a Bad Boy

Once I failed, it was like I had gone to Elvel and done nothing. Before, I had achieved my goal. I was finally being used as a good example. But then I failed. So now it was, "See, they gave this opportunity to Kevin. He didn't appreciate it, and he failed."

I went back to being a bad boy again. I didn't do drugs. I wasn't in a gang or committing crimes; I was just rebelling against everything.

My friends went through like fifty dollars to one hundred dollars a night. And I only got twenty dollars a week for buying my breakfast and lunch, nothing left. So, even if I smoke or drink, how am I going to pay for that? How? I didn't have any income.

My Sponsors Never Stopped Believing in Me

But my sponsors never stopped trusting in me, never. The people from Elvel School were like, "No, you've got to go. You've got only one shot, and that's it. You lost it. You're out." But my sponsors said, "We're going to keep supporting you. We want you to finish university."

So, I transferred to this program that lets you graduate from high school in one year. I was twenty. I wanted to move forward very fast, so I felt I was ready for this [accelerated high school]. I went for one year and finished high school. The best part was that I was a block from my sister. My sister used to wash my clothes. That was very good. I never washed my own clothes. [Laughs.] . . . So eventually, I finished high school. Only my sister went to my graduation. It was good to have her there.

I Wanted to Be a Doctor, but a Nurse Is the Next Best Thing

When it came time for university, I didn't know what I really wanted to do. I wanted to study something with numbers or in the medical area, so I was thinking about engineering or medicine.

But medicine is eight years, and if you want to get a specialty, it's two or three more years. That's too long, and it's the most expensive career in Honduras. You have to buy uniforms and medical things. My organization can't support scholarships for more than four years. In addition, I didn't study too much for the university admission test and didn't get high enough marks for the medical program. So, I had to choose a more certain career.

Trying My Hand at Teaching

I volunteered for a year, teaching English in a H4HC school, out in the countryside in Naguara. I taught from first grade to sixth grade, to get some experience. It was great. It was one of my best experiences ever.

Even though I was a volunteer, it was my first formal job. I had [a] responsibility to be there on time and to take all the applied tests. But I didn't want to do that for the rest of my life. I didn't want to teach. That's not my thing.

Nursing Is Perfect for Me

Then, I switched over to nursing. I tried to visualize how I wanted to see myself in ten years, not only thinking about life in this moment. I remember I worked in an office for three months, and I hated sitting like that in front of the computer and having the same routine every single day.

I thought a lot about what I wanted to do with the rest of my life. Then, I realized that nursing was the perfect career, because the training is short. It's in the health area. I would love that. I like meeting people. I like it so much.

I chose nursing because it's a way to help others. People have given me so much, and I want to give back something. And everybody gets sick . . . it's a way to help others. I remember when I was a kid, I hated people so much, and now, I love them!

People sometimes think that I'm immature, because now I love laughing. Since I found this laugh, since Karen helped me to laugh, I like it, and I don't want to stop. It helps me. Laughter is a way for forgiving everything and just feeling good with myself.

This is my second year of nursing. It's a five-year program. In one year I'll be licensed in practical nursing, like an assistant. If I study for two more years after that, then I'll have my master's degree. That's what I want.

How It Is to Be a Nurse Here in Honduras

I haven't worked as a nurse yet. I have been on medical brigades [charitable projects] as an interpreter. In Honduras, brigades are [nonprofit] organizations that bring groups and volunteers together to do work.

I love working with people. I love to help others, even though right now I'm not the one doing the medical work. I'm just an interpreter, translating for the doctor, just holding patients' hands. Maybe it's dental work and they're taking out their tooth. I feel so great, telling them, "Calm down, we're almost done." I love it. I feel so good doing this work.

In Honduras, nursing is traditionally a woman's career, but that's changing. I don't feel that you need to have a strong feminine side in order to be in nursing. You just need to love people and want to help others.

It's like, let's say, 70 percent of the men that study nursing are gay. So, a lot of friends make fun of me. "Oh, you're in nursing. Oh, you'll become gay." [Laughs.] And I just laugh. I *love* women. [Laughs.] I love nursing, too.

My Home and Family with the Guys at Casa Noble

I have been living at Casa Noble now for a year and a half. I am the second oldest. Alvaro is the housefather, the manager, and the older brother. When I came here, he told me that he was afraid to work with me. He had heard that I'd be the worst of everyone: I would not attend university, I would not get good grades, and I would act badly.

And then, it was totally different. I said, "I can start all over again, now that I'm away from Elvel." I said, "I'm changing. I'm going to shut their mouths again." And I was going to do it with my grades, with my classes. I took five classes in the first semester. I passed them all.

I also try to organize everything in the house. Alvaro doesn't spend the week with us. He only comes twice in a week and maybe for three or four hours, Monday and Friday. So, during the week, sometimes the boys leave dirty dishes. They don't do their duty. So, I'm like, "Okay, guys, you have to do this. Let's get it done. Let's start with this."

I've become Alvaro's right-hand man in the house. Everything's good with me. And my grades are finally good. Last year, I took twelve classes, and I passed all of them and with good grades.

My Dating Life Is a Secret . . .

Oh, I've been in love so many times. [Laughs.] No, just kidding.

At Casa Noble, they want us to focus on our studies and not get distracted. So, I can't talk about my love life. It's a secret, because we're not allowed to be in relationships. [Laughs.] But I just broke up with my girlfriend like three weeks ago. We had been together unofficially for two years.

I don't think that relationships are a distraction, because when I date a girl, I always tell them, first, God; second, studies; third, my family. Right now, it's actually my studies first. When I finish university, then my family is going to be second. Then comes friends, and then you. I'm clear with that.

Also, I love reading. I like having time with myself. I like thinking, and I hate like texting all day long, texting and calling. Then, I get bored of the people. I'm very clear about what I want and where I want to be, because I know where I come from, and if I don't do something with my life right now, I know what is waiting for me in my hometown.

I Go to School All Week and Teach on the Weekends

From Monday to Friday, I study and take my classes. I take the bus to my university. It's an hour bus ride, two hours back and forth every day. For example, tomorrow, I have to leave to take the bus at 4:30 a.m., because I have a test at 7:00.

Then on Saturdays, I teach English. I don't get paid. I'm offering community service. I wanted to do something for all the boys from Casa Noble and some of the boys and girls in Santa Lucia.

I don't have to, but I want to help. So, I'm teaching there. The kids have four hours of classes on Saturday, and I teach one of the four hours. It's learning for me, too—in nursing, you have to work with other people. Even though I don't have too much interest in teaching, it helps me to get along with other people.

Going to Church on Sundays, Just for the Positive Messages

On Sundays, we go to Catholic Church. At Casa Noble, it doesn't matter what religion you are. I'm not Catholic. I don't believe in religions. I believe in God, but I don't believe in religion. I don't care what church I go to, but I'm happy hearing good things on how to be better. It's not about the religion. It's about hearing good advice and getting along with the community and all that.

Now, what is sort of a trend is being atheist, not believing in God. If you're agnostic, you're cool. That's how it works with my friends.

At times in the past, I didn't believe in God. When I wanted to blame somebody, I blamed him. Now, I do believe in God. I can tell the difference where something is good and something is bad.

Sometimes, on Sunday afternoons, I go hiking. I sit on top of a mountain, and I sit there with this wonderful view. I appreciate it. When I go out, I don't take myself some drugs or smoke weed or something [laughs], because I want to have that reality landscape.

If You Can't Help Everybody, at Least Help One

A priest named Father Mike used to come here with Mama Karen. He told me, "If you can't help everybody, at least help one." So, my plan is, if I'm enrolled in the northern area, I would like to bring nurses and doctors to help everybody in my town.

My *abuela* [grandma] is still alive, but she doesn't really understand my life. The last time I went there, when she saw me, she said, "What are you doing here?"

I was like, "Vacation."

She said, "What [money] do you bring from there?" and I was like, "Nothing. They're giving me everything. I'm a university student. I don't get money from that."

She said, "So, you should stop studying and start working."

My grandma has nineteen kids. And I have tons of cousins. Sometimes, it's kind of hard to get along with them, because not one of them has been in university. Maybe two of them have graduated from high school, and that's it. And two of them went into the army. And then, the girls marry, have tons of kids and all that.

A lot of my aunts married at a very young age, between fifteen and eighteen years old. My mother married when she was sixteen. (She was married once before she married my father.) She had my half brother when she was around seventeen. I was born when she was eighteen.

I Miss My Mother Every Day, but I Don't Regret Anything in This Life

I hadn't realized that before: I am now right at the age she was when she died. [Cries.] But let me tell you this: I never complain about my life. Things happen for a reason. I'm the person I am because of everything that happened, and I love it. And maybe I'm crying, but it's of happiness. I don't regret anything.

I don't believe that my mother is still here [in spirit]; yet, last year when my sister and I went to see her grave, I had never felt so close to my mother since she died.

My sister was crying, and I was trying to be strong and help her. We usually go to the grave by ourselves, but this time we went together. When we were walking back to our house, I almost fell down, I was crying so hard. I couldn't handle it. I don't know. It was horrible. I had never cried so hard.

Right now, in my life, I have plans with my sister. First, she needs to graduate from university. She's moving fast. She will be finished next year with a degree in public accounting and finance. Susie is sponsoring her. She's the same one who sponsored me.

Best and Worst Moment: Being a Father Figure to My Little Sister

The best moment in my life, and somehow it was one of the worst, too, was on Father's Day, when Senaida was in ninth grade. The teacher asked her about a father role model for her, and Senaida told her teacher about me.

So, for me, it was like, "Okay, I'm doing what a brother is supposed to do," but then I started thinking, "Where is my family? Why didn't she talk about my grandpa? Why she didn't talk about my uncles?" I didn't like that. But I also felt so great that she used me as an example.

I have always been her hero. All her classmates know me, because she never stops talking about me. Three weeks ago, she asked me to help her write an English essay. It was "my brother this, and my brother that." Just like all her stories, it was about her brother. It was all about me.

So, she's not only my sister. She's my best friend. I'm there for her; she's there for me.

There is also a girl in the orphanage where my sister is. She doesn't have anybody, *nobody*. I don't know where her mother is. Her mother was on drugs the last time she went to visit her. Her mother went crazy and didn't recognize her. Since that last time, like since two years, we haven't heard anything about her mom.

So, we want to move in together, me and my sister and her. I told her, "If you need anything, just let me know. I'm your older brother." That's it. So, we want to give her a place to stay. When she has to leave school, okay, come here, stay with us. The plan is to move in together, start working, and rent an apartment, maybe in Tegucigalpa. We haven't decided where.

What My Pay Will Be as a Nurse

When I become a nurse, if I work with the government, the starting pay is 18,500 lempiras per month, which is a little over $800. If I work in a private area, I will get less. So, I will probably make less, because I want to work in a clinic. I'm not going to be rich. I'm not a very materialistic person, but that doesn't mean that I'm not afraid about the future.

I've Spent My Whole Life Being Afraid of the Future

I have been afraid all my life. My biggest fear in life is the future, what is going to happen tomorrow. When I think about that, I'm like, "Oh my God." Even though I see myself how I want to be, I still have anxiety about losing this opportunity that I have right now.

It's like not having somebody in my life that I can depend on, hold on to. I have my sister, but one day, she's going to get married, and then, I'll be feeling alone. I don't know. It's horrible for me.

I like to have everything planned out. I hate leaving anything to chance. My biggest fear in life is the future.

I am afraid to have children. For me, it would mean that somebody's life is going to depend on me. I have been through horrible things. I don't want to give them the same thing, that same legacy.

I'm a giving person. When I like someone, I'll die for them, you know? And so having a kid, it will mean that responsibility. I don't think that I will ever have children.

What Hondurans Are Really Like

We have wonderful people in Honduras. After not loving people, now I do. When I go to the north coast, to my town, everybody's like, "Good morning. Good afternoon." You don't see that in other countries. We use our hands when we talk. We are very expressive. I'm not talking badly about gringos [white people], but really, they just talk like this [hands down at his sides].

We have so many wonderful vistas—to the north coast, to the mountains and everything, and we don't appreciate it. When I go to my hometown, I wake up in the morning; I take my book and sit on the beach, waiting for the sun to rise. I love doing that. But people from my town don't do that because they live there. They've forgotten what they have.

What I Would Do If I Could: Help My Hometown

If I had all the money in the world, I would open my own clinic in my hometown and help all the people. I would go to work there.

One of my biggest inspirations in my current work is my town. I don't want to go back there with my hands empty, not making a change, and having the same role as my family has been through, as everybody has been through: marry, have tons of kids, and then give them the same future. It's a cycle. I don't want to do that. I would love to have a clinic so everybody can have access to medicine and care.

The people there don't make more than $5 a day. With that, you can buy a pound of rice and one of beans, and that's it. That's why they don't go to the doctor, because they don't have enough money. I'd like to be able to give them free healthcare.

I want to practice preventive healthcare. That's the secret. Normally, you only go to the doctor when you're sick. You never go for checkups. For example, in our community, we don't have electricity there. But if you boil your water, you're going to have fewer problems than just drinking it from the river.

I think that for a town to have good health, it takes prevention work with massive teaching, like how to prevent all the common illnesses in the town, and then to have a clinic there so that they can go there for emergency situations.

If we don't have roads there, only boats like now, if someone gets sick, it takes three hours to get him to a hospital. They take you in a hammock, then they cross the river in a boat, and then, you have to call someone to come get you, because nobody has a car there. There is a community center where a doctor goes once in a week, but that's it. And my grandma is the midwife there. She's in charge of the births.

My Dream Job: Village and Motorcycle Medical Care

In my dream job, I would spend part of my time in my local clinic, and then, for the rest of my time, I would ride a motorcycle to the forgotten towns that nobody visits and somehow get support for them.

I like the investigation part of nursing. I would love to study new illnesses, to do research and figure out how to cure them. I would love to focus on infectious disease.

What I Would Do with Tremendous Wealth

I don't consider myself to be a material person—so if I had all the money in the world, I'm not going to buy like a fancy car and all that. I do love motorcycles. I'm going to have one someday, even though Susie told me that, in America, people who ride on motorcycles are called "organ donors." [Laughs.]

I would want a house. I got my own bedroom last year. That's my paradise. I can do whatever I want there. I think that, because I'm insecure about the future, I like to be secure in my present.

My Favorite Book: *The Alchemist*

I haven't thought about what my dream house would look like. I know I'd have my own library. I like nonfiction, like autobiographies of people that have been through things and finally made something big in their life. One book that I love, and that helped me change, is called *The Alchemist*. I felt related with Santiago. I'm a dreamer, too, and I think dreaming helps you to mark the way where you want to go.

In the book, Santiago's parents wanted him to be a priest. He didn't want that. He wanted to travel around the world. So, he became a shepherd. He passed through a lot of things. He had a dream that he wanted to follow. He had to sell his sheep, because that was the only way to get money to travel. He got robbed. Then, he went to this oasis, and he fell in love with this girl, Fatima. He met the Alchemist.

When he fell in love, he thought his life was realized. That's how I felt when I was in love with my girlfriend. I was like, "Oh my God, this is going to be awesome."

But then, there are your dreams. Like with *The Alchemist*, okay, you're in love, you're going to marry her, life in the first days are going to be so beautiful. But then a few years later, you're going to start to remember about your dreams, and it will cost you this emotional thing that you couldn't accomplish them. And everything is about following your dreams, and at the end, there's always a solution.

My Generation Faces Rampant Unemployment and Crime

We don't have too many opportunities in our country, even in Tegucigalpa. You see tons of people graduating from university, and they don't do what they graduated from or studied. There's underemployment, too.

Do you know how I define the word "poverty"? Not having opportunities. Two months ago, I was on my way back to the house, and I saw these homeless guys, feeding from the garbage and all that. I was looking through the window, and I was like, "Oh my God. How'd they end up like that? What was the reason?" When you start thinking about how they end up like that, it's about poverty. They don't have opportunities. It's not because they want that life. That's something horrible about our country. We don't get many opportunities.

I'm a dreamer, and since I started university, I can't stop thinking about finishing. But what happens then? I don't know, but I have to do it, because I know how my life is going to be, with or without it.

There's also a criminal element here. You can't walk free in the streets, because you're going to get robbed or going to get shot. This is true especially in the city.

Honduras has a reputation for the highest murder rate.³ I watch the news every morning. And I hate that it's like entertainment on the local news. People won't buy the newspaper if there's less than eight people killed last night. They consider it entertainment. It's crazy. It's like the more people who died, the more fun it is to watch the news. That's why I'm afraid to graduate from university. Then what happens if I don't have any opportunities or I'm shot and killed?

The Politics of Blame Needs to Change

In Honduras, we always blame politics. But what are we doing to change that? And it's horrible that if you're a person who likes to talk and create stories, people say you should be in politics, because you're a liar.

People think there are two reasons for being in politics—if you're a liar and if you like money. They don't have another idea for why people would get involved. But in Cuba, you see like zero level of people that can't read. What was their secret? They made a revolution. It's not that I'm a communist, but I think that to make a change, you need a revolution.

Let's Start a Revolution of the Mind

Since I moved to Casa Noble a year and a half ago, I'm becoming more independent, and I love the person that I am becoming. If something happens, I make my decision. If it was good, I take the praise. If I do something wrong, if I make a bad decision, I don't have a problem saying, "I did it, and I'm sorry. How can I change that?" I'm the owner of what I do. I take responsibility. Ninety percent of the decisions I make end in a good result. When somebody asks me, "How are you doing?" they will hear my answer, "110 percent positive and increasing."

If we had a revolution here, it would be about everything in our mind, in the way that we think. We have to be more positive in how we approach life. I think, with the news, if their entertainment wasn't all about rioters and dead people and all the bad things that happen in our country, we'd realize we have so many good people here.

We have to start with ourselves, to look at how we treat our neighbors, how I treat the person who lives in the house next door, and not to blame other people. In the Bible, Eve blamed Adam, and Adam blamed Eve. Throughout history, we've always blamed somebody else. We need to take responsibility for our own actions.

If we want to change here, we need to have a change here. [Points to his head.] Individual mental.

My Life Is Not a Failure, and I Wouldn't Change a Thing

I've omitted a lot of things about my life, because then we would never finish our conversation, but I just want to say that going through all this stuff like I have, it's not a failure. Everyone falls. It's how you stand up from there that matters.

That's why I love my life so much. People ask me, "Would you change your life for something, for another life?" and I say no, because I'm the person I am because of everything that has happened in my past.

52

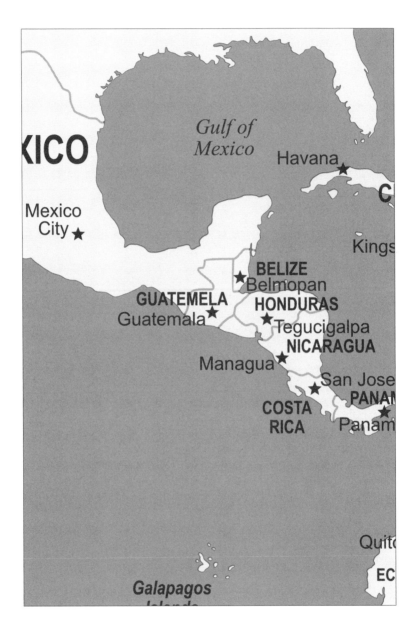

three

———

SANDRA

MIDWIFE CLINIC DIRECTOR

Ciudad Vieja, Guatemala

Editor's note: Sandra López[1] wants to ensure that every woman has quality healthcare and a beautiful birth. As the single mother of a special-needs son, Sandra has gravitated away from the *machismo*[2] strictly religious culture of her childhood and into an independent life of her dreams, with "the child, the house, the VW Bug . . . even the dog."

Sandra discovered she wanted to become a midwife in the middle of her own son's birth. She counted herself lucky to receive gentle care in an area where most give birth at home, unattended.

This tropical Central American country (about the size of Pennsylvania) has all climates, from humid coastal plains to chilly inland mountains. It sits just south of Mexico. More than half of its citizens live in poverty and 23 percent in extreme poverty.[3]

The clinic serves low-income, indigenous women; over 70 percent of their patients work in the agricultural sector and are of indigenous Mayan descent. They serve 3,500 clients in town, and women from remote areas come in by bus, or staff members go to them in a "mobile clinic" pickup truck. Sandra educates women on reproductive health and family planning. Her favorite part of the job is attending births.

For Sandra, life begins and ends in motherhood; not just for the women she serves but also for herself. She absolutely lights up at the mention of her son, Juan Sebastian, or "Juansie," as she calls him.

She's had a hard road in her personal life, surviving domestic violence in her childhood, a contentious long-term partnership, and single parenting of a son with Asperger syndrome.[4] Despite these challenges, she's created a stable home and good schooling for her son. And now, having spent years slugging away at life on her own, she may be just about to write a new chapter in an old love story.

Coming from a Macho Family, Ending Up as a Midwife

My name is Sandra Maribel López Ordoñez. I'm thirty-six years old. I'm a midwife and the project director of Open Hands in Ciudad Vieja, in Guatemala. We believe that all women have a right to dignified healthcare—yet only 31 percent[5] of women giving birth in Guatemala have an attendant to help them through.

My Family's Religion Caused Fear, *Machista*, and Double Standards

One part of my family is native to Guatemala. And from my mother's side, there are some who came from Spain, and they have been here for a very, very long time. I imagine my ancestors were Catholic. All of my family was Catholic before my father decided to become a Jehovah's Witness when he was eighteen. I was brought up in a family of Jehovah's Witnesses.

I am the only daughter. I have three brothers. My father fixed all kinds of electronic equipment and machinery. My mother was a housewife.

My father was extremely radical in his religious views, and he was very *machista*.[6] He lived a double life with double standards [morals]. He had other women, and he mistreated my mother a great deal psychologically. That was terrible, very difficult. I thought there must be a better way to live.

My childhood inspired me to want to support women in their own lives, to educate women about their rights, and to treat them well. I think that's why I do what I do.

My mother was very much influenced by religion. For example, [my parents would] tell us that the Smurfs [dolls] were little devils. My mother went to her sister's house once, and one of my cousins had toy Smurfs, and my mother threw them into the fire. In our home, there wasn't any type of literature, just biblical material from the Jehovah's Witnesses. It was as though a fairly large part of my life was stolen away from me, because I didn't know about culture. It was as if my eyes were covered.

We couldn't speak to my grandparents or aunts and uncles, because they weren't Jehovah's Witnesses. We didn't celebrate birthdays or any other special days such as Christmas.

Once, my grandparents in concealment [secretly] took us to the fair in the village. My father found out, because a Jehovah's Witness saw us there. This man went to tell my father, and my father hit us, all four of us. And there was a friend of mine who also was a Jehovah's Witness who couldn't stand this type of pressure. She committed suicide when we were about fifteen years old.

When My Father Discovered I Had a Boyfriend, He Beat Me

I had my first boyfriend, Samuel, when I was fourteen years old and he was eighteen. He was a very good person. I had a lot of problems at home, and Samuel always tried to take care of me. But because he belonged to a different religion, I suffered a great deal of violence from my father.

When my father found out that Samuel was my boyfriend, I received such a beating. He broke one of my fingers. That was the type of person that he was. He would bring the elders from the congregation into my room to talk to me and punish me or tell me off because I had a boyfriend, things like that.

So, Samuel and I decided to separate, because obviously I wasn't going to get married at fourteen. We didn't see each other again. We might see each other on the street and say "hi," but that was all. Then, he got married, and I went on with my life as well.

It Took Me Three Years to Leave the Jehovah's Witnesses

I quit being a Jehovah's Witness when I was between nineteen and twenty-one. It's not something that you can leave just like that; it took three years. When I managed finally to leave that behind, it was very difficult for me to recover.

I was afraid of dying. I was afraid that God would punish me. I was afraid of Armageddon.[7] I wasn't the only one. If we'd see Jehovah's Witnesses out in the street, we'd feel afraid, because they were very hard, really strict with adolescents. For example, if you wore an ankle bracelet, they'd tell you that that was a sin, things like that.

Now, I think my brothers are mostly like my father. They've lived through a great deal of violence, too, and that had a negative impact on them.

My Parents Separated, and Now My Mother Works with Me

Although my father and mother have been separated since I was born, they have never divorced. My father doesn't want to give her a divorce. He and I don't visit each other very much now, because he doesn't agree with the work I do.

My mother, Carmen, works here at Open Hands with me. She studied nursing for three years—before I did, actually. And she was lucky, because she worked for the nonprofit association WINGS,[8] and that started to change her way of thinking.

She's had to struggle through a lot of macho patterns as well, but I always tried to support her from when I was young. Now that I'm older, I want to continue. It's been a blessing having her work here, because she knows a lot about sexually transmitted infections, and she also helps me a lot with my son, Juansie. So, we're a good team. We've been working together for four years.

The "Princess" Who Had to Sell Bread at 5 a.m.

I studied at a public school, all of my primary education. My father didn't want me to study. That was another thing. My father's parents were people who had economic resources. In the village, people used to say that they were the wealthiest people in the village. They just had two children, and all of their grandchildren were boys. I was the only female.

People used to say, "Well, aren't you lucky, because you're the princess," but I wasn't. I had to work from the age of eight. I worked at my grandparents' bakery. I'd get up at 5:00 a.m. to help them to sell bread.

With what they paid me, about two hundred quetzals [$26] per month, I used that to pay for my studies. When I finished primary school, my father said, "No, I'm not going to pay for your studies." I had to pay for my own junior high school.

When I finished that, I had to go to a private school, because I couldn't work and go to the public school at the same time. So, I went to a private school. When I studied for my high school diploma, my father changed his mind and said, "Well, I can see that you want to study. So, I'll open a bank account for you, and I'll give you two thousand quetzals [$258], and we'll see if you can finish your high school diploma with that."

And I did. I finished. I got my high school diploma. I've always had ideas for selling things and making a bit of money, business ideas to help my money grow. And I continued working with my grandparents in the bakery early in the morning, and that's how I managed to study.

But after that, I felt a bit frustrated, because I wasn't able to go to university. It's very expensive . . . Later, when I was twenty-four, I planned to have a baby.

I Loved My Son's Father, but He Changed after We Lived Together

My son, Juan Sebastian, was planned. He was wanted. That was because I met the birth attendants here. I had never thought of being a mother and going to the national hospital to have a baby. I was afraid. But when I met the birth attendants, I said, "Well, now I want to have a baby," and I was in love with Juansie's father, too.

Juansie's father had been my friend for years. I met him when I was an adolescent, and he knew a lot of things about me, things about my childhood and my family. But when we decided to live together, he changed. He used the things that I told him to hurt me and to manipulate me. He didn't work, and he didn't want me to work. We had a lot of money problems.

Training as a Nurse and Working Odd Jobs to Support My Child

When I was living with Juansie's father, I wanted to do something to acquire knowledge and progress. So, I studied nursing for a year to become an auxiliary nurse. I didn't have any work then. Sometimes I had to work as a domestic, as a maid. I also prepared food that I put in a basket on my head to sell, like the women do in the communities. And with that money, we survived, the three of us. Of course, Juansie's father ate more than we did, the two of us.

I started studying nursing with the small amount of money that I had, and that opened doors for me. I worked as a nurse in three different places; then, I was told about a job in a nearby town, Chimaltenango, with an NGO [nonprofit]. They hired me as a project coordinator over women's projects. I learned a great deal there about sexual and reproductive rights.

My Partner Began to Be Violent with Our Son

Finally, I had a job. My partner didn't want me to work, because he wanted me to stay home, and I hadn't wanted to work before that, because I was looking after Juansie, up until he was five. But then I had to go out to work.

Juansie's father began to be very violent with him and also with me if I got back late from work. So, he started to hit me, things like that. I started to question continuing to live with Juansie's father. He beat me several times.

How Could I Tell Women Not to Take Abuse When I Had Bruises on My Face?

I had visible wounds on my face, and I was really ashamed when I went to work like that. I said, "No, I can't continue like this, because I'm going out to speak to women about their rights, and here I am, obviously hurt." I decided to leave him. And it's something that doesn't hurt me anymore, but it really did then. It was very difficult. I think I cried for two years.

We had lived together for six years. We were never married; we just lived together. Thank goodness for that. Otherwise, it would have been terrible. He would have wanted me to give him alimony.

To this day, Juansie's father continues to be irresponsible. After we separated, he didn't call Juansie once for a year. Right now, they only talk if Juansie calls him. He doesn't give us any money, either. He went back to another woman, and he has another son now. I heard he works in an organization called Namaste, which gives microloans to women. For me, it's ironic that he works there, but there it is.

Training to Be a Midwife

When I was working at the women's NGO, I met Hannah Freiwald, the founder of this project. She chose the name "Open Hands." She was thinking about the fact that women need to be welcomed, but also the way that we receive the babies, with open hands.

She said, "You have to work with me one day." I worked there for nine months, like a nine-month pregnancy [laughs], and then, I came to Open Hands in 2009. Initially, I was just an assistant in family planning. Since I got my high school diploma with a specialization in computers, I would help Hannah to record the client data.

But then, she started including me in other things, too. I was fortunate that she taught me how to become a midwife. Hannah still works here. She is the vice president of the board of directors. Now I'm the president of the board of directors: the boss! [Laughs.]

What We Do Here at Open Hands

At Open Hands, I am responsible for attending births and following up on all of the patients. I'm also the director, responsible for looking at our projects and general services.

Despite the fact that there are only four of us working here, we do have days when we go out to work in the communities, as well as attending births and providing all of our services here.

We also work with family planning a lot. We always need to make sure we've got the supplies that we need for our patients. We have to do fundraising to try to get donations for projects, and we also have people working here as interns. These internships help them feel comfortable in this work and give them a chance to get involved. There are always a lot of things to do.

Educating Families about Their Contraceptive Options

At Open Hands, in the last quarter, we had 190 gynecological consultancies. We had 150 prenatal consultancies, and 500 users of family planning. We cover a lot of family planning that the public health services can't because of the lack of resources on their part. We educate the women about how their body actually works, so they can understand how the hormones and other types of contraceptive methods work and then decide which method they want. This guarantees they'll use this method for a long time.

We have hormone methods, long-term ones such as a Jadelle, which is an implant under the skin, and three-month injections and monthly injections and pills, too. The three-month hormone injection, Depo-Provera, is the one that is most accepted by the women. They call it Depo. We're also educating the women about intrauterine devices, IUDs. The copper-T IUD doesn't have any hormones in it. We've been promoting it, because they can use it for up to ten years.

Our patients don't often use condoms. I think it's because the men don't like to use them. Some men will come in to buy condoms, because they're cheap here. But there are other couples that come in, the man and woman together, particularly for prenatal, and so we take advantage of that opportunity to educate the men, because it's difficult sometimes— this business of educating men.

We haven't really had the opportunity to have men's classes. What we have done, in the last two years, is we've operated on men so that they couldn't have children. This is the voluntary surgical method. It was very successful, because the men had their own private space during the vasectomy procedure.

We Work in the Clinic and Take Our Truck Out to the Villages

We work in Ciudad Vieja and the surrounding areas. We have a pickup truck that we take out and about to several small villages or hamlets, and villages around Antigua, too. I really don't know from how far away they come, how many kilometers.

We organize sessions for fast tests, rapid tests. It has really generated a lot of publicity for us. We do screenings for uterine cancer. But when we do these screening days, we also see if we can detect any other needs that the women have. The women know where the screenings are, and so they come for the other services.

Ultrasounds, Pap Smears, and Births

Typically, we have fifteen patients coming into the clinic every day. Each visit takes about thirty to forty minutes of our time. We do a bit of everything. Some days, we do ten ultrasounds, and other days, it's all family planning. There are a lot of days when everybody wants to do their Pap smears all at once. So, it varies a lot.

We try to organize ourselves each week, but working as a birth attendant has shown me that you can't follow your agenda normally when babies want to come! Maybe you calendar the whole week, but then there's a long birth or a long labor, and all of your plans change.

On average, we assist in one birth a week. So, we assist in fifty to sixty births a year. These are usually births in the clinic. But in some emergencies, we've had to go to the patient's house.

What I Earn as a Midwife

In my work, I earn eight thousand quetzals, which is $1,000 a month. With my salary, I don't have a problem. My problem is actually to *get* it.

I am responsible for fundraising for paying our own wages. That's the difficult part. For the last few years, though, we haven't had any problems with that.

But for me, it's also a bit difficult because I'm a single mother. Juansie needs special education. That's something that doesn't exist in public education, so I have to pay for Juansie's education. That's 2,600 [$336] quetzals a month, and I pay about two thousand [$259] in rent. My salary isn't a lot, but it's just enough each month.

The Number of Midwives in This Country Has Dropped

Unfortunately, we are not in collaboration with the Ministry of Health. It's a little bit complicated actually, because the doctors don't want to work with midwives.

In Guatemala, the number of midwives has actually dropped. In the rural communities, which are more remote, there are still quite a lot of traditional midwives. But in our area, there are not very many. The Ministry of Health doesn't want to train or certify any new traditional midwives. I think they are afraid of losing their market. In my point of view, they're trying to eliminate us.

We've Started Our Own Program to Train Midwives

At Open Hands, we started a project to train midwives, in collaboration with one of the universities. It's a three-year technical university course. There are fifteen young women studying. But there have been quite a few obstacles that we've come up against from the Ministry of Health.

We train midwives in both the old ways and in modern medicine. We believe women are prepared for natural birth, and that it's something that's natural. So we try to avoid it being invasive. That is the work or the labor: We let it happen . . . and it often takes days.

They [the Ministry] have protocols of how many hours a woman can wait, and if the labor doesn't advance, then they do a C-section or use medication to induce birth. Women generally have to lie down on a bed for giving birth. But with us here, women can decide what position they prefer.

Another example: If you can see in the ultrasound that the umbilical cord is wrapped around the neck, then they do a C-section. And normally about 40 percent of births have the umbilical cord wrapped around the neck. We don't believe that that should be an indication for doing the C-section. We just attend the birth and loosen the umbilical cord. We can feel when the head comes out, we can feel the cord. It's really simple to loosen it. It's not complicated at all.

One Patient Calls Me "Doctor Sandra"

My patients honor me. Most call me Miss Sandra, but one girl calls me Doctor. I say, "I'm not a doctor," but she says, "Well, for me, you are my doctor." That's really a compliment.

Everyday, I also see the satisfaction of the mothers, that they were able to give birth. That is a huge reward for them. It gives them incredible power to have overcome that test, and for me, just knowing I've been able to help them during that time is really a huge reward.

The Best Birth I Assisted Was Scary but Peaceful

I'm not sure how many births I've assisted in my lifetime, but I've collected about two hundred, maybe. I can remember nearly all of them . . . but I remember particularly one that was a very special family.

The labor was very peaceful. The baby was always happy; we knew this because we monitored the baby's heart. When the baby was born, he was pink and very nice, but he didn't breathe. The husband was there providing support during birth.

They immediately were affectionate with the baby, and they spoke to the baby in such a soft way and cuddled the baby and put him close to the mother. After about five minutes, the baby was breathing and quite happy and calm.

It was a beautiful experience, particularly because the parents were very patient and very calm, too. It was a stressful moment, but there wasn't any stress. That's one of the experiences I remember the most. Since then, the parents haven't had any other children, but they are planning for another. Baby Oscar is now three years old. He still comes into the clinic.

The One Baby I Lost—during an Earthquake—I Still Feel Guilty

I have lost one baby. It was July of last year. There was an earthquake in Guatemala. That experience was very hard for me. There was a friend here, a midwife from Germany (Julie), and she was with me attending the birth. She had a lot of experience. I have a problem with delegating, but on that day, I did delegate.

The birth mother was also a friend of mine, from when we were quite young. She and her husband, we all grew up together. They're a very poor family but very special people. They have good energy and are spiritual and mature, too.

Julie checked the patient. I think she was four centimeters dilated. She came in at 4:30 in the morning, and the earthquake was at about 5:00. In the second examination, the tactile exam, we could feel the buttocks of the baby. But the first time, she had felt the head. So, the baby changed position, but it was her third baby. Hannah said, "There's enough space there for the baby to be born."

She was ready to push, but the baby wouldn't come out. We don't know why. So, we called the firemen to take the patient to the hospital, but they were fixing the road, and it took them a long time to get there. It normally takes five, ten minutes at the most. It took them seventy minutes to get there on that day, and they took them to the hospital, but the baby died on the way.

I don't know why that happened with them. I don't know why that baby didn't come out. I felt very guilty, because I hadn't been there from the beginning.

Learning Leadership with ALG

Thank goodness I was in the Association for Leadership in Guatemala [liderazgoguatemala.org/en] leadership course last year, because it was with their support that I was able to overcome this guilt. It was very difficult. My classmates in the course were incredible, very spiritual and with positive energy, and they have such interesting exercises that it fills you with positive messages. To have received that course was a blessing.

I thought I would learn about administrative things, and I did that as well, but, as a result of the course, my goal this year is to be able to understand myself as a person.

Sometimes we don't appreciate what we do. But after that, I looked upon my work differently. It *is* worthwhile doing what we do, and we shouldn't belittle our work. I started thinking that, when I first started attending births, sometimes I was alone, and nothing like that [death] had ever happened, ever. And on that day, there was a certified birth attendant, a well-studied one.

My thoughts now are that babies are born if they are meant to be born. There was no reason why that baby wouldn't be born. So, that's calmed me somewhat and helped my sadness, because I can't find any other explanation for all of the other babies to be born and for that baby not to have been born. I think God knows what he's doing.

I Rent a Little House with My Boy and Our Dog

I rent a little house in El Panorama. It's very close to Open Hands, only about five minutes. I live there with my twelve-year-old boy, Juan Sebastian. He's almost as tall as I am! [Laughs.]

When I was very young, maybe about five or six years old, I used to say that when I grew up, I would have a Volkswagen, a dog, and a son. I thought I'd be a vet, because I loved animals. I never included a husband in that vision—I don't know why.

One day, I was thinking about what I used to imagine when I was young, and I realized that I am a single mother with a blue Volkswagen Bug. We've got four cats, two that we've rescued, and two dogs that we've rescued. I thought, "Oh, God," and I told Juansie. I told him, "Dreams become a reality." It's incredible. I sometimes can't believe it myself.

Having My Son Changed My Life

When we decided to have Juansie, my life changed. Juan Sebastian has been my teacher in life. Everything that came with him is what I am now. The experience of his birth was with a birth attendant midwife, and it was very long—I was in labor three days, but it was a wonderful experience. I wouldn't change it for anything.

Juan Sebastian has Asperger syndrome, and he needs special education. But with him, I changed the whole pattern of bringing up children, the pattern that Guatemalans have.

I am a survivor of a lot of violence and a lot of machismo. I had to unlearn that form of bringing up children. So, I feel blessed to have a son like Juan Sebastian, because he's helped me to cultivate my patience and the more humane side of me. He's changed my life.

I hope, when my son is an adult, he will be able to live on his own. He's very good at painting, and he's done some oil paintings that are really good, but he likes a lot of other things as well. He is a good swimmer.

When he grows up, he wants to be a baker, because he's allergic to gluten. So, he wants to make gluten-free bread for children who can't eat gluten. He has some very good ideas.

Guatemala Is a Very Violent Society

I remember very little of the conflict of the civil war in my country. I think it was during the administration of President Arzú when the conflict ended, and I was eighteen. But we never studied about the conflict at school. I had the opportunity to go to the U.S. last year, and I received a class at the City University of New York, and they spoke more about the armed conflict in Guatemala than what I learned here at school.

I said, "How can that be? How can it be that in the States people know more about the armed conflict than the people living here?" If we want to heal, we have to start by knowing about our own history.

There's a lot of violence here. I have my own beliefs about this. Guatemala is a very violent country and society. I thought of my own experience, and I think we haven't yet healed from the armed conflict.

What Keeps My People Down? Religion, Government, and Alcoholism

But the reason is because most Guatemalans don't know their own history or story. It's as if religion has concealed that part of our lives. There's a lot of ignorance, and that's because religion wants to keep people ignorant. That's what I believe.

I don't know much about the influence of indigenous religions on our culture. What I've seen here is more the influence of the Catholic Church and the evangelical churches. There are some priests and pastors who are open-minded and want to help, but not most of them.

There are other factors as well. The rich people here are interested in keeping the people ignorant. For example, it's convenient that public services don't have contraceptives. People then will have more and more children and remain poor and ignorant. I think those are governmental strategies, because they're creating slaves, you could say.

My mother says I'm a bit crazy, but that's what I believe. And when I go out into the communities, I can see that too. There are people that have the power and control, and there are people like us who work every day to earn a living and don't have access to health services or family planning. They will continue having more and more children, and they're never going to progress like that. That leads to violence, too, and poverty and misery.

There's also a lot of alcoholism here. One of the most powerful families in the country owns the brewery. I think they want to keep beer cheap so that men are stupid all their lives. People are always talking about parties and parties. Men go to the corner shop every night and drink beer. We've lost the family values in which men contribute to the family. That part doesn't really exist here. Women have to work as well as looking after their families. So, there's a lot of stress in that, and that leads to violence.

Having a Peaceful Birth Can Change Your Life

In addition, most women go to give birth at the national hospital, and it's a traumatic experience, both for the mother and for the baby, and that will affect the future relationship between mother and child. I believe if you're born with violence, how can you hope to live without violence? The work of the midwives is very important, because it cultivates the awareness of the importance of where life begins.

One patient told me that, when her baby was born in the hospital, the baby didn't respond, and he was going blue in the face. He was weak and really in trouble. The doctor slapped the baby on the bottom, and the baby didn't respond. So, they poured cold water, water with ice, on the baby, and the baby still didn't respond. And do you know what they did for the baby to make him wake up and respond? They took a stapler and put a staple in his foot, and so the baby responded.

If you're born that way, how can you expect to have a pleasant life full of kindness? It's very different from the experience I told you about with the couple whose baby wasn't breathing. They respected their baby, and they told their baby how much they wanted him to be with them; they didn't slap or pour cold water on him or have a staple put in his foot. I think that's affected humanity in general.

My Wish for Myself and All Women: Resilience and Power

If I could wish anything for the women in Guatemala, I would wish that they could actually be owners of their own decisions and bodies. That would change women's lives socially and completely. That would help everything else to improve.

And for me, I'm not sure. There are a lot of things I want. I want a lovely family. I would like to have economic stability. But, most of all, I would like to take this year and find myself. I don't know why it's so difficult to really understand yourself.

People here never think about understanding themselves, women particularly. That for me would be really good. That would be a gift.

I believe God has always been with me throughout my life. Every time I had serious difficulties, I suffered a lot from depression, too, and I was able to pray to him, and I felt that he was with me. I feel his company wherever I go. And he has never separated from me. So, I believe in God and my family. I have no religion, but I do believe in God, and I know he exists.

There's a word that I like a great deal, and that's *resilience*. I think that's something a lot of women have. I used to complain a lot about having been born a woman. But I'm very grateful now that I was born a woman. We women have special powers.

I just feel that I've been very lucky, and that I am in the place where I belong, with the people that I need to be with. I have to be here.

If I had all the money in the world right now and didn't have to work, I would buy a big house for Open Hands, and I'd do exactly what I'm doing now for a very long time, for many years. This is my life.

And my legacy: I would like people to know that they can have a good birth and be respected in that birth. If I could achieve that, I think that would be a big change in the society.

There May Be a New Chapter in an Old Love Story for Me

Although I am single, there are many good men in my life. I have a friend who's like my mentor. He's a gynecologist, and he is already quite old; he could be my grandfather. He's my best male friend, I'd say, because I can talk to him. I can ask him about things related to my patients, and he's very respectful. So, I'm lucky. And Juansie, he's another man in my life. He's very sweet.

I would like to marry someday, but I think I'm not a very good person at choosing a partner. As you know, you can continue with the same patterns when choosing partners. It's difficult. So, I haven't been very lucky in that sense.

After I left Juansie's father, I met a friend that I'd known in high school. We tried to develop a good relationship for six years. At the end, he told me that he didn't want to get married to a Teresa from Calcutta, a "Mother Teresa." We tried for a long time to make it work, but he wanted me to resign from my job. He wanted to take care of me and of Juansie, but, no, I don't trust that. So, we separated.

Then, about a month ago, I bumped into my first boyfriend, Samuel, because of work. He works at a lab as a technician. A week after that we met again; he came by here with a bunch of flowers for me. I've been very excited about that over the last three weeks. We have a lot of things in common.

Samuel is now divorced. He has two children, a girl and a boy, ages twelve and eight. He's four years older than me. And thank God, he continues to be the good person that he always was and that I remember. So, it's a very nice part of my life, and I'm very grateful for that, too. We'll see where this goes . . .

We all have interesting stories. This is why your project [myjobstories .org] is very good.

Education
and
Finance

four

_____

NADINE

COLLEGE ADMISSIONS COUNSELOR

Kigali, Rwanda

Editor's note: When I met Nadine Niyitegeka, she was still a college student at the Akilah Institute for Women,[1] studying hospitality management, a major industry[2] in this verdant "Land of a Thousand Hills," nicknamed for its lush, hilly terrain.[3] She and a handful of other students facilitated my group's tour of cultural sites and NGOs (nonprofits), working on human rights and poverty alleviation; that's how I met her.

I would later learn that this poised, graceful girl with the beautiful smile had grown up with chronic hunger. Her mother worried that she would faint in the street during her two-hour daily walk to high school—but she persisted, because she felt sure that education was the ticket out of poverty.

"I want to help other girls to have the kind of chances I have," says Nadine. She graduated from Akilah and now works for the college as an admissions recruiter.

She says that 96 percent[4] of young women in Rwanda get married right out of high school without realizing they have other options. "If I share my story with other girls like me, maybe they will see that they can do it, too."

Actually, Nadine should not be alive at all. Just two years old in 1994 when the Rwandan Genocide[5] erupted, she and her family huddled in her uncle's home in Kigali, hiding from neighbors who wanted to kill them because of their ethnic heritage. This landlocked country, smaller than Maryland, in the center of the African continent—that already had endured centuries of occupation and poverty—experienced over three months of terror while the U.S. and the rest of the world stood by in feckless disbelief.[6]

Rwanda lost nearly half its population of seven million: one million killed[7] and another two million citizens displaced over one hundred days, from April to July. Nadine had been reported as murdered; she later found a photograph of herself hanging in the Kigali Genocide Memorial Centre, among the faces of other children slaughtered.

When you're Rwandan, I learned, you have to deal with three aspects of the genocide in every conversation with a new non-Rwandan acquaintance: where you were, what you lost, and how you've forgiven all people and nations in the years hence—that's if this person even has awareness of the atrocities, whose history spans far more than just those three months in 1994. You have to listen to people gasp in horror and imagine that *they* could never commit or endure such crimes.

Nadine takes us through her experience of the genocide, to frame the context of loss with which she began her early life. "I just wanted to reach my goal and to be able to help my family get out of their struggle," she says.

She's hardworking and sincere, equal parts unspoiled and idealistic. She sees her past self in every potential recruit she meets on her road trips across the high schools of Rwanda, and it breaks her heart to think Akilah cannot rescue them all.

I Went to College at Akilah Institute, and Now I Work Here

My name's Nadine Niyitegeka, and I'm twenty-three years old. I work at the Akilah Institute for Women in Kigali,[8] Rwanda. I work within the admissions department, recruiting students. I've had this job for a year and a half.

I was a student at Akilah. After graduation, I had an opportunity to work with the Kigali Marriott Hotel [an internship partner of Akilah], but at the same time, our college's country director and founder approached me and asked if I could go to work for Akilah, in recruitment. I decided to turn down Marriott and work for Akilah.

Akilah started its first class in 2010. I was in the second graduating class, and I'm now the second person to have this position. The person before me was also an alumna. She was a mother, and it wasn't very easy for her to go everywhere in Rwanda. I'm different, because I'm young and single. I'm very flexible to work any day, anytime.

My job requires me to tour the whole country, and then, I have to spend the night there. So, that's what I would say would be the difference between us. I learned a lot from her. She did a great job. She's still working for Akilah but in a different position.

I Go Out and Find New Students from All Over the Country

In my work, I make a plan on how to do recruitment, and then, I visit different high schools. I schedule appointments with high school headmasters and plan info sessions. I recruit students from all around the country and make presentations about our teachers and programs. We have diploma programs in hospitality management, entrepreneurship, and information systems (IS).

I'm responsible for all of Rwanda. There are a lot of high schools, but what I do is visit one whole area of the country in one trip or choose one kind of school to visit. For example, I recently visited fifty schools, and twenty-five of them were TVET [Technical Vocation Education Training[9]] schools.

Currently, we're recruiting them for our IS or information systems major. Those are the schools I've been targeting. They're coed secondary schools, but Akilah is dedicated to [only] women. So, most of the time, I was talking to the girls at these high schools.

I don't reach out to only the best-performing schools in Rwanda. I'm also trying to see the normal schools. I look for the best-performing girls in those types of schools, the girls who have potential and who strive to work really hard there.

How do we measure potential? By their grades and their strong desire to really further their studies. I meet with high school headmasters, and they give me this information. Some girls don't have good grades because of different difficulties that they've met within their home life, but I can offer them interviews so we can tell they have potential. So, we measure potential in three ways: the grades, the referral of the headmaster, and the interview.

What We Seek in Potential Students, and How We Find Them

Right now, we have five hundred students. I'm recruiting only 120 students for next year. I will interview at least five hundred applicants. Last year, we received 870 applicants for only 212 spots.

Those numbers don't come only from what I do. People can apply online, and it's also from word of mouth. Akilah is really becoming known in Rwanda.

In recruiting, I'm looking for confidence, basic English skills, and the ability to learn and study. I also had to do an interview to get admitted to Akilah; I had to meet these criteria. Even though I didn't really have confidence, I tried and tried to talk. So, that's why I say that you have to have a little bit of confidence, at least. There are a lot of girls looking for these opportunities at Akilah, and we want girls who really deserve them.

Our Sliding-Scale Tuition Helps Paying Students Support the Ultra-Poor Ones

When Akilah started, they targeted only low-income[10] students, but now we target everybody, because we saw that we were attracting a whole range of students from different backgrounds and families.

Now, they're paying school fees according to social status, economic data in our records. It is called *ubudehe*[11] [which means "collective effort" in Kinyarwanda] in my country. It is a socioeconomic status as demonstrated by the government. Everyone has to go to their local community leaders. According to an analysis, they will decide which kind of category you're in. And, if you're a student, you have to bring us this paper from the government, and then, we will tell you how much you will have to pay.

So, our students pay different amounts. We have three categories. It depends on how much per year the family earns and their living situation. There are people who have their own house. They're not struggling to pay rent or to get the basic necessities. They can eat three meals a day comfortably without any difficulties. Some of them even have a car. They are in the top category.

And then, you have the middle class who don't own a house, but they can at least pay rent, and they can get their basic necessities. They have someone in the family who works. So, that's the second or the middle category. They don't have a car.

Then, they have a third category in which people are struggling to get meals, to be able to eat, maybe having one meal a day, or having difficulty paying rent. When I went to Akilah, my family was in the third category, the low category.

My Typical Day at the Office or on the Road

On a typical day of work, I wake up at 6 a.m. I take a shower and prepare my breakfast. I pack up my work. I'm not always visiting schools. Sometimes, I work in the office, so I just go there. I use motorcycle transportation, like a scooter. I don't drive it; I get on the back. It's like a cheaper way [than a taxi or bus] and quicker. It's not very safe, though. [Laughs.] I try to tell them to go slowly.

I have to get to work at 8:00 in the morning. Then, I open my computer and check for emails. If it's Monday, I work on a to-do list for the week and see what are the priorities, what I didn't finish the previous week. I work from my calendars and check on my to-do lists, see what I have on my plate.

The busiest recruiting season is from October to May, because that's when the high schools are about to do their national exam tests. So, I have to make sure that they have Akilah on their minds before they graduate.

It's So Hard to Look into These Girls' Eyes and Say No to Them

The worst part of my job is seeing these girls looking in my eyes and asking me to help them. Everybody's like, "We want to come to Akilah." You can see in their eyes that they really want it. And then, we have to choose which girls are going to be admitted and which ones are not. And because I know what it means to be at Akilah, I don't really like seeing them not getting this chance. [Cries.]

I have to make the calls to tell them whether or not they were accepted. It's very sad. We can't accept all of them, because we're not so financially sustainable. We can't help them with their English or tell them why it didn't work for the next time they apply. Sometimes, we have to say no just because the places have been filled. The girls are good, and they have the ability to study, but we can't admit them because we can't exceed 120. Otherwise, we won't find classes for all of them.

The best part of my job is the other side of that coin: recruiting these girls and seeing them passing their interviews and getting admitted into Akilah. Sometimes, the recruits and even the current students come to me to ask for my advice. When I see their lives changing and not being the same as they were before, it makes me feel really good.

Growing Up in a Poor Family, with Chronic Hunger

I grew up in a poor family, raised by a single mother. My mother didn't really have the chance to study. She doesn't have a diploma because of different things, the history of the family that she grew up in. She was able to complete primary school and the first year of high school. That was it. She's smart, though. She can speak French. She can read and write, which is good, because that helped her to get housekeeping jobs in Rwanda.

She worked with foreigners as a housekeeper and cleaner, which helped her to raise us and give us the few basic needs. But sometimes, she didn't have a job, and we had to spend a period struggling to have lunch or dinner. That meant we could miss food for even two days.

It was kind of a tough childhood. Sometimes, we wouldn't have a house, because we couldn't pay the rent. Sometimes, I had to drop out of my school, because my mom couldn't pay my school fees. She didn't have only me: I have three siblings. I am the second oldest.

My Father: It's Complicated

My father is kind of a long story. I didn't get to know him. He's still alive, and he's still married to my mom. They had us, but they didn't get along. Even though he was in the country, he didn't want to take care of us. He didn't even want to come to see us. So, that's it. They never formally divorced, because they didn't get legally married.

My sister and I tried to ask our mom, "Did our dad die, or is he still alive?" but she would never tell us about him. She wouldn't even show us a picture, so I could see his face. She would say, "It's kind of complicated. Your father's alive, but he doesn't want to come and see you. I don't know why either."

I actually met my dad once. I tried to ask him why he didn't want to care about us. He had money. He was a very respected man in my country. But he didn't answer my question, unfortunately, and I still don't know why he didn't want to care about me even though he had the opportunity to do so. He was working for the government with very good titles. He was even once like an ambassador in one country.

How Do You Explain the Atrocity in My Country?

People who don't know Rwanda, it is located in East Africa, and it's one of the countries which had the biggest atrocities in the world, the biggest genocide[12] in the world.

It happened in 1994. The bad leadership that was there at the time was trying to differentiate people because of their ethnic background. We had two ethnic groups at the time, Hutus and Tutsis. Tutsis were the ethnic group that was supposed to be killed at that time, and Hutus were the ones that were supported by the leadership. So that leadership tried to sensitize them to show how Tutsis are very bad, Tutsis are rich and beautiful and trying to take over things. The Hutus kind of agreed, and they accepted to murder the other group without questioning.

I don't really remember a lot. I was two years old. We weren't living in the capital city [Kigali] at the time, but we had come to visit our uncles there that night before the genocide, before the president's plane crashed[13] and the atrocity began.

Surviving the Genocide as a Toddler

On April 6, 1994, we came to Kigali to visit my mom's brothers. They were so young, around the age I am now. The plane that carried President Habyarimana Juvénal[14] crashed that night, so things became very bad. Immediately, the roads were blocked by killers.

You started hearing people shouting, a lot of noise, and then, because it was on the radio, our uncles were like, "Maybe this is the time that things are going to be worse."

My uncles suspected that people were going to come to look for them, because it was being said on the radio; so, they decided to leave and go hide somewhere.

I saw my uncles leaving. They were so afraid, shaking and saying, "We have to leave," because with the genocide, they were planning to kill the young men first, and then the rest of the men, and then kids and mothers later. My uncles were very young at the time. They were the age I am now.

I remember one of them tried to carry me on his shoulders. He turned around and said to my mom, "I see you have a lot of kids here." We had three kids at that time. So, maybe they would take one—me. "I'll try to help you," he said.

But when he got in front, he saw the soldiers with machetes. He was so afraid. He brought me back. He told my mom, "I cannot. I don't want to be guilty of your daughter being killed."

Then, a group of soldiers came for my uncles. They were knocking at the door very strongly, loudly. They're like, "Where are the cockroaches? Where are the cockroaches?" That means Tutsis. Tutsis were called "cockroaches" at the time.

We were left alone in their house.

The next day, a group of militias with machetes and guns came and pushed in the door of my uncles' house. They entered and found my mom, my sister, my brother, and me in the house. They asked my mom, "Where are the cockroaches (meaning my uncles)?"

They were threatening her. She said, "There's no one in this house. There are no men. There are no young boys in this house, just me and my kids."

They tried to look all over the house. And then, they came out really angrily, and one of their leaders asked them, he was like, "I didn't hear any noise. You didn't do anything?" and they said, "No, there's no men. Just an old woman and her kids." I don't know why they called my mom old at that time, because she was very young. She was twenty-eight.

My mom thought to herself that, if they come back, they will kill us. She saw people running outside and asked them, "Where are you going?"

They replied, "Church!" They were referring to a Catholic church, which was a twenty-minute walk from where we were.

So, we followed them, hoping that we would be safe. When we got there, we learned that people were already being abused . . . But we had no other choice. We entered the church, because at least it had a roof. We spent three months there.

Killers came to that church every day to look for people to kill. Later on, a bomb was thrown into the church. My mom had taken my infant brother (who was three months old) outside, and my sister followed. I stayed inside, because there was a group singing, and I enjoyed it. My mom suddenly saw that the church was on fire.

She came running and said to herself, my kid is done I know, but let me go find her dead body at least. Inside the church, people started screaming; their hands were cut off. I hid in the corner.

When the noise quieted down, they heard someone sniffing. It was me, covered in dust. They took me outside asking, "Whose kid is this?" My mom was so surprised and happy to find me again.

Another thing I remember is that someone accidentally poured hot water on me, so my arm was burnt. My mom tried her best to find a way for me to get to the clinic. Luckily, a nun helped us get there, and I was given first aid and got some medicine to treat me. But my mom was almost killed on the way, because they kept stopping the car that we were in and asking the nun, "Where are you taking that cockroach?" She begged them and explained that she has a kid (me) who was burnt, so please have mercy. Luckily, we arrived at the clinic and got back.

My mom and two of my siblings and I survived. We lost our grandpa, and my aunts and uncles. I am glad to be alive and be sharing the story.[15]

Now [currently, by law[16]], you cannot ask me if my family was from one tribe or the other. It is not permitted. I'll say this: It's not okay to ask, because now my country's really trying to heal, and we don't want to see ourselves as one person or the other. People know the story, I think. People can tell.

My Stepfather Was Murdered

I was quite young when my mother fell in love again. What I remember about this guy is that he was so caring and so happy. He didn't care that we weren't his kids. He was really taking very good care of us. When we were sick, my mom would call him instead of our dad, and he would come and help. Unfortunately, he was murdered in the genocide.

Actually, they were planning to get married, he and my mom. They weren't married at the time because he had to get a divorce from his first wife. He went there at that time to get a divorce and clear out everything. He meant to come back so that they could plan what day and everything. But he didn't come back. We heard the story afterward.

But There Were Also Good Times in My Childhood

But there were also good times in my childhood. My mom was so caring and loving. She's still like that. Even though we really didn't have a lot at home—almost nothing—she would play with us and take us to church.

It was a Protestant church, and it was a big part of my life, because that was a place of love, where people cared about each other. We prayed, sang, and danced. I was part of the dancing group. It was a charge, a release. We'd be with other kids and also play in the neighborhood.

At that time, we rented a very small house made of mud with one bedroom and one living room, no water running inside the house and no electricity. But our house was just like the other houses around us, so we didn't mind.

There were times when my mother couldn't pay rent. Sometimes, she would ask her friends to host us while we tried to look for other means. We would then find a cheaper house, and she tried to look for other jobs, so she could be able to pay that. It was hard. Sometimes, the owners of the house would be civil. They would wait like three months, four months until my mom would find the money to pay them. It was kind of a struggle.

Taking Care of My Brothers, and Playing Sports with the Boys

As a young girl growing up, I had to take care of my young brothers. I washed dishes and cleaned the house. I had to go fetch water. I was kind of a tomboy. Sometimes, I used to fight with other kids on the playground. I don't know why, but I felt inferior or something. I tried to defend myself all the time, show them who was boss. Trying to get them to accept my idea and whatnot. But I wasn't always that way.

Other times, I was trying to be social. I really liked playing and dancing and all that. We had traditional games, with sticks and balls, on courts drawn in circles in the dirt. I also played football with the boys. I liked hanging out with boys. I was the only girl on the team. We made the ball out of plastic bags at the time. We couldn't afford anything else. We didn't even know about [manufactured] balls. I was so happy playing with that ball.

It would sometimes get unfixed, so everyone had to bring plastic bags or rubber bands or the ropes to tie it together. It was a very good thing, working as a team, trying to bring a piece yourself to contribute. And the boys accepted me, because I was trying to be a good football player. I kept playing football until high school, but then I switched and played basketball. I wasn't that professional; I was just doing it for fun.

I learned a lot growing up in that kind of life. As I grew up, my life started getting better. It's kind of sad to look back, but it was a lesson that no matter what kind of challenges we go through, you can get to a bright future. I was educated, and I got a job, a good job, after graduating. I'm able to support my family. That makes me happy.

Walking to School with No Food in My Stomach

I went to a private high school for just one year, and then, it was too much for my mother to afford. So, I had to stay in the public school. I really struggled with math and physics. But I was good at arts, languages, history, and geography.

When I was thirteen, I had to walk for two hours without food in my stomach to get to school. Other students would get dropped off. It was very hard to do such a thing.

At that time, my mother didn't have a job. The school didn't serve lunch. You had to get lunch for yourself, but I didn't have something to pack. So, I didn't have lunch. Then, I had to leave class at 2:40 in the afternoon and go back home. Sometimes, we didn't have dinner or breakfast. But I did it, because I just wanted to reach my goal and to be able to help my family get out of their struggle and help myself.

Where Did I Get the Drive to Carry On?

I had something inside me that told me to do this. Some girls in my neighborhood were trying to get a very good life, to put on nice clothes and just have an easy life. But what I wanted to do, since I was a child, was to be on my own and defend myself and be independent. So, I thought, to be able to reach that, I have to be educated.

I had dreams. Specifically, I wanted to become a lawyer. As a child, I always wanted to defend myself and others, and I hated injustice so much. I was thinking, if I could be a lawyer, I would try to help people who were looking for justice. I saw kids being abused or not getting their rights, or women who were abused because they were women or because of no reason. I thought those kind of people needed my help.

Wanting to Make Sure No One Gets Abused, Ever Again

I remember, when I was like twelve, there was a little neighbor boy. [Crying; takes a tissue.] Thank you. This one neighbor, her kid lost a coin, a coin of about one hundred shillings. That's not even a quarter. For losing that tiny amount of money, the neighbor took an iron, and she put it on this kid's belly and burned him.

This kid came to our house. His mother told him, "Don't tell anyone." He was about eight years old. He showed us. I tried to ask him about it. He told me what happened. He was like, "Don't tell anyone, because my mother will kill me."

I didn't know what to do at the time, but that image kept burning in my mind. I kept asking how this kid was doing. Recently, I heard that he didn't want to study. I think the damage done by his mother was very unjust and very bad. So, that's why I was thinking that maybe I'd be a lawyer.

Serendipity Sent Me from My Grocery Store Job to Akilah College

After high school, I immediately got a small job in a grocery store. I really liked working in an environment when I could see different people and go do things. And, of course, I was also contributing to my family income.

My boss's son Christian was attending university. The director of Akilah went and presented at his university, talking about Akilah and how it was coming to Rwanda. Christian immediately thought of me. So after the presentation, he came over to the store. He said, "Nadine, I want to talk to you." I was completely scared, in my heart. I thought, "What did I do?"

And he said, "Nadine, I have good news for you." I remember that I was very shy, looking down and playing with a bottle. It was kind of hard to talk to an older boy, the owner's son. He was like my boss. I'm like, "Okay, what's that?"

He said, "I was observing you, how you work for us, and I think you have potential." That was the first time someone told me that in my life, *you have potential.* I was like, "Okay."

I didn't believe him. He said, "I heard about a school coming here to Rwanda, and it's accepting women and girls who want to follow their studies, and I think you'll like it."

I said, "Yeah, I'd really love to study there. The problem I have is that I cannot afford it."

And he said, "This school is offering 85 percent tuition. You can try to get the 15 percent or try to work after school." And he said, "You have to do an interview and a test."

I said, "Wow. What test? Do I have to do the test *and* the interview in English?"[17]

He told me, "This school has been founded by an American. So, you will meet some foreigners. They will probably interview you."

I was like, "Christian, I cannot do this. I've only studied in French." My English, at that time, wasn't really that strong. I had only broken English.

And then, he said, "Yeah, you can just try it. I can help you, teach you how to behave during an interview."

That's how I got to know about Akilah. [Begins to cry.] Christian introduced me to his father, the owner. He invited me for tea. [Blows her nose.] He told me afterward, "My father really liked you. He thinks you're smart, and he thinks you have potential, too."

They trusted me. I was the person who took the money to the bank and helped them in the office. I was working as a grocery store assistant, but sometimes they also asked me to help them with other things.

So, I went to apply, and then, I did the exam, the interview, and the test. And I passed! They called me after two weeks, like, "Congratulations, Nadine. You are admitted."

I was very, very happy. Then, I told him, "Guess what? I was admitted."

He didn't seem surprised. He said, "Nadine, it's no big deal. You can go further than this. I believe in you." He was like, "You just have to work hard."

I was like, "Wow."

Then, I Became Christian's Wedding Planner

Christian did some of his studies in the United States, in Boston. And then, he came back, and he completed university. Then, he got engaged to be married. He asked me to help him with his wedding preparations.

That was in my second year of Akilah. I was studying hospitality management, and I was about to graduate.

On my graduation day, I had a party at my home. It was one of my greatest achievements. I invited the other girls at Akilah to help me with the hospitality and serving. I told them what the dress code would be, and I planned the decorations. Christian liked how my party came all together.

It wasn't that expensive, because I didn't have the money at the time, just these simple things—but he thought it was great.

After being at my graduation party, he said, "I really like how you're so organized. I think you are a good event planner." He said, "I can't even pay you as a wedding planner. I can't afford to—"

I said, "No, you don't have to." This would be like a gift to me, to be able to do something for him after he helped me get into Akilah. So, I became his wedding planner. I didn't know I could do that! I collected support [donations], because when you get married in Rwanda, people support you. And he liked it. Their wedding had seven hundred people.

Later, Christian owned a petrol station, then a fertilizer company. He's very, very smart and very entrepreneurial. At the fertilizer company, he asked me to be his assistant, to help him organize his meetings, receive calls, analyze the markets, and report to him.

I didn't know anything about office work. But he trained me. It was a part-time job, and it really helped me with paying my school fees, my 15 percent share. Even though it was only 15 percent, it was $500, and to my mom and me, that was a lot.

When I talk about Christian, I get very emotional. This is the person who believed in me for the very first time. He's my role model. He was the person who showed me the way. He kept pushing me. He was like, "Nadine, you can do this." So, that's why. [Cries.]

How Akilah Strives to Be Different in a Developing Economy

Akilah was the first college for women in my country. Now, there are five universities and other higher institutions.

[Nadine blows her nose, asks for water. "I'm sorry. I'm making a mess." Talking about the past seems to make her experience all of it again.] When I was a student here, no matter what they asked me to do, I had to do it. Eventually, I would graduate. So, I kept pushing myself, trying and trying.

Akilah has a very unique educational model. It depends on [donations from and partnerships with] the private sector. Akilah has a very, very good relationship with the private sector. They went and interviewed people who owned companies in different fields. They asked, "What exactly are you looking for when you're hiring someone, today or in five years to come?" These businesspeople told them what kind of skills and knowledge were necessary. So, Akilah built a model around that information.

Also, students can access various books and computers and do research on the Internet. Students study in groups, where they can help each other, like if you might be weak in math, and someone is strong in English. No one has to struggle alone.

A student has to contribute 70 percent in a class session. There is no lecturing where someone just comes in and stands in front of you talking for two hours. Everyone takes turns standing in front of a classroom and giving a presentation. We studied communication skills, business skills, and technology skills, which are very relevant to today's market, and everybody has to give an idea about the topic.

The education that I received at Akilah was more interactive than I expected. I wasn't used to that. In my primary and high school, the teacher would just stand in front of you and talk at you for like two hours, and you would write it down and memorize it, then you would go out.

Here, you get hands-on practice. You get to know what you're doing practically and technically. At Akilah, I've learned by doing. When you have to stand up in front of a classroom and present, you increase your critical thinking. If the teacher is asking you to talk about a new lesson, you have to think very hard to be able to participate.

Who's Inspired Me So Far in Life

Christian was the first person who saw my potential and taught me in my life. The second person was my leadership teacher here at Akilah.

According to our traditional culture, women didn't used to speak up, because we thought it wasn't socially acceptable. Then once, when I was a student, I gave an idea about the lessons of leadership in my favorite class. The topic was what makes a good leader. And I raised my hand. I was like, "I think a good leader listens to her followers and not only makes her own decisions but also according to what her followers need."

The teacher really praised me. She said, "Nadine, that is brilliant. Wow, you have good ideas." I reflected on what Christian told me. I thought: probably that's true.

Communicating Is #1, and Giving Back to the Community Is #2

I'm a person who doesn't like to sound like I'm talking nonsense. So, I had to really work hard and use my brain a lot so that I could succeed at Akilah. Our model creates and builds a team spirit, and it also teaches things, such as how to write a business email, how to communicate clearly, how to present yourself in an interview, how to be a group leader. Whether you have your own business or are working for someone else, you still have to know how you would deal with clients and other workers. So, this was a very good experience to me.

I also did community service as part of my program. I worked on two different activities as the team leader of my group. We worked with the Diabetes Association, where we helped create hope for people with diabetes.

We also worked with street kids in an orphanage, teaching English and hygiene. It's hard for some kids to stay there, because they feel it's like a prison. They're not free anymore. And you are telling them the importance of education, asking them their goals and their dreams and why they want to achieve these things. We'd help them draw a picture of what they want to become in the future.

I remember this one boy who made a snake. We asked this boy, why a snake? He said, "Because snakes hate people, and they can bite," and I asked him why. He said, "Because I want to kill people when I grow up."

It was a very powerful thing to hear from a kid. I kept asking why, but he couldn't tell me.

Turns out that when he was growing up, his stepmother abused him. So, he didn't feel loved. He felt like people were not nice humans. But we talked with him, and then, he kind of changed his mind. I saw how it's very important for us to give to other people.

How I've Changed Compared to the Girls I Grew Up With

When I began at Akilah, I was like any other girl who joined Akilah for the first time—not a lot of confidence, no English, no future goals or plans. I was a bit shy. I didn't want to talk in class, but my teachers kept insisting, "You have to talk. You have to give an idea" and all this.

Slowly, I did start to participate, and I saw a change in myself. I started thinking about my future, having plans and having goals, believing in myself. I worked hard, and pretty soon it was a big change. Even at home, my mom and friends would tell me, "I never recognize you anymore. You're acting differently."

To me, I took that as a compliment.

Like with my friends: They used to come over and talk for three hours. But then, I started seeing what's a priority and how to use time wisely. So, I would say, "We're going to do this for this hour, and then, you're going to leave. I'm going to read my book or watch this documentary, because I want to learn and grow."

Then, they'd go, "Oh, Nadine, why?" They couldn't understand. I started to see a big difference between me and these other friends who didn't go to college.

I remember once I went to a wedding, and there was a group of young men standing by themselves. The girls were on the other side. I was like, "Why don't I just go see what they're talking about?"

I went in and joined, and I said, "I disagree with you." And then, everyone looked at me like, "What is this girl doing here?" They were arguing about men and women. For example, in their home, they don't have to wash and help their wives.

And I said, "You are partners. No one is a slave of each other. You need to help each other. You love each other. That's not the meaning of a wife, some helper. It's someone you want to start and end life together with, if you're that fortunate." I made my point strongly. I said, "This thing has to end in every young man's mindset."

As a Result of Akilah, I'm Ambitious and Outspoken

As a result of my education, I would say I'm ambitious, and I'm more outspoken. I can fight for my rights. I'm courageous. I didn't know what it means to work hard, but now I understand. I now believe in myself, which is confidence. I respect time and authority.

To me, my diploma is a symbol of power. It's not only a diploma: It's the skills and dreams that I have now. I want to have a good job and be someone important for me and try to help my country. I'm very confident that I can be whatever I want to become, reach my goals and then make them bigger and bigger. Despite all the things that happened in my country and to my family, I think I could help bring a change.

I've Traveled to the U.S. and Asia with This Job

Since I've worked for Akilah, I have also traveled to four countries: Burundi, Malaysia, Hong Kong, and the United States. Akilah also plans to expand soon into Uganda.

Ten months after I joined Akilah, they were looking for a girl who could be a representative for the school to go to Hong Kong and help with fundraising. That's where Akilah's CEO and founder, Elizabeth

[Dearborn-Hughes], lives most of the year with her husband and little children.

I was chosen to go and help with fundraising. It was my first time to leave Africa. I was excited to help Akilah as well as explore other big cities of the world. I stayed there for two weeks. Then, I had to go to Malaysia for a week for a global conference called "Women Deliver."

All those experiences were like a dream coming true. I called Christian when they selected me. And he was like, "I told you." [Laughs.] He said, "Yeah, you can go even further." He says that to me every time I accomplish something: that I can go further.

I Support My Whole Family

I'm the only one who works in my family. My salary is $400 per month. So, I pay for everything—the food, rent, health insurance, school fees for my younger brothers, other necessities that they might need.

My family is not living in a mud hut anymore. I moved them after I got a job. Now, they live in a better house, right in Kigali. We were all staying in one room before, but now there are three bedrooms and one living room. My mom has a private room. The girls have their private room; the boys do, too. And we even have a room for visitors and guests.

Right now, I'm not able to save money. I would love to, because I really have a lot of goals and dreams to achieve. But I can't right now.

Compared to other Rwandan salaries, it's not a bad salary. It's a fair wage for what I'm doing. It's a starter. And Akilah tries to be fair in their salaries even though they're a nonprofit. They try to pay a reasonable amount of salary. It pays for a lot of things.

How My Life Will Be in Ten Years: Career Plus Family

I'd love to have a family in ten years. Professionally, I'm working to get to a higher position. I believe there are a lot of opportunities in Akilah, because it's a growing nonprofit. Meanwhile, I really want to further my studies, because I think my goals require more studies. That's why I'm worried that I'm not saving now, because I want to be able to pay for my school. Even if I'm getting a higher position or doing another thing, maybe in government or anywhere else, it will require more skills and knowledge.

For fun, I do traditional and modern dancing. I dance in church and also for fun. At Akilah, I was part of a dance group. As for music, I like R&B, classic, and country, Rwandan and Western and American songs: I like everything.

In many ways, more than just music, I guess I'm sort of a global girl. I'd say that's just because I had a big chance and a big opportunity to travel around the world. Not that many East African girls get to travel and see what I've been able to see, so far.

Achieve Power in Order to Empower

My vision is to be an advocate for other African girls. I want to keep advocating for girls so that they can be able to be educated and have the opportunities that I had.

I'd love to have my own business. That's one of my own dreams, to open my own business, maybe to become head of UN Women[18] in East Africa. I would be a big advocate for women and girls or any other people who may need my help.

In order to achieve these goals, I don't think I would pursue a law degree. I think I would take on another type of degree. I hope maybe one day I will be a Minister of Gender Inequality or serve as a member of Parliament for my country. I have met a few of these women leaders; they are very hardworking and inspiring. In this position, you can educate, empower, and care for women and girls.

Traveling the World and Helping Others — Starting with Education

I'd also love to travel to other countries. I really like to learn from different people. I'd like to travel to Haiti, Bangladesh, and Asia and see how life is different . . . Bosnia, Europe . . . Based on this trip that I made last time, I saw a big change. It was eye-opening to see how people in other countries or other feminists live their daily life.

If I had all the money in the world, I would help other people in need. I would use my time to get to them and see if I can help. Maybe I would found a loan refundment NGO [nonprofit], try to help people get loans for higher education.

I would also buy a house for my family. I would help my siblings to keep going to school, so they can have a better life. I would take care of my mom, because she's getting older, and physically she's not as able to do things.

I would also use this money to have a good time with my family! Not for myself; I don't really like living a luxury life. What matters is if I have all the necessities and to see my family happy and myself reaching my goals and dreams. That would be enough for me.

Nothing is easy. Every important thing has to be worked for, and a lot of time and energy and everything are required to achieve what we wish. It is always important, in my opinion, not to think of yourself only but also to think about others, how we can improve society and our surroundings, make the world a better place.

five

———

KELLY

ENGLISH TEACHER

Daegu, South Korea

Editor's note: Kelly Kang's country is smaller than the state of Indiana, population fifty million. It feels really small, and the funny thing about South Korea (hereafter referred to as "Korea") is that, except for about twenty thousand Chinese immigrants, just about everyone is Korean. It's the most homogenous country I've ever seen.

However, because Korea's success in trade and economy has required doing a lot of business in English, the study of the English language has in itself become a big business here. So, you also get a smattering of Americans and Europeans in their twenties and thirties, here on work visas, teaching[1] the sons and daughters of Korea's devoted parents to speak the language of commerce. My niece Brienne has lived here for two years, teaching English to earn good money that allows her to live abroad while paying off her U.S. college loans. Brienne works with Kelly: That's how I met "Kelly Teacher," as her students call her.

We tour the school, then walk next door to a place called The World Café. We order lattes and share some goopy sort of waffle. Outdated American pop music blares in the background, occasionally punctuated by the ring of a customer's cellphone or the whine of the espresso machine.

In some ways, Kelly seems classic Korean.[2] She's schoolgirl pretty, with long, thick, wavy hair and a blushing smile. She shows up to our interview all buttoned up in a lacy blouse with a proper collar. She's wearing a demure skirt with her legs fully covered in thick black tights. Modest and unassuming, prim and proper, she fits all my stereotypes of the good Asian girl. She seems utterly innocent and obedient, incapable of any sort of defiance and individuality that American children might express.

Born two generations after her country was decimated by the 1950s Korean War, and at the end of a postwar period of tremendous economic growth, Kelly and her peers now face such post-industrial challenges as a growing gap between the rich and the poor, environmental degradation, and low birth rates. She talks about low wages in comparison to rising prices and the difficulty she and other young Koreans experience in securing employment. Even though she plans to get married and have children, she's an anomaly among her peers: She says most young Koreans plan to stay single, simply because they can't afford to get married and support a family.

This summer, Kelly will marry her boyfriend of six years. Her fiancé, Cho-Kun, is in divinity school, studying to be a Baptist minister. Kelly had a conversion experience five years ago while in college in China. Many Koreans (46 percent) claim no religious faith at all—and that's how Kelly was raised. But her discovery of God, she says, turned her from a person who was chronically irritated and unkind into a perennially happy person who loves children, her students, and life.

Kelly is truly sweet, both loving of and beloved by her students. "My heart is sore for them," she sighs when she sees them lugging their heavy backpacks home and looking exhausted at the end of another long day and night of school. She worries about her students having no freedom and being forced to study by their overzealous parents.[3]

Although we conduct the entire interview in English, Kelly ends up apologizing. "I'm so sorry," she tells me. "If you return next year, I will study English so we can talk more." She often says "right" and "mmm" in agreement.

She blushes and laughs, with her hand covering her mouth. And what she does next will forever endear this girl to me: She invites me to her wedding in July. "Please; I really mean it. You must come back," she says. I sincerely wish that I could.

I'm an English Teacher

My Korean name is Jung Eun Kang, and my English name is Kelly Kang. I'm twenty-seven years old. I live in the city of Daegu, which is in southeastern Korea. My formal title is "student consultant." I'm a manager of students at Chungdahm Learning Institute (CDI).

My job is to manage the students and teach them English. I check their homework, their attendance, and their schedule. I grade their online homework and their tests. I also work as a communicator between the parents and the teachers. So, if there's a problem with a student, I'll tell their teacher, or the students will call me and talk to me, and then I will talk it over with the teacher.

I've worked here for eight months. Our city branch of CDI has

1,300 students. There are maybe fifteen consultants working here as the core teachers.

I'm in charge of several different classes at one time. Monday and Thursday, I have five classes, and Tuesday and Friday, I have four classes. Wednesday and Saturday, I have two classes, but those are very small classes. I'm assigned 125 students.

But I remember every student's name! [Laughs.] At first I worried about that, "How can I remember their names?" but I do. I really love them. So, I remember. [Laughs.] Also, they hang out together in social groups of friends, so I can think of them that way. Every time I walk into the classroom, it's like, "Kelly Teacher! Kelly Teacher!" I feel they love me, too.

I Had a Normal and Happy Childhood

I think I had a pretty happy childhood. I have a mom, dad, and a younger brother. My father's name is Sun-Kwang Kang. He is fifty-five and works at Sony as a computer programmer. He makes a lot of money—but it's not mine! I have to earn my own. [Laughs.]

My mom is fifty-four. Her name is Kim Young-Hee. When I was young, she taught kindergarten, and then, when I was eight and went to elementary school, she retired. She wanted to stay home with me. She helped me with everything. She's now a housewife. She's always cleaning, and she likes to cook.

I don't cook. [Laughs.] My mom cooks Korean traditional food, like *bulgogi*. That's a kind of meat dish, grilled marinated beef with side dishes. She makes bulgogi burgers. She also makes *doenjan jjigae*; it looks like soup and has tofu, vegetables, and potatoes. We also have a traditional dish, *banchan*, little dishes of boiled foods that you eat with rice. I think for people from other countries, it smells very bad. It tastes very hot. My mom cooks all these things. She's a really good cook.

My younger brother is twenty-six years old, one year younger than me. His name is Jung-Min. He graduated from university and works in a city just outside Daegu.

When I was a kid, I played the piano and read books. I liked reading novels. [American] Noam Chomsky was my favorite author. I liked hanging out with my friends, talking on the phone and on Instant Messenger.

I went to public schools before university. In middle school, I went to a math academy and English academy and then a public high school. We didn't have time for anything but studying. I went to school at 7:30 a.m. We finished and finally went home at 10:00 p.m. We had classes where teachers taught us from 9:00 to 6:00 p.m. From 6:00 to 7:00 p.m., we ate dinner at school, and then from 7:00 to 10:00 p.m., we just studied by ourselves at school. Then, we went home.

The Problem with Education in Korea

Some parts of my education were good; some were weak. This is typical for my country. The teachers stand up in front of the students, writing on the blackboard. Students just look at their notes. They are just writing, remembering, then testing.

If their test grades were good, the student went up to the next level. If their test grades were bad, they were simply considered to be bad students. I think this is a problem caused by the government here.

Ideally, there should be communication between students and teachers. Students should be able to share what they think. In my elementary school, middle school, and high school, everybody felt that all of the students should study hard and go to university. That's okay if you *want* to go to university: Everyone who wants to should be able to go. But if I wanted to learn to play the piano or the violin during high school, I didn't have a chance to study that. There was no time for extra activities or physical education. I just had to study math and science for university.

It's Gotten Even Worse for Students These Days

Now, the students at CDI work even harder than I did at that age. At least I got to choose my job, but they don't choose their life! Not at all. Their parents choose their schedule. They just go to school, eat, go to bed, and sleep. When my students finally finish their academic classes and leave to go home, I look at them as they go. They are very tired. They don't have any power [energy] left.

They move very slowly. They go, "Bye-bye, Teacher." They have a big bag, and they take all their stuff and go home. When I look at them, I feel like their life is very sad. My heart is sore for them.

It's Different Here: Interactive and Fun

But I also think that, compared to regular schools here in Korea, our program at CDI is so fun! The kids have much to do. The students and teachers have so many communications. They talk together all the time. The teachers are not just in front of the blackboard writing, like in most schools.

Often, we teachers get very tired, because our students are noisy and active. The students here are generally interactive. They have many chances to speak and participate in fun activities. For example, when we studied *The Arabian Nights* [a collection of Middle Eastern and South Asian folklore tales], they got into small groups to debate or discuss what wishes we would ask if we would ever meet a genie. A lot of them wished to go home. [Laughs.] Some others wished to have no more retests.

At CDI, if a student misses a certain amount of points on a test, they have to take a retest on that material. They really hate that. They have to take the retest up on the sixth floor, and then, after that, they can go to their [usual] class.

Also, in our classes, they go in front of the other students and make presentations. Sometimes, we take pictures, or we use a tablet to record a video that we then send by email to their parents. I think the students like this a lot.

Going to University in China and Contemplating Life

I went to a private school for university. I was on a scholarship that gave me a choice: One was to go to America; the other was to go to China. But I didn't want to study English! [Laughs.] So, I went to China to study at Shandong University. I was twenty-two when I went there. Shandong is just across the Yellow Sea from Korea, in between Beijing and Shanghai. I was about an hour-and-a-half airplane ride from Korea. My father wasn't near me, but he was also working in China at the time. When I was twenty-five, I returned to Korea.

I have more freedom as a woman in Korea, but in China, I had more freedom of time. I had long periods on my own. So, I read many books and thought about *me*. For example, who am I? Why am I here studying Chinese? If I graduate from university, what do I want to be? Do I really like this major? Why did I choose to major in journalism and advertisement, and so on.

After I Got a Degree in Advertising, I Discovered I Didn't Like It

For my first job out of university, I worked as an advertising executive (AE) at an agency in Daegu. I had majored in advertising and journalism. But as it turned out, I don't like advertisement agencies. I think advertising says the good points, but they don't say the bad points. I think this is not right.

For example, if we have a coffee, say this coffee [gestures toward her cappuccino], some part of it might be good, and some part is bad. But advertising would say that the good part is *very* good, but the thing is that it's just okay. I think this is not right. So, after I worked a while at an advertisement agency, I left and changed my job.

It was not a big agency. The director was very young, just thirty. There were so many drinkers there! I hate that. I just wanted to finish my work and go home. When I'm all by myself at home, I get comfortable, take a shower, read, listen to music, and meet up with my boyfriend. But with this advertising agency, I didn't have any time, *my* time. We would finish work, and then, everybody would always go out drinking. I didn't like this. So, I changed jobs.

I Worked at a Travel Agency That Made Me Sick

Next, I worked at a travel agency. I translated for them from Korean into Chinese. Nowadays, so many Chinese travelers come to Daegu City: They come here for healthcare and medical treatments. So, I used to translate for them. We had a passport/visa program. I assigned them their visa, their airplane, and their hotel.

At the travel agency, we worked in a very small office. We had just three rooms. In one room, some directors smoked. It was a very bad, stressful environment. I had so much acne. My face was so red. It was really serious. I had to visit the doctors at the clinic for four months after that. And I had heart problems due to the stress. My heart was enlarged, and my heart rate was elevated.

It was very stressful. I didn't know what I could do. It was just stress, stress, and more stress. All I wanted to do was sleep.

So, I left that job last year, in July. I lived with my parents, so if I didn't work for a while, they would take care of me. But it was only a month in between that job and this one. I took a holiday in Singapore, just for fun. I liked Universal Studios—I loved the *Transformers*[4] ride. [Laughs.] And then, I started working at CDI in August.

My Day as a Teacher, from Start to Finish

At 9:00, I wake up. I go to the gym and exercise and then eat breakfast. I might take a little rest time to read a book. Then, I take a shower, and I take a bus to work, or sometimes my boyfriend drives me here. I arrive at CDI at 2:00 p.m. to start work.

First, I check the students' homework. I tell them, "You didn't do your homework. So, start studying. You need to finish your homework." I call some students' moms and consult with them every day about what the students are studying, what grades they're getting, and how is their attitude.

At 4:00, the junior classes start. These are kids from third to sixth grade. I check attendance and check in with their parents if need be. At around 6:00, I eat some dinner. I just bring in food that my mom cooked at home. At 7:00, the juniors finish, and the seniors, the sixth to eighth graders, start their time. I check attendance. We have a five-minute rest time. During these five minutes, we use the time to call on some students to ask them why they didn't do their homework or ask how was their day, how is their stress level. We finish at 10:00. At 11:00, I arrive at home, and I have my time. At maybe 1:00 or 2:00 a.m., I'm asleep.

We have a TOEFL class. TOEFL is the English-language preparatory course for eleventh graders' entrance exam for college. It's the test for non-English speakers that you have to pass in order to go to an English-speaking school abroad.

And then, we have master's classes, which are higher-level classes. Basically it's for kids who are almost fluent in English. The master's students are better than me. [Laughs.] I also assist with a class called "English Chip." It's like they're putting the English chip in the brain . . . that's what *I* want!

My Students Sometimes Misbehave and Act Rude

The worst part of my job is when I have to go to the parents when the students are bad. Moms always think their students are different than what I'm telling them. They think they're perfect. They don't really believe me when I tell them their student didn't do their homework or was misbehaving.

Some students don't want to do anything. They're just being hyper, or they're drawing pictures [doodling]. Others are just leaning on their desks and sleeping. If the teacher has questions for students, they don't answer anything. They're just sitting there while the time is going, sitting and waiting to go home.

This is a very big problem, but their parents don't want to believe the situation. I tell them the truth, but they don't believe their children have that attitude.

Some students hate their moms . . . so if they don't do their homework or they're neglecting their studies and I call their mom, maybe she'll talk to her son or daughter. Now, their relationship gets much worse. So, this is one problem.

Some students' tests grades are very bad. They aren't up to their class level. Their test grades are down. Their parents get so angry. They say, "Not my son or my daughter—their test grade is fine!" Some parents yell at us. They doubt our word, and they think we made a mistake about the students' grades.

Don't Call Me "Kelly"

My worst problem with students has been when a boy was rude. In Korea, if someone is older, you don't just call them by their first name. If we are friends, I will call you by your first name. We have a very important tradition that if one person is older and the other one is younger, you address them with respect. But some students call out to me, "Kelly!" No "Teacher." Just "Kelly." This is a problem. It should be "Kelly Teacher." Here, that's considered very rude.

I've also had a problem with students lying. When we have a retest, they fix their answers. I've already checked the incorrect answers. Then, they say, "Kelly Teacher, you made a mistake."

Outside the classroom, the teachers are checking their work on-camera. We can see them erase their answers. You see, we have cameras in our classrooms that record everything. So, if we think a student is cheating, or we think they're misbehaving, we say, "We're going to show your mom this camera, this video," and they listen.

Some days, there are many problems. Today, in [my colleague] Lyle's class, three boys were very bad. These boys, they were just very big and mean. They were yelling, and throwing erasers, and giving incorrect answers on purpose.

The young girls in that class were so upset that they couldn't study. When they left school, they were crying. I could tell that they were just going to go home and continue to cry. So, I think this is a very stressful situation for the girls! They just want to study and get their work done.

I talked to these boys in the hallway. First, I just gave them a warning, and then the second time, I told them I will go to the seventh floor and tell the head of the school. I didn't yell, but I was angry. They were smiling. I told them, if you want to do that one more time, I will call your mother. Most of the students are afraid of their moms. The moms here are very strict.

The Upside and Downside of Caring about My Students

I worry about my students. I worry all the time. Sometimes I worry if this is the kind of life I really want to build for me. I think, though, that some students' lives are much harder than mine. I don't really know how it is for them.

The best part of my job is every time I get to know a child and watch the students grow up a little bit, in their English and in their thinking. They improve a little. I like to see their progress in their learning. So, this is a very good part of my job.

I think they know my sincerity. So, if I give them just a little praise and a little bit of snacks, they are very happy. So then, I look at them, and I just feel so happy.

And, in my work, I have received praise from some of the students' parents. They told me or messaged me, "Thank you for your concern."

There was this one girl, when she first came to CDI, who was very embarrassed. She didn't want to come here. But over time, she started to love her class and began to love English. Her mom and dad came in and said to our director, Sonia, that they are happy with me. They gave me praise. "You work very hard. You love your children."

My Boyfriend Is Studying to Be a Minister

I have a boyfriend. His name is Cho-Kun Woo. He can speak English way better than me! We've dated for six years. We had a long-distance relationship when I studied in China; I would see him on holidays. For summer vacations and winter vacations, I went to Korea, and we would date. He studies theology at the university in Daegu. He's going to be a Baptist pastor.

Cho-Kun's father is a minister, too, a pastor. My parents are Christian, but when I was young, I didn't want to go to church. So, I didn't.

Cho-Kun and I are secretly engaged. At CDI, nobody knows the situation. I think I will tell them in March. Right now, it's a very busy term, and we are in the middle of academic testing, so I don't want to bring it up yet.

We will get married on July 11th at 11:00 in the morning, at a reception hall. I plan to wear a Western ivory wedding dress; we borrow these from a wedding shop. According to our custom, my parents and grandparents will throw peanuts at me, and I will try to catch them.[5] This means their son and daughter will have a baby soon.

I would like to have children someday. I would like two or three. But Cho-Kun wants eleven children—really! Like a real-life soccer team.

After the throwing of the peanuts and eating some foods at the reception, we'll go on our honeymoon to Paris. My dreamland is France, so we're going to Paris. I can't wait! We'll stay there for just one week.

I Found My Faith as a College Student in China

When I was twenty-two, at university in China, I had a chance to go to the church there. I changed my heart. Before I had religion, I was a bad girl. I was very selfish. I didn't want to do anything. Much of the time I was very annoyed and irritated. You could see it on my face; my face looked hard and cold.

My mom said now that I have a church and I have a faith, my face has actually changed. I'm very happy. My mom says that's why I love life and people so much now. I think it's because I know God's law. That's also maybe why I love kids.

So now, everything that happens, if something goes wrong or I hear some bad news, I just pray. I think God has given me the best of things. I think everything is his plan, and everything is going to be okay.

What I Do When I'm Not Working: Read and Sleep

In my free time, I don't like watching TV or movies. I like Korean pop, *Shinhwa*; that's a Korean boys' group. I also like listening to the *Begin Again* soundtrack. You know Keira Knightley? She was in that movie, and she sang, and she has a beautiful voice. I love it.

For fun, Cho-Kun and I go to a café. I read books. He takes pictures. He's very like that. He's a part-time photographer. But cameras are very expensive! My most happy time is when I finish work and come home, take a shower, go to bed with a book, and sleep.

My Father Is My Hero

My father is one of my heroes. He is very good in his work, with his family . . . really with everything that he does, he does it so well. He went to China to work there and study Chinese. This was not an easy thing to do at his age. I think my father is very much my hero.

In my family, we communicate a lot. Every day, we talk and share our days and our feelings. We have a family Instant Messenger chat room for my parents, my brother, and me. I can tell them if I had a bad day at school. If some of the parents are yelling at them or at me, I can just talk to my parents about it. They are very understanding and supportive. And then, during breaks and rest time, we also travel together.

I also admire [my boss] Sonia. I have had three jobs in my life. With the first and second, I didn't have a role model. But Sonia is very professional. I really want to be like her. I want her language skills! She's very smart and influential at work. When she is in the office, my heart feels calm and comfortable. When everything is happening, if there's a bad situation or someone says bad things, if Sonia is in the office, I still feel comfortable. I don't worry. It's no problem.

The Challenges of Being a Young Adult in This Country

One of the challenges here, in my opinion, is finding a job. When I first graduated from university, I didn't know who I was and what I wanted to do. Everyone is in this situation, especially when we are just graduating from university—we find it very hard to find a job. We don't know what these jobs require, and we're just writing and writing so many resumes and still not getting a job.

In Daegu today, the wages are not much higher or lower than when my parents were young, but the economy has gone down very much. We have wages that are a little, little higher, but we have other things that are much higher—like coffee, food, and rent. It's the consumer price index. Prices are going up, but the wages are staying flat.

Many of my friends say they don't want to get married. They don't want kids. They just want a single life, just to be single and be very comfortable.

They think that in order to have kids, they need too much money. So, my friends, both here in Korea and in China nowadays, they don't want to marry and have kids.

The Political Situation in the Koreas Is Not Good *or* Bad

I think North Korea is . . . I don't say just good or just bad. But the situation is that their president has a problem. [Laughs.] It's their Communist society. They don't have freedom. This is a very big problem, I think. They are starving and dying, some kids. They don't have anything. They're just working for their country. I think the situation is very bad for the people there, and that is the president's fault.[6]

I do think South Korea has a responsibility to help. Giving money is very simple, but this is not good. It's not reliable; it could end up in the wrong hands. So, I think it's better to give rice or cows or medicine that gets to the people. That's better than money.

Here, we should have freedom. We don't. I feel our freedom is becoming very much like Big Brother [with constant government surveillance of its citizens]—the government looks at our emails, our Instant Messenger, and our Internet activity, all our communications. I feel this is a very serious problem. The government is like a certain kind of CCTV. Everything is being watched and monitored. These are very big issues. We don't have privacy.[7] We're like China! It looks like China here.

I Want to Travel the World and Buy a Lot of Books

If I had all the money in the world, I'd travel the world. [Laughs.] I would just go and travel. I've already traveled to Vietnam, Hong Kong, China, Singapore, Malaysia, and Mongolia. So, next, I would go to France, Italy, Greece, New York, Seattle, Greenland, Germany, and Switzerland.

I don't really like to go shopping, but if I had a lot of money I would buy many, many books. I would spend money on books and travel. I also like going out to eat.

My Goal Is to Help Poor Children by Building a School

But for my work, my end goal is to go to another country and help some children. If I had money, I'd go to another country in America or Africa. I would go and build up a school, and I would teach there.

I have done this type of work before, as a volunteer in Malaysia and Mongolia. I worked with an NGO [nonprofit] there. I played with the kids and taught them things, like how you have to wash your hands. I thought, when I was teaching them, this is awful, because they have so much poverty here. When I went to Malaysia, I taught in Chinese, and in Mongolia, I taught in English. I would like to teach like this again in the future.

It takes a lot of money to open a school. To reach this goal, I'm saving my salary. In Korean dollars, I make 1.8 million Korean won per month. That's around $1,500 a month. I think other teachers are more experienced and might receive more money. My salary is pretty average.

Nowadays, many foundations help to build schools. And my boyfriend is working on his degree, and he is going to be a pastor. Some pastors are just in charge of their church, and some pastors go overseas and help people and teach about God and the Bible. Cho-Kun wants to be a missionary pastor. I want to go with him and do that too.

What I Want the World to Know

For people who read this book, I would want them to know that I want to keep going with my job. I really love my children and this job.

If I have a chance, I want to return to Malaysia and help poor people, poor children. They need to teach English there, and the kids really want to learn. So, I will keep studying English, and I will teach them. If I have a baby, my kids, I want to teach them first to know God and second to know other people. I would want them to also love their work and our Earth.

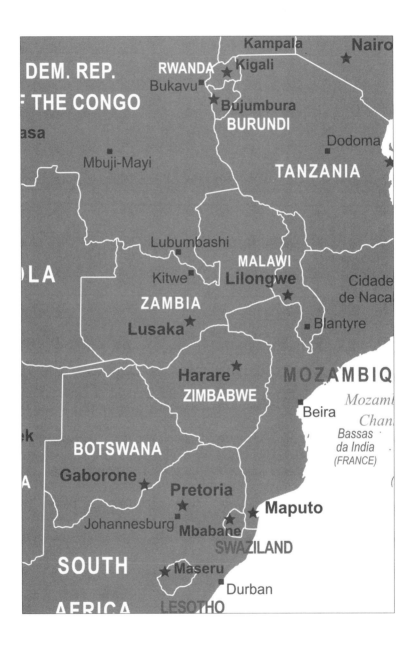

six

———

MISOZI

MOBILE-MONEY AGENT

Lusaka, Zambia

Editor's note: The four friends in this photograph work together at a mobile-money booth in Lusaka, Zambia, in southern Africa. Misozi Mkandawire, an independent mobile-banking franchise agent, is the third one from the left. She's the boss.[1]

Their names sound like a plaintive haiku: Misozi (which means "tears"), Mercy, and Memory. I'm fascinated by the poetry of people's names here, many of which convey spiritual qualities that perhaps their parents wished upon them at birth: Faith, Chastity, Prophet . . . Misozi, who says she doesn't care for her name, got it because everyone was weeping on the day of her birth[2]—also the day her aunt died.

We're in a tropical, landlocked country with a population of fifteen million. It's a former British colony that acquired independence in 1964; anyone with a secondary education or urban exposure speaks English. Misozi does, and she also happens to speak three other local dialects, which serves her work in the rural areas, where she's opened three of her eleven mobile-banking kiosks. I meet her while on a storytelling trip with Grameen Foundation (grameenfoundation.org), when we check in with their partner, *Zoona* (pronounced *zoh-na*; means "it's real;" zoona.co.za).

This social enterprise provides financial services for the unbanked (85 percent of Zambians, according to Zoona), through their mobile phones. More than a thousand entrepreneurs work as franchise owners of and tellers at banking kiosks, where customers get help sending and receiving mobile money. Agents conduct bill payments, cash deposits and withdrawals, transfers, loans, business-to-business (B2B) payments, and business-to-consumer (B2C) payments. They've expanded into Malawi and South Africa and plan to take over the mobile-money market across the entire continent.

We[3] find Misozi in bustling downtown Lusaka, with her three employees dancing around each other inside a tiny, bright green-and-white painted booth. They just can't keep up with the lines that snake down the sidewalk . . . Business is better than ever.

Misozi started off in the sales department at age eighteen and acquired her first franchise banking kiosk at twenty-two. She's worked her way up in two short years to owning eleven outlets, employing nineteen young people, mostly female. She supports her mother, siblings, cousin, niece, and nephew and is on the verge of becoming a millionaire—in the local currency, anyway.[4]

The unstoppable Misozi seems far older than her years in wisdom and discipline. Yet she's a Gen Z-er through and through: She likes rap music, she streams her TV over her laptop, and she believes in the infinite power of technology. She's become a technophile-philanthropist with a new venture[5]—to empower Zambian youth and end poverty through financial services and business support. How will she do this? Through an app on her mobile phone, of course.

My Childhood Had Humble Beginnings

My name is Misozi Mkandawire. I am twenty-four years old. I am the youngest in a family of five and grew up in Lusaka, the capital city of Zambia.

My childhood had humble beginnings. My mother worked as a tailor making women's clothing in the house we grew up in. My mother always pushed hard work and education on me, and that had a positive impact.

My father had TB [tuberculosis] and passed away when I was eight. It was a bit difficult. When my dad passed away, my older brother had completed school, and he was the only one who was working. So, he had to make sure we all went to school. I think he sacrificed most of his time and money to make sure we were okay.

I attended a local public school in my area called Kabulonga Girls High School, then received my diploma from National Institute of Public Administration in accounting.

I Do Not Like the Meaning of My Name

I speak four languages: Tumbuka, my language from my dad's side; Nyanga, which is common in Lusaka; a bit of Bemba, which is more widespread in the region; and English.

In Tumbuka or Nyanga, my name means "tears." It is a common name, mostly for women. At the time I was born, my dad had lost his sister. It wasn't a happy time, so they called me *Misozi*. I don't like my name very much. [Laughs.] I often thought I should have just changed it. But right now, I don't have a problem with it. I'd never give it to my child, but I don't mind it now.

My sister has a worse name [laughs], which means, like, "you hate me." I think at that time my parents were having problems in their marriage. I'm not sure who gave her the name, whether it was my mom or my dad. Another sibling's name means "keep each other." So, that was on a good day.

How I Got Started Working in Mobile-Phone Banking

I work in mobile-phone banking. My work entails providing financial services to primarily unbanked consumers in urban, peri-urban, and rural areas of Zambia.

Most banks, people are dressed up, and they speak really good English, and that can make people from the countryside feel a bit uncomfortable. We're a local brand, and we haven't really gone corporate, so people feel very comfortable just walking up to a Zoona booth. In the past, low-income and rural Zambians would use a bank [if they could get an account—which requires collateral] or send money on a bus. Now, they have another option.

I do money transfers, bill payments, bulk payouts, vouchers, airtime sales, and international remittances. My first Zoona outlet was opened in October 2012, and I had one employee. The first few months were very challenging. I had to work hard to bring in customers, since very few people had heard of Zoona.

Through hard work and determination, I have been able to build up the business the past two years. Now, I have nineteen employees: seventeen females and two males, all under the age of twenty-eight.

I also work to train my employees with basic business skills, so they can move up in the business and eventually become Zoona agents, go back to school, or start up other businesses. I've empowered five employees to become Zoona agents, operating their own shops independently, which has allowed them to increase their incomes.

Currently, my focus is on growing my business and seeing new opportunities in the mobile-payments market in Zambia.

How Mobile Banking Serves the Unbanked

People who live in urban areas are educated and have bank accounts, but people in rural areas do not have bank accounts. So, they use services like Zoona to pay their bills, transfer money to their family back home, and maybe even save a little bit. Zoona has a user-friendly system; it was designed for anyone.

I have eight shops in Lusaka, two in Kitwe, and one in between Lusaka and Kitwe, in Siavonga, in the southern part of Zambia on the coast of Lake Kariba. Before I decide on a location, I see the population that's there, the number of people, and also I look at the services that are provided in that particular area. When the bank is down or has long queues, they can easily go to Zoona.

Zoona Works Just Like M-PESA in Kenya

Zoona is like [Vodaphone] M-PESA, a very well-known mobile-banking platform in Kenya. They're designed for the urban and the rural parts of the towns. You can find Zoona and M-PESA at the supermarket, or at a shopping mall, or in a very small town. I think Zoona will become as big as M-PESA. We're already taking up some of the models that they did, like the aggregator model. I think Zoona will kick M-PESA out, eventually. [Laughs.] We are a lot alike.

I Live with My Mom and Siblings in the Suburbs

I live in Lusaka, Woodlands Extension, with my mom, my sister, my cousin, two nieces, and a nephew. Right now, my mom's into farming. She farms mostly maize, and then, she also keeps chickens. On a small scale, she does sweet potatoes and vegetables. We have a farm in Kabwe. She doesn't go there every day. She goes there mostly during the weekends. We also have some other people who are working there.

I support the family. I have an older brother. He lives in the Copperbelt, a province in Zambia where most of our mines are. He supported us for a very, very long time after my dad passed away. But then, later on when we were about eighteen, he was like, "Okay, you guys, you need to fend for yourselves."

So, he's with his family there. Whenever we're stuck or we need help, he does come through, but most of the stuff, I do myself. I work six days a week.

Church on Sundays, and Then, I Zone Out with American TV

On Sundays, I go to my church, Mt. Zion. The main service is two hours, but sometimes I stay four more hours for the youth service. The youth church is usually more fun than the main church. It's not only praying. People do poetry, sing, and dance. It's a way to keep the youth from doing harmful things. It's really nice.

When I get home after church, I take out my laptop and watch all my television series: *Heaven, Agents of S.H.I.E.L.D., House of Cards*, and *The Big Bang Theory*.

I also love music a lot. Mostly it's pop and a little bit of soul. Eminem is a favorite of mine. His was the only international act I've seen, and also groups from Australia and Nigeria. But locally, I've seen a lot of artists. Sometimes, you find concerts very close to home, and if there's someone performing nearby, I do go watch.

My Sweetheart, Abraham, Supports Me a Lot

I have a sweetheart, Abraham. He's nine years older than me. I met him through work. He's really supported me a lot, always guiding me. If I have an idea, he's usually the first person I tell, and he'll say, "Okay, this will work. Maybe if you do it in this way."

Marriage is not yet in my future. It's a good thing, but I just feel right now it's not the time, because it can draw me back a little, and I have this target. I need to be alone for now, and then, when I'm finally there, I think then I can get married.

Zambians Are Friendly but a Little Backward Outside the City

I have done some traveling in Zambia. Cities like Lusaka are more developed; people are educated here. We have people who have master's degrees or at least some formal education. There are a lot of business opportunities here. But, on the outskirts, life is a bit slow there. Some people are not even able to speak English. The opportunities are very rare, and people often end up not doing much with their lives.

Zambians are very friendly people. We have a lot of ideas. You know, we're brilliant people with few opportunities. That's what I think. So, it's a friendly country. When you come here, you always feel at home. And like other countries, there's a lot of segregation or racism, but in Zambia, it's relatively minor.

The infrastructure in Zambia is not very good. The hospitals are not top notch. They're just not as effective as they're supposed to be. You find people dying in queues while they're waiting to be attended to. At a maternity ward, you find women that are actually giving birth on the floor, because there's not enough bed space.

And then, for education, at least now, you can go from grades one to seven, and it's free, and then, you only start paying after eighth grade. So, I think in the education sector, we're trying, but for the hospital side, a lot needs to be done.

When I Was Young, People Teased Me about My Nose

When I was young, I was teased. People would laugh and say, "Oh, you've got a big nose." I was always so shy. I would wear a hat; I never used to take it off.

That's why I like Michael Jackson a lot. I think he suffered a lot in his young age. He wanted to feel normal, and he never got that chance, and he was always teased. He was always in a shell. The only freedom he had was when he actually went onstage. I have this big poster of him in my room. I know people find him a bit weird, but I do like him a lot. It's not that I look up to him, but his story is a unique one.

Sometimes, I feel when you're looking at people from the outside, you might easily judge them. But once you get to know them and spend time with them, there's more to them. With the right direction and the right help, people can always get to where they need to be. That's how I feel, like I have a lot inside, and I haven't yet reached my full potential.

Then, I Discovered Myself and What I Can Do

Fortunately, when I was in tenth grade, I met my friend Memory. She helped me develop a process to discover myself. When we were in secondary school, we worked for a man who had an advertising company. He told us to go out and look for clients who wanted to collaborate. Usually, we'd just go out and find people and tell them about the company, give them ideas, or tell them we can make a jingle for them. It never really worked out, because we never managed to get anyone to actually do an advert [advertisement].

Then, when I was eighteen, Memory told me about Zoona, and I applied. She told me they had openings in the sales department.

My first job was handing out flyers on the street and telling people to open up an account. It was called a "One Account." For every account we opened, if they made a deposit, we were given five kwacha [not even a penny].

Sometimes, we'd stand in the street under the boiling hot sun. Sometimes, we'd go office-to-office and ask people to open these accounts. If you were lucky, you would have five people open and deposit, but sometimes, it would be so difficult. They'd open the accounts, but then, they wouldn't make deposits.

It was on a day-to-day basis. One day, it's good; the next day, it's not so great. The most I made was in a group, four of us. We reached our separate targets, and we each received 850 kwacha [16 cents]. That was pretty exciting. Whatever money we'd make, I'd put it away or give it to my mom. I was saving for school.

I currently carry two Kiva loans of fifteen thousand (kwacha) each [$3] and two Zoona loans of twenty-five thousand (kwacha) each [nearly $5]. Right now, I make fifty thousand [about $10] a month. I may be a millionaire by next year.

My Boss Pushed Me So Hard That I Hated Him a Little Bit

My boss, Graham, I think he saw something in me, and he started to teach me things. I began to work in the main office. He showed me how to use [Microsoft spreadsheet program] Excel. He showed me how to use [word-processing program] Word, and he was always on my back, telling me, "You have to learn how to do this." He really, really pushed me to learn. At that time, I think I hated him a little bit [laughs], but now I appreciate him, because what I learned is because of him.

Then, after that, I was making a little more money. After 5:00, when we'd close for work, I'd go to night school. It was pretty close, so I just used to walk there. It took me two years, but I graduated with an accounting technician's diploma.

The Skills a Mobile Banker Needs to Have

In order to do this work, you need to have a bit of accounting knowledge, and you also need to understand how figures work, because you need to know how to calculate for your commission, your profits, and your expenses. And you need to learn how to separate business from personal issues.

I think that's where most of the agents are failing, because they immediately spend the money they make for personal use. I put the business money aside. I don't tamper with it. When I have enough money, I invest in another shop. I'm always trying to expand.

I create a budget for the things I need to get for home. So, that would be bills, groceries, and everything. Then, if I need any new clothes or if I need to change my hair—nails, yes, I have that expense as well. I put the rest in an account.

This discipline comes from both my parents. My dad was a statistician, and my mom was always there, guiding me and telling me, "You don't need this. You should always get what you *need*, not what you want."

Sometimes, I'll get something, and she'll say, "Was this really necessary?" You know? So, I'm always thinking, "Should I really get this? Is it something I want, or is it something I need?" I always have to have a balance between the two.

I Start Every Single Day with a Prayer

The first thing I do every day is pray, because so many things happen. You always have to pray for protection. And I believe behind everything that happens, there's a Greater Being. Things don't just happen. So, I pray.

Then, I have to figure out what I'm going to wear. That's always a mess. Sometimes, there are a lot of people who come in from different sectors, asking you questions. You need to look presentable. But I do have very bad days where my hair is everywhere, and then, on those days, I don't want to see anyone.

After I figure out what to wear, I take a shower. I'm always running a little late. My cousin pushes me all the time. "Hey, we're running late." Finally, we get off to work. Usually we leave the house by 6:15, because there's a lot of traffic.

My Typical Workday

We get to work before 8:00 a.m.—usually by 7:30. We clean up the shop, and then, the girls start reporting, plus the two guys. While we're cleaning, I'm giving them what I call "the black books," small books where we keep the records and some of their cash. Then, we'll clean up, and then, at exactly 8:00, we have to be open for business.

We have customers waiting sometimes at 7:30 who say, "Oh, no, I wanted to do this earlier, because I also start work at 8:00."

And then, most of the time, you do work overtime. We have a lot of customers. It's very difficult for us to tell them, "No, we're closed now. Come back tomorrow."

All day, I'm mostly monitoring, because I have a lot of accounts. I have over twenty transaction accounts with Zoona, so I need to make sure everyone is managing their accounts and that they have enough cash. If any [kiosk manager is] in trouble, it's easy for me to either transfer flows to them or send them cash, or I have to drive over and take cash to those who are not in town.

At my outlet, I have three tellers. Here, I have one person, Mercy, who helps me out. When I'm not around, she's able to help the other tellers. For the other shops, I usually have one person who's in charge. I decide who's in charge by the way they perform and also by the way they just interact with the customers. I'm able to tell if a person really, really loves their job and if they're serious about it.

My Protégé, Mercy, Has Become a Dear Friend

I first met Mercy a year ago when I trained her. She wasn't actually working for me in the beginning. She was working for one of the other agents in Kitwe. Then, later on, she needed to come back [to Lusaka], because her son and her husband were here.

From the time she started working with me, she's always been on time, and she always asks how she can help. You can tell that this is one person who wants to learn. She always asks questions. When she doesn't understand, she takes time to ask you. And for me, that's a sign that this person can be great. Mercy has a great mind. She's one of those people who really, really wants to learn and can be a leader. I think there are a lot of people in Zambia who have the intelligence but have not had opportunity.

Technical Glitches and Temperamental Customers Get Me Down

The most challenging part of my job is when the banks are down—when we're having bad Internet or our system is down. There have been times when a person is using Zoona for the first time. They'll walk in, and they'll want quick service, because they have this expectation that Zoona is fast and easy.

So, they're walking in, and maybe we're having a bad network, or they didn't show up with an ID, and then, they start badmouthing the company—"This is a bad company"—and saying we need to close down, and they're yelling, and we have a lot of other customers in there, which makes it pretty embarrassing sometimes, because you don't know what to say . . . but I've dealt with a lot of those customers.

In a case like this, first, you try to talk to the customer. You tell him, "Excuse me, sir, please calm down," and you try to explain to him, "This is the process. Did you receive a message?" That happens if he doesn't have an ID.

He says, "Yes, I did."

"Did you go through your messages? Did you read it?" and he'll say, "Yes, I read it."

"Can we read it together?" and he'll say, "Okay, okay," because now he's feeling a bit embarrassed, because you're not shouting.

What happens is, if they're shouting and you're also shouting, it just makes things worse. So, you need to always look a bit apologetic, and eventually they cool down. And then, we do have customers who never want to cool down, and they just storm out, but then even those, you just let them be, because you can't really follow them and say, "Hey, I'm sorry." Just let them go.

In this work, I've also had a teller who defrauded me, but that was just once. We managed to catch her before it went too far. And customers have harassed me. Sometimes, you get people who are just angry. They'll just take out their frustrations on you. So, yes, we've had very bad cases where someone is yelling, or they want to get physical, but it's never gone that far.

There's a man who sits in front of my shop, Mr. Moses. He must be in his forties or fifties. He's pretty old. He sells envelopes and pens and stuff. So, when I feel overpowered, I'm able to call him. And most of the guys around there know me, so it's pretty easy for me to get security.

The Competition: Western Union, the Post Office, M-PESA, and Shoprite

We use either MTM or AirTel as our [cellular] network. When MTM is down, we usually shift to AirTel, but we've had days where both sites are really, really bad, and there's nothing else we can do. We just try to talk to the customers, but then, they're not very happy. They have to wait, and, you know, competition for us is next door. [Laughs.] Just last month, the post office reduced their prices. Western Union is also in the post office.

And Shoprite is starting a pilot program. Right now, they are making us a bit nervous, because a lot of our customers have actually shifted to Shoprite, but I'm not too worried. If they stick to lower prices, then we need to get worried. But right now, I'm not. Shoprite is not everywhere: Zoona is. And, with Shoprite, there is a lot of paperwork. Zoona doesn't have paperwork.

Worst Day So Far: The Competitor Stole One-Third of My Monthly Profits

My absolute worst day was when Shoprite started transacting last month. My business dropped a little. When I have a lot of customers walking in, I'm able to provide that service, and at the end of the day, I'm also making a profit. That makes me very happy.

But on the last day of last month, when I looked at my profits, I think it broke my heart a little, because I saw that those guys were really pushing us. That particular shop was making nine thousand, but then, it dropped to like six thousand; I lost about three thousand.

I was a bit nervous, and I wasn't very happy about that. I was also doing the accounting. I needed to pay rentals and salaries. And that shop has a Kiva loan, and I needed to make a loan repayment as well. So, I was like, "This month was just for expenses, no profits." That really broke my heart.

What's the Best Is Being My Own Boss

I love working with Zoona. I love the fact that I get to be my own boss, that I'm able to account for everything I make, and they provide me with the system and the tools to be able to do all the accounting for the month. I also love that it helps me help my family. My brother, the one I mentioned earlier, he's also got his own Zoona outlets in the Copperbelt, and I think I inspired him into opening them. And I'm also employing my cousin and other tellers. It's been a great journey for me.

In the six years that I've worked with Zoona, I've become more independent. If you met me a few years ago, if you asked people, they would tell you I was very shy and I often kept to myself. So, yeah, I've changed a lot. Most people who knew me then and see me now, they say, "Wow, you've really grown out of the shell." Being with Zoona has been really awesome. It's worked out better than I thought it would.

As a Top Agent in a Multinational Company, I Got to Go to South Africa

Recently, I was selected to be one of twenty Zoona agents countrywide to become an Aggregator Agent. Now, I will be working to bring in new Zoona agents to the business, train them, support them, and help them build a sustainable revenue stream to enable them to live better lives through their start-up mobile-money businesses.

Earlier this year, Zoona brought me to their headquarters in Cape Town for a week.[6] This was a reward for the top ten agents, and I got to go with my friend Memory.

For the first few days, I sat down with the IT [information technology] team, and we looked at the problems I was facing as a customer. I was able to explain to them, "Okay, this hasn't worked for me, and this works for me," and most of those changes, I'm very happy to say, I was able to see.

And then, for part of the time, they told me, "Now, go relax. Go have fun." So, I went to the beach. I went to the waterfront. I also went to watch the Eminem concert. I got to see Eminem!

I Find a Lot of Inspiration in the People Who Work Here

The managing director, Lelemba, is a role model for me. She's really awesome. She has her own organization. She does motivational speaking for accountants and other businesspeople. She hands out financial literature. And she's young, in her early thirties, and she already has a master's degree. She's a very nice person to speak to as well.

I think every Zoona agent has a unique story. We all have different backgrounds, how we're brought up or where we live or where we're situated, and every time we meet and interact, we all have our own views and ideas of how Zoona should work or how we manage our business. We all have different success stories. I'm really, really glad to have found myself where I am right now, and I can't wait for what the future holds.

Visioning My Next Venture: Mobile Loans and Start-Up Support

Sometimes, when I just sit, I will get an idea. It just hits me. I'm sort of going in a zone, and it hits me. Sometimes, it's through conversation with people, like someone might have an idea but it's not fully developed. I can look at it from a different angle, and I tell them, "Okay, but what if you did this?" I'm able to open up and present what I think. It doesn't always work, but at least I try.

Recently, I have been trying to invest in microfinance, giving out small loans to people I know, people who can easily pay it back. So far, I have no complaints. It's going well. I'm not fully into it: I don't want to lend out a lot of money and then have trouble getting it back. For me to go full-scale into that, I need to find extra help so that at least we split the responsibility, and then, I can concentrate on building it.

As an entrepreneur, you don't always want to get a loan. If you have a loan, as you're making a profit, you always have to put at the back of your mind, "I need to make a repayment." Although you use the money and it's helping you out, you also feel like, "I don't really want to have a lot of expenses at the end of the month, because then I'm just working to pay off bills." But then, when you're starting out, sometimes you do need to borrow money if you don't have funding.

Starting Out Small, Experimenting by Loaning to Friends

I have a lot of friends, and we talk about business, and mostly the challenge that we have is finances. So, I thought to myself, "If I can make this much and save this much, why not start up something of my own? Why not start up a microfinance?"

As of now, I've loaned out to five people. The biggest loan I've given out is for ten thousand. My entire portfolio is about fifty thousand [$10]. I haven't gone into it on a full scale. I'm just trying it out. Usually, I just give them for a month. We have a written contract. When you're with friends, it's very difficult to just have it said in words.

I told them, "You can pay it back in a month, and if you have any issues, you tell me before, and then, we can extend the time." Most of them are comfortable with a month. And right now, I'm very cheap compared to most people, because I'm just trying it out. I charge 10–12.5 percent, depending on the person. For the banks, it's 16 percent. And most of the other people, the other microfinances, they charge 30 percent or more.

How Fappis Solutions Will Be Different

Next year, I need to make sure the microfinance takes off. I actually have two ideas of how I want to tackle this. It's not going to be your ordinary microfinance. You say, "I want a loan," and you fill out the paperwork. That's not how I want to look at it. What I want is a product where someone can actually access a loan instantly. I want to design a system that would only be for people who are employed, people who can pay.

So, they will log into their phone or their computer, wherever. Then, depending on how much they get paid, they'll have access to a certain amount, and they'll have a time frame of how long they want to borrow that money. They'll click that amount, and then, they'll click the term agreement, and then, they just press "okay," and that money is credited instantly to their bank account.

They won't need to fill out any forms, because, once we have a contract to that company, you're entitled to actually access an amount. And then, we would get our money back on a monthly basis. A certain percentage is cut off [from your income]. We would be paid back automatically, with our payments deducted from your salary.

Our platform will make accessing loans as easy as mobile banking. Through the use of a computer or web-enabled phones and unstructured supplementary service data (USSD), employees will be able to access direct business loans, cutting out all the paperwork.

And then, the other one: I want to help entrepreneurs, providing financial services and small loans to youths and women. They would come up with a business plan, and, if it's viable, we'd give you one person to guide you. You keep your idea, but they would guide you on accounting, on how to work in a business. You would have sort of like an angel to guide you for six months, on mentorship, training, business networks, and management guidance. And then, when they feel you can stand on your own, they let you go, and see how your business progresses.

The company will be called "Fappis Solutions." It is named after my dad.

Supporting Zambian Youth and Women

Fappis Solutions will enable youth to present business plans that are viable and realistic, in search for financial aid. The business plans will be funded fully by the company for 50 percent of the company as standing surety until the loan is fully settled; then, the new business owner will return to full ownership.

We'll also provide small loans and empowerment programs for women in rural and peri-rural areas. These empowerment programs will provide women with solar products, such as lighting and heating. The products will be obtained from the company to be resold on a loan basis. These loans will give women not only employment but also a chance to run their own businesses.

The company would work on a worldwide basis, including training and support from inception, business management and cash flow education, online and on-the-spot monitoring. It would help young entrepreneurs like me, who have little to no capital to start up a business, so their ideas can make a change in their lives.

Come Back in Five Years: I'll Have a Thriving Business and a Foundation

I believe that, five years from now, Fappis Solutions will have already spread throughout the country and possibly into other countries as well. Maybe take it international. In ten years, I will start a foundation and have a great team supporting people who want to be entrepreneurs.

I've had a lot of success in my life, and I think it's because I haven't given up on the dreams that I've had. Also, the support system I've had of people who have encouraged me has really, really helped me.

Agribusiness
and
Food Processing

seven

SREY POUV

RICE MICROFINANCIER

Siem Reap, Cambodia

Editor's note: Sometimes, when you take a chance and a long flight to a faraway place, you wind up finding your soul mate.

That's what happened to my photographer friend Karl Grobl.[1] He'd spent decades traversing the planet, snapping pictures of people working their way out of poverty while running photography classes and tours to support his nonprofit work.

Then, once upon a time, Karl found himself in the small town of Battambang, Cambodia, shooting for Seva Foundation, an organization providing eye care to those in need and working to prevent blindness.

Pulling up in the back of a bicycle rickshaw to a restaurant, Karl caught in a flash the silhouette of a young woman with piercing eyes.

She took his breath away. Srey Pouv (pronounced *Shray Poov*) Kai and Karl exchanged a few stilted words through his driver/translator, and then, he left.

Two years later, Karl returned to Cambodia to court her. He'd learned her language, Khmer, and discovered that she'd studied English with the hope of communicating with him. "He was different," she says. "He was kind."

"She's amazing," Karl beams. "I'm playing catch-up on a lot of stuff. It's incredible. There's a lot about my second half of life that I never ever thought I would find." Karl and Srey Pouv have been together nine years and share a son, Kevin (age six) and an adopted daughter, Eher (age seven).

Srey Pouv was born in the year that the Communist Khmer Rouge were defeated by Vietnamese allies in the capital city of Phnom Penh— after four years of the "Killing Fields" genocide that left nearly two million people dead. She spent her childhood in a refugee camp near the Thai border, where violence still raged around the families huddled in tents. They felt lucky to get an occasional can of tuna to supplement their diet of rice and beans. Srey Pouv's earliest memories are of hearing bombs exploding near the camp.

Her father went missing; rumor had it that he was murdered by the Khmer Rouge. Her mother never really recovered from that loss: A shell of a woman, she could not work, could not care for Srey Pouv, could not hope. Srey Pouv had to drop out of school after eighth grade, since no one could pay her school fees.

But by the time Karl met her, Srey Pouv had worked a string of menial jobs, survived a severe case of tuberculosis, landed a job as a field agent for a global nonprofit, and earned enough income to shelter and care for her mom.

Years later, Srey Pouv and Karl have built an elegant, serene home they co-designed. They run two businesses—her rice microfinance[2] and his photography—from the abode where they also host and support her mother and a handful of cousins. Like the unshakable gaze of Srey Pouv's luminous brown eyes, their love remains unwavering. Being in their home with them on a sunny afternoon in early spring when I visited Siem Reap, I could feel the love between them. It's palpable.

No Cash Required: Reaping Profits from and with Rice

My name is Srey Pouv Kai. I was born here in Cambodia, in a little village west of here called Battambang. I am thirty-six years old.

In April 2002, I started my own business with just twelve dollars. I loan rice to the farmers in the countryside. I give it [rice seeds] to some families at the beginning of the year. They grow the rice, keep some for their own family, and sell any surplus, once they pay me back in rice for the loan. One year later, in January and February, I collect this loan in rice [in 100kg or 220lb bags] and then sell those bags of rice for money. The first year, I made $12.50.[3] The most I've earned in a year was just last year: I made $3,400.

The first year, I just gave money to one family, one woman who needed some money to provide for her extended family. We also lend money to people for the food they need or to give to their children to go to school.

I also assist World Vision with their microfinance lending side, which is called Vision Fund. In the initial stages, they were trying to find customers in rural areas, and Battambang was one of their target markets. They would go out to a village, and they didn't know whether there were potential microfinance customers and who would be able to pay the loans back. They were looking to hire someone from the village.

My job is to provide information about the people that would like to borrow money. In other words, are these people likely to be able to pay the loan back, or are they not? I've been the "eyes on the ground" for Vision

Fund. Since I lived in the village for twenty years, ever since I was a child, I know all the families and all the people.[4]

Sometimes, I know whom you *don't* need to give a loan to. These people are lazy. They do not want to work. They're also drinking. They always borrow money; then, they spend all that money, and they start to borrow again. I know exactly about people like that. They have many loans from many people.

But, if I know a person whom you *would* want to give a loan to, if I say, "Okay, this person you can give to," then I try to help. I tell the borrower, "You need to pay money every month. You will be charged every month for the interest."

How I Got into Microfinance

Before, a number of lenders in the community were charging high interest rates for loans.[5] People would receive a loan as high as $1,000, and they would pay something in the neighborhood of $500 a year just to borrow that money.

Vision Fund came in and said, "Our rates are a lot less," but they needed someone like me to explain, "Vision Fund is another option for you," rather than going to the "I'll break your thumbs" moneylender guy[6] who is in the village.

If that customer gets a loan, Vision Fund says, "Thank you very much for bringing us a customer. Here's a small commission." Currently, I am responsible for recruiting fifty to sixty people. My biggest customer is the man who's painting the [local Buddhist] pagoda.

Right now, I have two jobs. One, I work as an independent consultant for World Vision and Vision Fund; the other is my own rice-microfinance business. Both of these, I run out of a small house I still have in Battambang. Some of my family members still live there, too.

How This Work Compares to What I Used to Do

Before I had these two jobs, I had to get up at 3:00 a.m. to work. I sold sweets from a cart on the street. They didn't pay me money; rather, they gave me food that I could eat anytime.

Now, with my own company, I take interest payments in rice rather than in cash, because rice is harder for the customer to spend on the way to giving it to me. If this year I took in 160 bags of rice, I could sell it for $3,500. But I will not sell all of this rice. I will give some to my aunt, to take care of her. And with World Vision Fund, I am paid $8–$10 every month on commission. In all of this, what's important for me first is my business—I want to help myself first, and then, I can help someone else.

My current business is difficult. I have to be clever, and I have to know how to handle the people. Also, I must know the person outside there loaning money. I have to understand the process of paying interest on the loan and how the borrower must pay the money and interest to the lender every month.

Growing Up a Refugee of Communist Terrorists

I was an only child. My mother, Timalai, told me this story: When I was three months old, our family didn't have enough food to eat. My father, Kaimong, went away to earn and bring back some money for the family. Someone told my dad there was food near the border of Thailand. In those days, if someone went to anyplace without permission, they would kill him.

He'd planned to come back to take my mother and me with him, but he—he never came back. We didn't know clearly, but most people said that he died or someone killed him. His closest friends thought he'd been murdered by the Khmer Rouge.

My father was a good person. He worked hard to take care of the family, not just our own family, but also his sister, his brother, and his relatives. He was always working to take care of the poor people.

Earlier, he actually had been forced to work delivering stuff for the Pol Pot [Khmer Rouge] regime. In other words, Pol Pot said, "You need to do this. Otherwise, we're going to kill you." He wasn't a sympathizer with Pol Pot, but like everyone else, he was given a job by them.

His job was to take something like rice or soil or some food to give to the people in other villages. When he brought the rice, he'd cut a small hole in the bag. Then, some rice would fall out. The family would know, in this area, that there's some rice on the ground. They would go and get that rice, because my father was smart! He knew if he gave rice to his family, he would be killed, but he could cut a hole in the bag, and some rice would fall out along the way, and then, the family could get it.

Nobody from the Khmer Rouge knew that he put a tiny hole to make the rice fall down. But all his relatives knew the way that my father would go on his path and the way to collect the food from the ground. If the Khmer Rouge knew what he was doing, they would kill him. But that's what we think happened to him, anyway.

My Mother Was Never the Same after That

My dad just left us alone, me and my mom, with my uncle. We still had no food to eat. It was a difficult life. My mom and uncle and I then escaped from the province to the refugee camp by the Thai border. I was three months old. And my father was gone.

My mother is a good person, too, but after her husband went away, she changed from that time. She wasn't interested in anybody. Her heart and her brain were now different than before. She didn't work.

We spent another ten years in the refugee camp. In the refugee camp, they educated the kids. Where I went to school, I had to walk about four or five kilometers [three miles] from our house, alone. Every Saturday, we went to collect our food from the United Nations, rations that they provided for the people who lived there. It was not an easy life.

I felt scared of my life over there. One time, when I was eight or nine years old and walking to school, somebody [a man] wanted to catch me. I was very scared. Very lucky for me, I was close to the school, and they had a guard there. I ran and then began to shout. I was not sure what he was going to do. Maybe he would have raped me.

I was just a little girl, living in Site 2, our refugee camp, walking several kilometers to school. But my mother wouldn't buy me a bicycle, which would be safer, because bad guys can't touch you when you're on a bicycle. So, this problem remained, with me thinking maybe somebody's going to try to grab me on the way to school.

Then, the time in my life came when menstruation started. My mother didn't tell me anything about that. I was totally afraid about what was happening. And my mother didn't provide me with tampons or pads or anything like that. So, it happened when I was in school, and I tried to cover it with my notebook, because I only had one pair of underwear.

[Her mom didn't take care of her at all, Karl adds. Srey Pouv cries when she tells this story.]

My mother and my aunt were around, but they didn't care.

We Heard Bombs in the Night and Had to Run and Hide

It was difficult sometimes, especially at night. We would hear bombs at night, and all the people in the villages escaped and were running away. My family also escaped. We went to somewhere that had a hole and hid there, to protect ourselves from the bomb.

And thieves would come to our house. They wanted to steal something from the family and break into the house, and so my mother and I

escaped to somewhere else to protect ourselves. Sometimes, my mom and
my uncle would lose each other and then later have to search the refugee
camp to find one another again.

After ten years, we came back to Cambodia, to Battambang Province,
where I was born. When we came back to Cambodia, the organization
UNHCR [the United Nations' refugee committee] gave each person $50
to help us get back home and start a new life. We also got one bag of rice,
50 kilos, and enough beans for cooking for one year.

When I came back from the refugee camp, I continued to go to school,
through the eighth grade. My favorite subject was Khmer [the native
language]. I still walked to school, about three kilometers a day.

I Wanted to Be a Nurse When I Grew Up

When I was a little girl, I wanted to be a nurse. I wanted to help the people
to recover in the hospital. In Cambodia, you go to a government hospital,
and, if you want the nurses or the doctors to do anything to help you, you
have to pay first. I would like to help the people without extorting the
money, like they did. In other words, I would like to offer healthcare that
is free.

I'll give you an example from my own life . . .

My First Experience Borrowing Money Was to Save My Own Life

In 2003, I had TB [tuberculosis]. My cousin and I had to get up at 3:00
every morning to do the housework. I had to work really hard, all the time.
We would sell sweets in the market. We worked outside all day just to get
some food. Working nonstop, not taking time for sleep, not to take a nap
or sleep at nighttime.

One day, I got sick, and I started coughing. I didn't understand why,
but it was so bad that I couldn't work anymore. My cousin gave me three

thousand Cambodian riel [75 cents] to pay for a taxi to take me back to the house and then to the clinic.

Then, I went to the clinic. This guy took an X-ray, and he said, "You need to take this medicine."

I said, "Okay. How much?"

He said, "How much do you have?"

"I still have five hundred Thai baht from my cousin," I said. (My cousin had pawned a gold bracelet to come up with the money for my medicine.) That's equivalent to $14.

The guy said, "That will do for three days'" [worth of medicine].

He gives me medicine for three days. He does not tell me that I have TB and that I can get the medicine free by going to the NGO [free clinic]. Now, I go into debt to my cousin for the five hundred Thai baht that I had to pay to this guy . . . five hundred baht is a lot of money! And ultimately, I end up at the NGO clinic that gives me enough medicine that can cure the TB.

The Doctor Told Me There Was No Hope for Me

My health was still not better. I went to the other hospital [the clinic], and the doctor told me that I would not get better in the future. I was scared about my life. I was afraid that I wouldn't recover.

Every night, I heard an owl shouting. We call this a bad omen, this bird. When an owl shouts at nighttime, that means somebody is ill. It means that the bird came to take the life of someone. Someone who's sick is going to die.

My mother came to take care of me every night, and she heard an owl shouting, and then, one other person in my house passed away. Then, I felt okay. The owl wasn't signaling for me.

I took my medicine every day for eight months, but my health was still not better. It was very serious. And my mother didn't cook rice soup for me every morning or give me some food. We were a very poor family.

My health is still not 100 percent, but I feel better. But now I no longer want to be a nurse!

How My Job Brought My Life Partner to Me

Later, I found a job in a restaurant called the Aseans in Battambang. I said to myself, "I'm ugly, but I can get a job back in the kitchen or something," and then, I would be happy. But they wanted me to work as a waitress. They paid me $16 for every month.

I met my husband after I had been working in this restaurant for about one and a half months. One day, I stood by the door, and Karl saw me. He had just arrived in Battambang. He was taking pictures for the Seva Foundation, which is an eyesight NGO. When he got off the bus, there were all these *tuk-tuk* [bicycle taxi] drivers, all saying, "I'll take you to a hotel."

And, out of all the tuk-tuk drivers, there was one disabled guy. His name was Mr. Savon. He had polio as a child. His one hand doesn't work, and one foot doesn't work. Karl said to him, "You get the job."

So Karl got in a tuk-tuk with a disabled guy, and Mr. Savon took Karl to the hotel. Then, Karl said, "Where's a good place to eat?" and the driver said, "There's this new place. Let's go." So, they came to my restaurant, and as they were driving in, Karl saw me, and he says that there was something about me . . .

They sat down for dinner. I talked with the tuk-tuk guy. I couldn't speak a word of English at all. I couldn't communicate to Karl except through a translator. He was just sitting at dinner, and I was bringing the food, and he talked to me.

Karl was different from the other tourists. He dressed nice, from top to bottom. He was kind. Karl also went to visit my house. I told him that we didn't have anything in the house, that we were a poor family . . . and then, he had to return to work. This was in 2004. He didn't get back to Cambodia until 2006. During those two years, I learned English, because I wanted to talk to Karl.

[Karl interjects: So, I have to go back to work, but I have this idea that I need to find out more about this woman, because it was like this *thing* that I understood. I knew there was something special about this girl, but I couldn't communicate with her. She apparently thought maybe similarly.]

Karl's always doing something, like especially helping people. He has his camera. Working in the restaurant, I'd seen a lot of people who are crazy, but Karl was a different person. But I didn't know if I would ever see him again.

In 2006, Karl came back. For some reason, the tuk-tuk driver's phone number stuck in his head. He memorizes certain numbers, and that number was in his head. When he came back in 2006, Karl made a phone call to him, Savon the driver. For the second time, the tuk-tuk driver met him at the bus station. Karl asked him to take him to my house.

I was still not married. We thought a long time before living together. There were cultural differences. It's much more difficult to understand the nuances of what people do and say, and whether or not they're sincere, when you don't speak the language and you don't know the culture. So, we were a little bit skeptical about each other, and we took a long time to really come to the decision.

Instead of a Wedding, We Invested in My Business Venture

Around November or December of that year, we did start to live together. In 2007, we traveled together to Thailand and Vietnam. We talked about getting married. I told him that in order to get married, I would have to send a lot of money [$200] to the district, because a wedding in Cambodia, especially to a foreigner, costs a lot of money. The wedding would be over in a day, and it would have cost the equivalent of several years' salary for a Cambodian. I would prefer to invest this money in my business. So, we decided to live together without marriage.

My husband also didn't look to me only that one day. It took a long time before he decided to live with me, and me with him also. With us, up until we married, husband and wife, our hearts were different, and our ideas as well were different. I have my own business, and I didn't want to depend on my husband.

[Karl: There was a whole period of time when we were both looking at each other like, "Is this the real thing?"]

So, Karl gave me the money, $200, that we would have spent to get our marriage license. I took this money and used it to make loans to people in my village.

Our partnership is different from other marriages in Cambodia. A lot of people here are married to people from other countries. With us, there is a seventeen-year age difference. In Cambodia, generally the older husband doesn't take care of the wife.

Traditionally, the men always go outside to find another lady. My husband never goes to drink beer alone or spend time outside or overnight. He always stays here at home and spends time with our family. For fun, we stay at home. We turn on music and dance.

And most Cambodian women, they just find the job to pay for what they need, one day to one day. They don't try. They're just waiting, passive.

And when their children get sick for one or two days, the mothers take them to the hospital and drop them off to be cared for by someone else. They think that caring for them is very boring. If my child is sick for even one day, I am very worried. I am more of a hands-on mother. In my family, we have no problems. We love each other. We are much happier than the other people around us.

The Family I've Created with Karl

Today, I live in Siem Reap, Cambodia, with the following members of my family: my husband; Kevin, our six-year-old son; Eher, a seven-year-old girl that we've had since birth whom we are officially adopting; my mother; two cousins and the wife of one cousin; and a girl that's a friend of the family that we're helping go to school. So that's nine people. I always thought that I would end up taking care of all of them.

[Karl explains about Eher: Okay. So, this young woman who's walking around that you may have noticed or not, she's actually the mother of the girl that we're adopting. She is, to put it mildly, a train wreck, and she doesn't really feel any connection with the kid.

But the child gravitated toward Pouv and me, and, certainly by default, she considered herself to be our daughter. And her mom was fine with that, too, because she just went back to where she was a dealer at a casino. Finally, I said, "Why don't we just make this official?" And we adopted her.

Not a tear was shed when she was signing the paperwork to give her kid away. Many of the mothers in this community display an inexplicable lack of maternal instinct toward and connection with their children. Maybe it's poverty, or culture. It's hard for people to understand the lack of connection. But it was good for us.]

I am Christian, although I still go to the pagoda. My mother is a Buddhist. During the Buddhist ceremonies in Cambodia, my husband and I go see my mother and spend time after the ceremony.

At home, I speak English with Karl. I cannot help the children with special English like grammar, verbs, things like that. Karl helps me with my email. He knows. Sometimes, there is a word I cannot understand exactly. I make an attempt, and he will explain. He's learning Khmer. We teach each other our languages.

How Cambodia Compares to . . . Chicago

I have been to the United States one time. Karl is from Chicago, and he took me there. First, when I arrived, I thought this would be a new world for me. I thought it would be very nice to live there, but then, I realized that it would be difficult to get a job, because I only had an eighth-grade education.

Most people like to go to the United States to look for a job, because they think over there, they can get a lot of salary compared to Cambodia. But if we own a little bit of money, we spend it differently here than in the USA. If somebody tried to work hard here, they would get more money here [comparatively]. And in the life over there, most people try to work very hard every day to get their money.

People think that my wealth comes from being married to a rich American husband, but that is absolutely wrong. Karl understands this: His money is *his* money. I work for my own money. I'm the lady, and I'm not waiting for my husband to give money to me.

I have my own ANZ bank account. I roll all of my profits back into the business. But even though I have a husband, I still manage my own business. The money I earn goes toward getting other customers. They need loans to buy some land. They do not have the money on their own. I don't want to put money in the bank. I like to put money in the business.

I handle my finances by myself. You know, this guy, he's my person, but I told him, "You need to save your money. You need to take care of yourself, not me."

If I Had All the Money in the World, I Would Still Work

If I had all the money in the world, I would still work and spend my time the same way. I would take care of my children, make sure they went to school, and look after my husband, my home, and my relatives. I would try to be a leader to my relatives. I want to help my family to stand up, like me.

The people in our home are family, and the reason they're here is because I'm trying to model for them and help them. Maybe they can make a life the way they want it to be, as I have.

It's not an easy task. Not all of our family members or people in my community have my kind of forward thinking, my initiative. Many are just okay with, "Well, I'll get something to eat today," and not thinking about tomorrow. And so, by sharing my story here, maybe they'll get the idea, "Well, maybe I can do something."

I have tried many, many times with my own family members. I bought my cousin Chia the chicken coop and the chickens out back. I bought their pigs. I bought the cows. I said, "Look, try to start your own business." But it's very difficult to get someone to really take the initiative and start up a business, even when you hand it over to them.

We Hired My Family to Build Our New Home

I said, "Let's hire my family to build this place," and so, for a year, they lived here, ate here, and worked here. I oversaw the construction of our house. I translated the plans and managed the workers. I got all of the cement and rebar and glass and wood and everything to make this house. It was a family project. My cousins and extended family are people that can build things.

I tried to encourage them, "Don't take the money. Wait until the end so that you have a big chunk of money, which you can start a business with."

Along the way, they'd say, "Oh, can't I just take a month's wages right now and buy a cellphone?" And I was trying to say, "Just save money; just save money."

At the end of the construction, in summer 2014, we had a little session. We said, "Okay, here's the money that we owe you. Please do something smart with it." I still worry about them—my relatives, as well as my kids.

I try. I try to be fair with money, even if everyone cheats me all the time, even if people tell me not to care so much about my family.

I've Made All My Dreams Come True

Everything I dreamed about before, I have now, and yet I also feel that I've had a difficult time. My goal over the next ten years would be this: I want my loan business to grow. I remember how it feels when there is no one to help you, and so I want my loan business to be able to help as many people as I can.

For myself, I want my children, Kevin and Eher, to go to the USA for their education.

Earlier in life, I felt like a slave or something like that. I was thinking: Now I need to stand up and save money and put money in the hand. Save, save, save, save, you know? Then, I can stand up and save someone else . . .

Maybe someone will read our story and will see what they can do to make their life better.

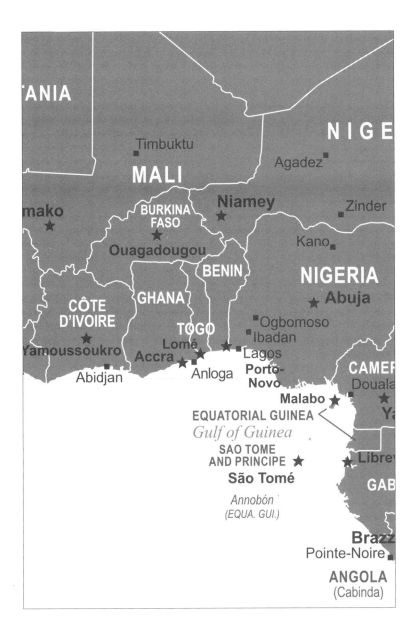

eight

SENA

TOMATO CANNER

Anloga, Ghana

Editor's note: Traveling to Africa with Grameen Foundation (grameenfoundation.org) as a storytelling consultant, I arrive into Ghana a day early to interview a Skees Foundation partner, Sena Ahiabor, a social entrepreneur who's concocted a cheap way to solve a centuries-old Ghanaian problem—the seasonal glut and roadside rot of thousands of tomatoes. Using machinery he devised himself in his small, home-based factory, Sena preserves those tomatoes in an organic purée he calls "TomaFresh." He named his company Tip Top Foods.[1]

I cannot wait to meet Sena. Jet-lagged and wilting in the humid, tropical heat, I end up pacing. Sena comes late to our meeting—by two hours—with no phone call heads-up.

I later learn that his old-style mobile phone lacked the minutes necessary to call anyone other than his wife (to let her know he made it all right). He's been gravely ill with malaria and had feared he wouldn't make our meeting at all, but Sena rallies. He splurges on a three-hour taxi ride, which costs twice as much as the six-hour bus ride would have done, [2] and he bursts into the hotel a bit rumpled and sweaty but beaming with joy at the chance to tell me all about his tomatoes.

Ghana is a tropical West African country a bit smaller than Oregon. Sena comes from a long line of farmers from the Volta region, [3] but he's more than a farmer: He's a full-fledged agronomist, who studied soil science at the University of Ghana at Legon School of Agriculture and completed a three-year internship with a mentor through the University of Zürich in Switzerland. He's always pondering problems, like how to reap more produce from the sandy local soil and ways to process other crops grown by his small-scale neighboring farmers, to even out both their incomes and nutrition.

He's an intellectual, constantly brooding over technical and social problems, for which, "I have a write-up on that," he often says.

Sena's studies have taken him abroad, yet his vision remains local. Beginning and ending each long workday with the desire to make his corner of the world a better place, Sena and his wife, Apollonia, barely earn a subsistence salary from the many jobs they cobble together (such as cleaning, gardening, and laundry). They give food to neighbors in need and support local students by paying their school fees.

Sena hopes his company will make it big and make him rich along the way. He'd like his children to take over the company, grow it into a successful "turnkey" operation, and become the number one tomato-sauce supplier to Shoprite grocery stores and the Eastern Ghana school system.

This slim man with a professor's demeanor exudes optimism about the capacity of humans to hunker down where we were born and tackle problems of hunger through simple solutions of supply, packaging, and distribution. He talks for hours about his inventions, then grins broadly as he presents me with a parting gift—two bottles of tomato purée.

Later, when I lug home my precious TomaFresh and stir it into spaghetti for my own family, we taste the simplicity of Sena's pure intention, and we feel—for those few bites—that we're dining with our global kin in Ghana.

Born into a Long Line of Farmers

My name is Sena Ahiabor. I'm forty-six years old. I live and work in the Volta Region of Ghana, in West Africa. We're on the farthest southeastern coast of Ghana [on the Gulf of Guinea], in the town of Anloga. We share water with the coast, just about one kilometer from the coast. It's a large town. We have a metropolitan status of 100,000 people.

I was born a farmer's son, and I have always been a farmer. My grandfathers were all farmers. I have six brothers, no sisters. My mother worked with my dad on the farm. In those days, shallots were the mainstay. They grew all the vegetables you can think of, the African vegetables, maize, small onions, okra, pepper, and tomatoes. They owned the land, and they hired sharecroppers to work on the land.

I wouldn't say my parents were well-to-do. They were poor, but they made sure they met all my needs. They got me anything I wanted. I was never hungry. I never lacked for anything.

I didn't grow up in Accra [the capital city], but my primary education was there. I moved back for secondary school in my hometown, then back for the tertiary in Accra. I migrated between the two towns.

I Thought I'd Be an Engineer
When I Grew Up—and I Am

I attended the University of Ghana at Legon, in Accra. At that time, the university was free. You just qualified through the exams, and then, you enrolled—but it's not like that anymore.

I thought I was going to be an engineer, because I liked designing equipment. I considered studying this at [the] University of Ghana, but their engineering department was limited. I also realized that, as a farmer's son, I am expected to farm and help the family. So, I majored in soil science.

I trained as an agronomist, but I'm into agri-processing. Soil is so important to me because I grew up in a sandy condition [adjacent to Lake Volta]. My hometown is full of beach sand. To grow crops in such soil is so demanding. You need to improve the soil and water it daily.

We use a heavy application of organic manure, especially cow dung and chicken droppings. And then, you have to leave plant stubbles over the manure and incorporate this mixture into the soil to improve the strength of the soil. At the end of the day, the whole thing drains out. You have to apply it all again. Few farmers have used this composting method in my area. That's how I got interested in that. I wanted to see what I could do to improve the lot of my people.

Canning Tomato Sauce the Italian Way

I finished university in 1994. My father passed away two weeks before my final-year exams. I was twenty-four. After university, we used to have a one-year mandatory national service program. I was assigned to a university farm where they grew rice and did some cattle rearing.

At the tail end of my national service, I left for Switzerland. I had an internship with the International Association of Agricultural Students (IAAS). I didn't go to Switzerland to make money; I went there to see their farming methods, so I could bring these ideas home and modify them to suit the environment here.

My Swiss boss was so impressed with my work, he asked me back three times. The agriculture university in Zürich ran the program. They placed the students in farms. But thank God for this man who decided to take me on. Each year, he invited me, and a local family bought my air ticket. I came home to Ghana every year at the end of the fall season, because I was already preparing the ground for my tomato-processing project.

In Switzerland, my boss's sister had a one-acre greenhouse, and they were growing tomatoes. The large ones were discarded, because they couldn't fit the size of what he wanted, and they threw them away. They wanted to collect them and use them as purée.

The tomato farmers would call this neighbor, an Italian, to process the tomatoes, so they would have purée for household use. One day, we had just come back for lunch, and there was this man doing the tomato processing for my boss.

The Italian asked me if I was interested in learning. I said, "Yes, why not? We have a lot [of excess tomatoes] back home."

So, he taught me how to do it. It took him only about fifteen, twenty minutes. I tried the equipment. It was this handheld pulper. I asked him if he could get one for me. He went to Napoli, across the border to Italy, and brought one to me, and I had to carry that in my hand luggage. I didn't want to lose it! It was close to ten kilos [twenty-two pounds].

When I got back to Ghana, I bought a crate of tomatoes and did as the Italian had taught me to do, and everyone liked it. We were all happy. And from then on, I looked at other ways to do it and then to do it on a larger scale. This is how Tip Top began.

When I came back finally, after Switzerland, I opted to do landscaping alongside trying to grow my tomato business. So, I worked with the German Embassy and a few expatriate people taking care of their homes, growing their gardens for them, until I realized that I couldn't stay in Accra and nurture my tomato business in Anloga.

I'm CEO of a Tomato-Processing Factory

I am the CEO of Tip Top Foods, which is a tomato canning company that I founded in 2005. The factory is right across the driveway from our house. It's about 60 x 60 feet. We intend to move our home when we get bigger, but at least for now, that's okay. The factory is totally separate from the living area. They both share the driveway, but the factory's to the left and our living area is to the right. If you drive in, you get to the office, in one of the warehouses, and the main shed is on the other side.

We employ thirty to forty local farmers for the inputs, and in season, we hire around fifteen migrant workers to help process the tomatoes into purée.

My Vision Sustained Me When My Dream Seemed Impossible

Life is, like they say, how you make it. I would say my top skills are my ability to resolve issues or problems using my ingenuity and to look beyond today, into the future. For example, once when I returned home from Switzerland, I had two vehicles—vans completely loaded with items to sell and some to keep, but I lost it all in a fire.

Within three months, I lost my three vehicles. I had an accident and spent three weeks in a coma from a motorbike accident. Then, I thought I was going to go back to Switzerland, and my boss wrote me that the house there burned down. I was stuck here. So, I said, "Let me just see what I can do with all that I gained from Switzerland."

We did a sample with the hand crank. It was good. I said, "Let's make it five-star."

So, I coupled an electric drill onto it. My wife helped out. We were not married yet; she was then my fiancée. We made the sauce in the kitchen, a small place. We gave out samples to people, and they liked it.

I got a contract [for the new company]. I started buying more of these bottles. I didn't have even a new cap to put on them. This cap was important. So, we started, and people were buying it gradually, but to go big was becoming a problem until the orders came in. That's when we had a boost.

The Problem: Our Tomatoes Rot While We Import Canned Sauce

Ghana is not poor. Ghana is not wealthy, either, because things are not properly done. I'm sorry to be saying this, but that's the truth. There are so many potentials here which are not harnessed. Every year, my people grow vegetables, all kinds of vegetables and tomatoes, and they go rotting in the field, and I see all that go to waste, and I feel the pinch of it.

Pricing of tomatoes fluctuates so much. You could pay about five hundred times more when tomatoes are not in season than when they are in season. Why haven't we been able to stabilize the price of the tomato, the fresh tomato used to make the paste?

Currently, I think, in Africa, we are the largest importer[4] of foreign tomato paste, of the whole continent.

Another Production Challenge: Organic Versus Chemical Fertilizer

I also intend to run an organic manure project. I have a write-up on that. The main challenge of the farmers here is the sandy soil. At the time when they're just about to do the major farming season, most of them are broke. Then, the rain sets in. The first rainy season is around May to July. Then again, rain can return in September, October, but it's erratic. It's about three months of the year.

During the rainy season, farmers can't go to the market to collect their dung [fertilizer]. And even if they do, they don't have trucks to bring it down, because they become very heavy and bulky. So, they plant without fertilizing, and then, the yields go down. If we had an organization that could collect and store and give and sell [dry] dung to them just before the planting season, a lot would go very well with my farmers.

Also, the cows eat grown grass, and they ingest it with the seeds. So, not only are the farmers applying those fresh dungs, they are also applying weed seeds. You have to do a lot of weeding. But if you heat the dung for a very long time, that sterilizes it and kills the weed seeds that the cows have eaten. You can do this with natural sunlight, if it beats down so that it becomes hot enough to actually sterilize it.

What is actually hampering good food production is the inability to apply organic manure in good quantities. A lot of small-scale farmers are going for chemical fertilizers now, which are leaching up into our lagoon and killing the aquatic flora and fauna.

Secondly, the land-use system is not favoring those who want to do organic manure. You could just fertilize the land for a season of three months to plant. So, in that way, you don't want to do organic manure, because the organic manure releases minerals slowly, more slowly than the chemical fertilizer.

I wish we could provide available organic manure all year around. Even now, you have to arrange with trucks. It takes so long for them to bring it in. The crops are wet. People have money when the dung isn't transportable, or they don't have money when it is, and their crops are in, and the production is lower. So, it's a vicious cycle every year.

My Wife Came to Ghana Because of Civil War in Togo

My wife, Mrs. Apollonia, is from Togo. I first met her in 1986 when she was sixteen. She came with my auntie, and we became friends, although she only spoke French, and I couldn't even speak French. Then, she left for Togo. I tried writing French to her once, but I don't think the letter got to her.

In 1993, they had a political upheaval in Togo, and her whole family came down to Ghana. I met her, and then, I asked her to come over and attend school in Ghana so that she could learn to speak English. She accepted. So, she came over and started at school.

After she finished, she went to Accra for a computer hardware program. I was then going on and off to Switzerland, and she was here in Accra. Then, on January 22, 1999, we got married.

We have five children: three boys and two girls. The eldest boy is home with us right now. He likes football [the sport Americans call *soccer*] so much! He plays very well. I bought him his first football when he was three years old. He was the team captain for his class, and he's gotten to a junior team now in college. So, we marry his time for winter training and then for studies. We are very strict about him. But he's doing well.

Our eldest daughter is also at home. She runs errands for people. She's also very good in the kitchen. She's a homemaker. The middle son is young, very, very energetic, easygoing, and open. Then, we have a little girl who's just started school; she says things which are far ahead than what she should know at her age. And the baby, he is just coming up, just starting to speak. We don't know yet what he's going to be. I think he's also doing well. So, what I can say in a nutshell about my family? I think I have a wonderful family.

When the kids are older, they will all go to college—of course. They will go wherever they find themselves . . . but I hope one of them will eventually take up the business.

We Hire Local Farmers and Migrant Workers

We produce canned tomatoes each year from late August into early November. Migrant workers come to work with me during the season. Right now, we have about fifteen workers. Some are from the area, and some are university undergraduates from the University of Togo.

We house and feed them, and at the end of the day, they take three thousand CFA [$5.20/day]. But I don't think we will be able to pay that much this year because of the exchange rate. We have targeted a bit less this year. My work is on contract. For example, the women who clean the bottles, we pay them based on the quantity that they clean.

Our workers are men and women. We don't have youth working here. Honestly, I don't like children being exposed to money at an early stage. They go wayward. They don't want to work. They want to chase after the money. So, I look for people who are old, who are not in school. Or, even if you are in school, you have to go to school first, that day, before you can work.

We are the highest paying [local] organization, because our work is so laborious, and it's a work that you cannot put away. Once the tomatoes are ripened, you need to process them. So, we then do day-and-night processing. When they are ready, you need to go.

When the tomato season is about to begin, things are generally not in place. We are not ready for processing in terms of equipment and all of that. But the fruits have started coming in, and you must make a move and begin. There are so many tomatoes. The farmers are calling you. If you don't start working, then problems begin to occur.

When we are processing, I wake up early. I sometimes sleep only three to four hours at a time. We sometimes do two shifts, day and night. The season is only three months. So, we do as much as we can and store the sauce, and then, later on, we can transfer it into smaller containers.

When the season is over, we close down. We intend to go into other items processing, and we're getting a contract with Shoprite in Accra [the capital city] to package some of the vegetables that we grow there. Then, I can get a few of the workers to be full time. But, currently, we close down. In the offseason, we occasionally clean around and within the warehouse. Then, we call the workers to come and clean for a fee.

I'm Still Mad at Myself for the One Rookie Mistake I Made

My worst day was when we used dirty cans. The cans were not properly washed, and then, they were not properly pasteurized and re-sterilized.

We lost around seventy-five cans—the large jerricans that serve our local schools. That was a big loss to take. We sold those cans too early, and then, we had to do them again.

In that situation, I didn't get angry. I just knew that I needed to concentrate more. My weakness is when I lose concentration in an overwhelming situation. I have to leave the scene quickly and stay away for a while. But my wife helps a lot. She knows my moods. She comes in; then, I come back.

Government Bureaucracy: Ten Years to Get Certified

I came back [from my training in Switzerland] bubbling with all the energy to change the agriculture for at least part of my country, but then, I struggled to get a certification from the government. It took me from 2005 to 2014 to receive certification from the Food and Drug Authority [Ghana's FDA] for my product, but now that's not a problem anymore. I have my certificate, and I can finally sell my product.

The government awarded me the Certificate of Merit, National Food Processor, in recognition of the outstanding contribution toward the development of agriculture in Ghana. So, now I would like to collaborate with the Ministry of Agriculture to improve my equipment and get a bigger volume done. For example, right now, we have inefficient boilers. It takes so long to boil the tomatoes. The amount you can do in a day is reduced.

Pasteurizing is also problematic. We need state-of-the-art equipment to get all the microbes out. If you don't cook them very well, you lose them, and that's what we sometimes do. It all amounts to getting some money to get the equipment.

Right now, we provide the product in two sizes: the big jar holds one kilo, a thousand grams. The smaller jar holds three hundred grams. We are currently limited with the packaging material. We want to see how we can do bulk packaging so that, when the tomatoes are in season, we put them into these big jars to later be put into small jars.

Our Market Is Growing, but It Could Be the Whole United States!

We currently provide canned tomatoes for about four schools. One school orders 150 jars per year from us, about fifty jars per term, depending on the number of students. But our biggest client is the secondary school in my hometown.

We wrote proposals to a lot of schools and gave them samples, and they are interested in getting the product from us. We have limitations to finance large-scale production. I can't produce to meet the needs of the school. I need new and better equipment, which are energy efficient.

The shopping mall wants our TomaFresh, but the big shops need us to provide a label with a bar code. I just got a certification, and the bar code will appear on the new label. Soon, we will be able to supply the shops and the schools.

I'll speak to you bluntly: I don't see our product on the market here. I haven't seen any of this type of local packaging on any of the shelves. Those other canned sauces you see are imported from elsewhere—from Europe, mostly from Italy. So, I think I have a virgin market here. If I'm well packaged, I think I'll make great strides here.

I had my best day last year when I ran out of all my packaging materials. Then, I knew I had met my mark!

I imagine that Tip Top is going to be very huge. It will be a player in the region for organic food, food from our own soil and toil, locally grown food to be used here, with the excess going out to anywhere else.

So, for now, we'll get all the vegetables to be close to organic-certified produce. Then, we can also start marketing this tomato purée as organic. And that's when we can have a market share in the United States. We have the labor here, so we can produce here and export there.

Sweet Potato Project in Collaboration with U.S. Universities

We source our tomatoes from neighboring farms. I have a farm, too, but it's mainly for research programs. Currently, I'm the southern coordinator on this horticulture collaborative research program for Tuskegee University, Pennsylvania State University, and the University of California–Davis. I got to know them through a friend of mine. We were roommates at the University of Ghana at Legon. Then later, he had a chance to study for his master's at Tuskegee. That's how they contacted me.

We are studying the sustainable technology of an orange and purple sweet potato project. We're trying to multiply these sweet potatoes to use for canning to remedy vitamin A deficiency here in Africa. They brought samples from the States. They're trying to match them with the local ones. I took two of the American varieties that were brought to me plus two of the local ones. I'm trying to compare the way they grow and the timing and all that.

We are currently working on a sweet-potato bread. Sweet potatoes can be grown year-round. They want to develop the dry ones to make into chips and be ground into flour. We could also clean vegetables like okra, pepper, and cabbages to meet the shops' demands. Then, we could supply the shops with this food.

I'm Both an Entrepreneur and a Social Entrepreneur

I consider myself both an entrepreneur and a social entrepreneur. People come to us for food. When we have extra potatoes, we give them out to people who are hungry, because they cannot be sold easily.

And currently, I am paying school fees for two students. They promised they would come back to work with me and my factory in exchange for money they needed for registration for their exams. I went to the head of the school. I said, "Let me just pay," and then, they said it was not even a formal agreement—but the students will be coming back to work at my factory to pay for what I'm giving them.

These farmers are doing everything they can; they are dedicated, but you know, the challenges of living that they face . . . most of them are peasant farmers. Some of them come to us for money to buy cow dung to fertilize their farms. We sometimes give them interest-free loans, because that's the way we get to work hand-in-hand with them. Others need money to buy the inputs for planting, especially the organic manure. So, if we have the means, we look at our finances.

A farmer might say, "I need about twenty or fifty sacks of cow dung." If we are sure we can afford it, we'll give you the seeds and manure. Then, we take that tomato crop back [once it's grown]. We are doing this with a few of the farmers. So, that brings cohesiveness between us.

There can be thirty to fifty farmers [who supply to us], depending on what we get from them. The women, especially, they go to the market, but they can't sell their tomatoes there. No one wants to buy them, and so they just rot in the sun. I say, "Bring them to me." They bring them. If they meet my quality, I take them.

My wife is very open, very friendly. She is always ready to make new friends and to share whatever she has. I think she's a family woman. A few people who are known to us and who are close to us, she goes to visit them to help clean their homes. When we meet people and she sees them, she tells me, "Oh, this man or this woman, I think she needs that or this. Can we help them?" If we can, we give a helping hand.

We Work Other Jobs to Make Ends Meet

Right now, Tip Top is not very big. I take a small stipend from this work, three hundred to four hundred Ghanaian cedis [$75–$100] per month. I want to see how I can grow this business before I can start giving a good salary to myself. And Tuskegee University also gives me a small stipend.

The money we make, we plow back into this project. Half of our business is in direct services, like laundry, which is doing so well. My wife owns a laundry facility, and I help her. We have five washers. We don't use dryers; they are too expensive to run. We do all the laundry. We bring it in and weigh it. If you want it ironed, we do that for a fee.

On a typical day, when I wake up, I may help my wife with the laundry. If there's a crop, I work on the farm. Actually, with these sweet potatoes, we have to have the vines there all year round. We water almost every day because of the sunny nature of the soil. I don't have a big farm. So, all my work is centered around the house. My normal day plan is I do this, this, and that until the day's ended.

I also do landscaping horticulture. We clean people's homes. Anything that I think will bring me money, which I want to do and do very well, I go for it!

When I'm Not Working, I'm Reading, Designing, or Cooking Tomato Sauce

When I'm not working, I'm either reading or designing something. I do a lot of designs or have ideas that I want to work on, or I'm repairing something in my house or doing some cleaning or something. I'm always busy doing something.

It occurs to me, I don't know if it is in my dreams, when I'm eating, or in the middle of something else, but all of a sudden, something comes up, and then, I don't waste time. I quickly put it on paper. I think of our problem, and then, I get a solution to it.

I also like to cook, using our tomato sauce. My specialty is stew, made of fish or poultry or meat. It is made with onions, ginger, tomatoes, sweet pepper, and green beans.

This Job Has Me Creating and Refining, Night and Day

I go to bed very late. I am the last one to go to sleep in the house, close to midnight, because I'm on the Internet, or I'm writing, or I'm reading. I'm always thinking about my projects . . . Then, I don't wake up very early in the morning. I'd say I wake up around 6:00 a.m.

I designed most of the equipment we use currently. For example, I did a gantry [see chapter-opener photograph]; it's just a metal beam like a tripod with a long bar across which is strong enough, then stuff that rolls on a wheel over it so that I can move it from place to place. Then, we have these hoists, a chain-linked pulley system, and a cage-type thing in which we pack the bottles. We then immerse the whole thing into the hot water.

Actually, when the Italian taught me, he said we should allow the water to cool before we take the bottles out.

I said, "No, that would be a lot of energy going to waste. So, why don't I just finish with one batch, and then, I pull it out and bring in another one?"

We have a lot of the cages packed with bottles. When one is ready, we take it out, using the chain hoist, put it by the side, and then, we put the next one in. A few things like that, that I did myself, I realize as days goes by, that some are not efficient. So, I just reinvent the machines. They're already there. But whenever I see there's a problem that we can actually deal with, I do, with my ingenuity.

My Dream, My Company, My Legacy

I think thirty employees could work on ten key projects, and then, the output depends on the equipment and the farmers. We could have about twenty trucks filled every four days. If you have capacities of producing two tons of tomato sauce per hour, in a day we could do about two tons per hour all day; that's sixteen to twenty tons of sauce per day.

So, what I want to say is, "What you see depends on what you look for." It's just like that quotation by John Lubbock. Because I had already prepared myself that I was going to go into this, and because, despite my problems, my mind was already made up, I was undeterred and moved on.

People get disorganized as a result of a small break in the free-flow of whatever life process is there, but I was not shaken. So, what I tell people is they should package whatever they want to do very well in their mind and go over and over it again so that, when they have to start, there'll be very few mistakes. You can start very small.

I don't believe in plagiarism. That's what is scarring the whole world now. People want to just copy anything. It's not about the copying: The guy who makes a copy doesn't have a foundation. Start at the root. Grow it, and get the branches and the fruits.

The whole thing is in the mind. You go to bed at night, and you sleep over it, think about it, how to improve upon it. You cannot look at it later and go back and redo it. You will mess up. So, I believe in whatever you do, you go at it slowly, and then, you improve upon it steadily until you get to where you want to go. That's what I would want to tell people.

176

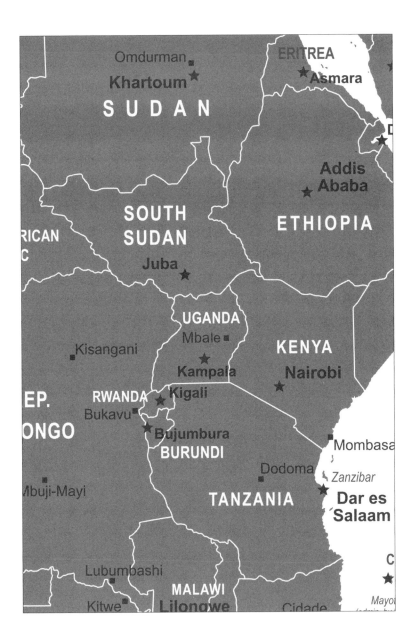

nine

———

MARY

BANANA FARMER

Mbale, Uganda

Editor's note: Uganda sits nearly smack in the middle of the African continent with a population of forty-two million in an area slightly smaller than Oregon. Thirteen tribes comprise its 99 percent African population; the country gained independence from Britain in 1962. It's known for its struggles with political corruption, HIV/AIDS, and human rights violations, especially against homosexuals, and for years of civil war and ravaging by the Lord's Resistance Army in the mountainous north. Its major export is coffee. Here, almost everyone works in farming, although 82 percent of Ugandans cultivate tiny plots by hand as sharecroppers and own no land of their own.

I meet Mary Gibutaye,[1] a sixty-five-year-old self-made farmer, on a visit with Grameen Foundation (grameenfoundation.org). Having pieced her farm together like patchwork, little by little, after a midlife divorce, Mary had found herself in a field full of infested banana plants. Panicked, living hand-to-mouth, and supporting three grandchildren, she had no funds to start over and no idea what to do.

Then, she found a simple tool to help her eviscerate the infesting worms and transform her farm into a leafy haven of seventy thousand bunches. It wasn't insecticide or a tractor. It was a mobile phone.

She rented it, equipped with a "Community Knowledge Worker" farming-assistance application, and became a volunteer advisor to one hundred local farmers in her county. She walks several hours a day to visit their nearby homes.

Mary turns to her mobile phone to research crop and livestock diseases and their solutions. She also can access weather, almanac, and fair-market-price data. She knows when and where to sell her bananas at the best price, so she doesn't have to settle for whatever the peddler coming through her village on any given day might offer.

One word describes Mary: *jubilant*. She never stops smiling, punctuates the end of most sentences with a throaty chuckle, and answers questions with her own unique, charming affirmative: "Yes, please!" She has eagerly adopted crop rotation and organic cultivation on her farm. Mary's farm has no plumbing or electricity, so she charges her phone through a solar station. She's become a local icon and a role model in a place that's not exactly known for respect toward women.

Frustrated with a lack of work ethic around her, Mary worries about rural youth turning to "idleness" and adults wasting away drinking. She and her phone, which she calls "the computer," are on a campaign to teach her neighbors how easy it really can be to grow a surplus of varied crops for consumption and sale. Mary calls her mobile phone her "secret weapon": It's the sharpest tool on her farm.

To Mary, bananas equal cash, and trees are an investment in the future. And proof of her success hangs right over our heads: The bananas on her trees are five times the size of the neighbor's next door.

I Grow Crops Just to Sustain Myself

I am a farmer. Monday through Saturday, I work on my farm. I diversify my production. I grow bananas and coffee, also maize, various cereals, such as millet. I also grow legumes, like beans.

On a typical day, my family does a lot of farming. We make a plan, a kind of farming calendar, that we discuss in the morning. Right now, we are busy planting. But the other crop, beans, is also ready for weeding and spraying.

Early in the morning, we don't have water. [Mary's farm has no plumbing or electricity.] We have a barrel for water behind our house and a borehole for the well that we share with the community. I have to go early, by five or six in the morning, before the water is all gone. Then, from there, we've got to dig. We go planting, then weeding, then we make lunch. The whole day we are busy.

When I'm tired, I go back home. I have to relieve myself; then, maybe I take a snack or make a meal. Then, when I feel that I am rested and OK, I go back to digging. After that, I come home to bathe.

When I have free time, I am on my phone, studying agriculture. I don't listen to music. I like to look things up on the Internet! For example, I can find out what country is the smallest, and which one is the largest. Or how old is [former U.S. President] Obama? Let's look that up . . . [Chuckles.]

Or you will catch me in my banana plantation, pulling up the weeds or organizing my mulch, or looking after the weakened plants that I have not wanted to fail.

I plant the new crop just after I have harvested the old grain crop. I grow vegetables to sustain myself, because the crops are my food and, at the same time, the household income. The vegetables reach maturity faster than the beans, and then, as you are waiting for the bananas to mature, the beans are ready. So, that is what I do.

On my farm, the trees are very important. They help as windbreakers. That is point one. Point two is that my trees, like this *grevillea* tree here, are for drainage. Behind them is a swamp, but this grevillea has drained the soil, and so now I have planted vegetables near it. The leaves that drop down from the trees help to improve soil fertility. Meanwhile, their root system allows for minimal tillage, so we don't have to disturb the worms, which make the soil aerated. The trees' root system and the worms' work prevent me from having to dig out the soils, so they are very useful.

Right now, I have three acres of land. My plan is to have another two acres, one for banana production and another for trees. You see, trees are a sort of passive income. I use them for firewood and also sell the trees for firewood and [the trunks as] poles. People here like poles. We use them for building construction. You have to remove the branches, which are another source of firewood.

I Used to Be a Bad Farmer

When I first started this work, I was a bad farmer. I didn't plan my farm. I would just come out and grow everything. The income was very poor. I was selling, and transport was a problem. You had to spend a lot of money on getting the produce to the market. Then, you had to just sit there at the market, and you couldn't leave until your supply was finished. I used to be very poor.

Before I was with Grameen, I worked with another NGO [nongovernmental organization or nonprofit]. I went to a class on conservation agriculture to learn how to improve the soil.

When I started improving a bit, the Grameen Foundation thought I was the right person. They promoted me and made me a Community

Knowledge Worker (CKW).[2] Later, I realized that with conservation agriculture, I had done very little. But then . . . Grameen came with that phone!

What a Little Mobile Phone Can Do

Grameen gave us very nice phones, full of applications and technology. They also gave us ReadySets [solar charging stations]. I don't have any electricity here, so I just put out my ReadySet and charge it in the sun. Then, in the evening, when it has power, I [charge up] my phone while I am sleeping.

When I first received the phone, I didn't even know how to operate a computer. They told us how to operate the phones and how to use Google. The first time they taught me, I was scared! I wanted to run out of the class. [Laughs.] I thought I was a poor performer because of my age.

But [the trainer] Madame Sarah, she was very much on my side. She said, "You are smart. You look bright. Now, if you leave this work, I will not be happy."

She had a mandate: I had to learn how to use a computer. And then, later, it turned out that I was the one teaching people how to use it! [Laughs.]

These phones are full of information. There's a "CKW Search" where they will tell you about the production of different crops and how much product you can get from your land. The phone advised me to grow two-thirds of my land for perennial crops and, if I plant trees, then also to plant annual crops. So, that's my plan: I am now doing crop rotation.

When You See a Banana, You See a Piece of Fruit—But I See Shillings!

Yes! [Laughs.] That's what I see. Right now, we have a respite from the rainy season, so I want to remove some of the fallen leaves. I want to make room for new seeds, because I know by planting a banana plant, I am saving at least five thousand shillings [$1.50] in the future, or more. The price will depend on the size of the plant. That bunch you see hanging over there: It's worth five [thousand shillings]. But the other big ones should be seven to ten, because, when they are mature, they will produce bigger fingers [fruit]. So, the price ranges from five thousand to fifteen thousand [$1.50–$4.45].

I love my banana trees! I love them like my children. They're a source of food and, at the same time, a source of income. Here, it's very difficult to go and borrow money, even if only five thousand, from a friend. But I can easily borrow money from my banana plantation, because I just go to the trading center, and I say, "Can you raise [an advance of] five thousand?" And they'll give it to me immediately.

So, the friend who's always there, whether I'm tired or not, is my banana plantation.

Then, the phone will tell you what varieties to plant, fertilizers to use, and production costs to expect. Just today, I read about the production of bananas. It was telling me how much I should invest in land preparation: $3,344,000 [$992], for the digging of the holes and so on and so on. Then, the gross income would be $6,000,000 [$1,780]—the difference is over $2 million. So, before I grow something, I look at my phone.

Before this, I was not getting any income, apart from the bit I got from the market, as I mentioned. First, there was this disease called the BBW (banana bacteria wilt). It was a terrible disease. It was wiping out the bananas, and I was giving up.

The mobile phone told us how to control the disease. The simple technique that saved my banana trees was to improve my management. The phone said the [BBW] disease was being spread by not cleaning your tools. After weeding a banana plant which is sick, you would continue to a normal one—and so then you would transfer the disease to a healthy plant.

Now, the Internet was advising us first to weed the healthy plant, then go to the diseased one [so as not to cross-contaminate]. When you go to the diseased area, you cut all the diseased plants into smaller pieces. Then, you disinfect your tools.

This area suffers from three deadly diseases. Besides the banana bacteria wilt (BBW), there's also banana fusarium wilt, which makes the banana have yellow leaves and brown spots on the fruit. It's not very common, but we realize the importance of avoiding it. There's also bunch-top disease; that's when the leaves grow together. They are very short and closed like a bush. This too can be spread by cutting healthy plants after your tool has touched a diseased plant. But it has not yet intensified in Uganda.

My plants had banana fusarium wilt and banana bacteria wilt, both of which are now controlled on my farm today. And so, my income has improved.

I Employ Five Local Farmers

My cash-crop farm employs five local farmers. They need money, so they come to work here. Even in my family, there are also people who've worked for me. If I'm going to pay them, where's the money coming from? From my bananas.

Five people work here for me; each one is given three thousand shillings [90 cents]. That's $15,000 [$4.45]. When I sell my bananas and firewood, I am already indebted to these people. At the same time, I'm making sure, if they are doing the weeding, they are getting paid.

The money [I pay out in salaries] is being returned to me by my bananas and my trees. That is how I am surviving. The money I earn makes me have whatever I like!

How I'm Different from Other Farmers around Here

I think I'm different from other farmers, because now the performance of my crops is better than theirs. I've got this weapon—my phone. They don't have one. This phone is ever-alert. Tonight, when I'm in my bed, I can say, "Now, I am going to grow maize. How do I do it?"

I am very proud as a CKW, because I have done a lot of the activities [that the program teaches] on my own small plot. More farmers trust me, and I'm teaching even more farmers to get on board. We have over a hundred farmers who join my meetings.

I Opened My First Bank Account in My Sixties

Grameen also introduced us to Opportunity Bank. I opened an account. I currently have over two million Ugandan shillings in the bank. I can even use my phone to send mobile money with MTN.

Now, in the community around us, they have formed their own savings groups. They save every Saturday. The minimum is two thousand shillings [60 cents], and they just keep it locally in a box. They usually share that money [back with contributing members] after a year. Let's say they start in January; they're going to share it around December, for Christmas shopping and so on.

There are very few people here who have got a savings account like business people, in town, in the bank. Some are saving money in a sack. But in general, people in this community, they don't bother. People are scared. They say, "Ah, we might save, and then, people will steal our money!"

Sometimes with local savings groups, you lose your money over issues of accountability with the cashier or the treasurer. Some of the treasurers are not trustworthy. When they look at the money, it's disorganized, and it does not add up, or they've decided to give the money to their friends. Or, if the treasurer doesn't have any money, he has to sell his land and then give out the money to the owners. In the end, the sharing is very poor.

Others saved for just a short period, and then they wanted loans, or they wanted to withdraw. The culture of saving is minimal. They think of the short term, and then end up unfortunate. That's the problem. The culture of saving here is very poor.

Orphaned, Pulled Out of School, and Married at Eighteen

I was born here in the Mbale district, in a county in the central area that's adjacent to this one. I grew up there as an orphan; my father died when I was very young. My uncle was not very happy to see me come to live with him, because he had grabbed my father's land. When I tried to complain about that, my uncle was not happy . . . so I did not proceed with my complaint.

I attended school until Form Four [fourth grade]. When I reached Form Five, I no longer could go to school, because I didn't have the school fees.

I wanted to get away from my uncle. I left his house when I was eighteen years old.

A gentleman picked me [out, as his bride] from school. He promised to take care of me and help me out, so I married him. He even went to my uncle's home for an introduction. He paid a dowry. I had to join him at his home, in another district.

Then, I had a problem with my husband, because I could not have a child. When I was with him, I was unfortunate in that I had many miscarriages. In that culture, they don't want a lady who cannot bear children. A rich man fears to die and leave his resources with anyone other than his own biological child. So, we had problems. We were not cooperating, not getting along. And I was not treated as a proper wife, so I left him.

Divorced at Forty, I Began to Build My Own Life

I was forty when I left my husband. I had stayed with him a long time [twenty-two years]. Because my husband had paid a dowry, and he would have wanted it back, I could not return to my uncle.

Since I couldn't go back to my uncle, I had to come this way and settle here. I got some relatives to help me buy a tiny patch of land. Then, in 1993, I bought another small portion of land. As I sold a few crops, then I would buy another portion of land. Then, eventually, I bought this site [with the house and barn].

I came from nothing and was growing whatever I could, learning along the way. Whatever did nicely, I would grow more of it.

And then, another thing: I received salvation. I went to a Protestant church. With salvation, you're all the time hoping, hoping, hoping. There were believers at my new church advising me, "We are married to Jesus." So, I became excited. I wanted that, too. In fact, I had already converted myself to the way [lifestyle] of a true Christian. So, I said to myself, "I'm accepting of myself. I accept what has occurred."

I said, "Our life is like that." In the Bible, after all, there are people who don't have children, but they are happy. They excel in their labors—I am like that. I didn't have children, but I was excelling at farming.

My Children Came to Me as a Surprise, Later in Life

I am sixty-five years old. I am single, but I have four adopted children. I adopted one boy, Wepuhulou Ronald, when he was about five. I adopted him and supported him. He's now twenty-four. He's not yet married, no children. He graduated from academy and is now living in another district, teaching biology and chemistry in secondary school.

I also have three other adopted children: a grandniece who is eighteen, and two of my brother's grandchildren. He's incapable of looking after them. One is thirteen, and the other is eleven.

When we are together, there's a nice company, because we are all different ages. I give them advice. When I talk with the nieces, they like it, because I am really their mother now.

I do not have a television. I am not very much interested in acquiring one. I feel it's better, because, first of all, I am alone. That is my fear. You might buy a television, but these [local] boys, these thugs, once they know it is there, they will come in, and, even during the day, they will come and steal it.

This Beautiful Village Is Plagued by Robbery and Alcoholism

I live in a beautiful place, and it seems like a peaceful village. But actually, there are many robberies around here. Most of the men don't value the work of digging [farming]. They imagine that it is not a job. They are just idlers. For them, when they see a [white] person like you, they think that you are going to just give them money for free, not having to work for it.

How did it get to be this way? . . . I think these boys learned their behavior from their parents. The parents were not at all serious at teaching them at the time of bringing them up. Some parents say to these boys, "Ah, after all, you'll soon be on your own. If you don't want to work, you're free."

The father may be a negligent farmer who doesn't work hard to train his own child while he's still growing. Some of the parents also take a lot of alcohol. Early in the morning, they go drinking. They drink homemade beer made of maize, mostly. After it's brewed, they add juices from meat. To make this beer, they ferment it for one week, then roast it, then start to brew it by adding the millet yeast. After three days, the beer has become mature. It's very strong, so it gets them drunk.

Most of the people who enjoy drinking don't have an activity [a job], a serious activity to take up their time. They play cards, sometimes for money. They try to survive like that.

The men go to these drinking parties. They stay there the whole evening while the wife is busy doing the farming. It's not OK! My farmer group ran the numbers, and we calculated that a family whose parents are drinking lose about two million shillings [$598] per year.

Do the Math: Drinking = Lost Income

Every day, they start drinking after 4:00. Then, they end up coming home around ten. That's about six hours wasted. Now, multiply those hours by 365 days, and if he drinks throughout the year, you have spent roughly two thousand per day for the brewing barrel, bananas, pork, and yeast—more if the man wants to show off to the neighbors that he's powerful and can buy rounds of beer. Add to that the lost income you could have made during that time. Any small profits they make on your farm they use to frontload their pockets to go and drink.

So, money is wasted. Time is wasted. The parent is also not there to watch out and make sure the children go to school or to organize a meal for the family. The children come home to an empty house and have to get their own dinner. So, it's not a good activity.

Other people don't drink: the women and the schoolboys. The boys who've progressed past "A" level have realized the importance of education. You don't find *them* drinking. The mothers don't want to drink, either.

In fact, in our community, the mothers are overworked. They're overloaded, because most of the time, they are busy planting the beans. From the beans, they go to fetch the water. From the water, they will have to go and till the land. Then, they have to go back in the afternoon to plant and weed whatever is remaining.

My Neighbors Form a Network to Watch Out for Me

The chairman [mayor] gives us security. Then, my neighbors, they're also very good. The one that lives over there, he's going to help me plant the beans. So, there is plenty of security to keep around me. Let's say, for example, when I go in to rest, they will look after this land for me.

But then, with a farm, even as strict as I am, they [the thugs] also know how to disorganize you. There was a time when I was away, and I still don't know how, but this kid got up into my house and stole my radio. So, that is sad. But actually, at my age, I think the phone is quite enough, because it gives me all the information I need actually.

What We Need: The Fulfillment of Work

What should be done? The local government should come up with a program to engage our young people. They are very bright and active. Then, at the same time, we CKWs are trying to bring some of the youths on board. I take my phone to them and say, "Friends, you grow tomatoes. What activities are you using to help them grow?"

They say, "Oh, we don't have any money for buying [fertilizer or inputs]."

And I say, "Let's look at the computer."

I get my device, and we look up their crop or disease, see how they could reinvest with their spending money. I read [for those who are illiterate] or translate [from Swahili, for those who don't understand English]. For others who can read, after I open the computer, I give it to them to read it. Some of them get really taken up with the device. They start to tell others, "Right now, we are learning about agriculture." Or, "Let's go to Mary—she has it in her computer."

So, we are starting our own gradual process of outreach, because I am alone in this area with this phone. If we could have several farmers [as CKWs] to use it and walk around, they can be convinced from this that it's a good thing to go in for farming.

Chickens and Cows Make a Farm a Home

Right now, I've got ten birds. We used to have many more, but they were stolen. So, these ones I just bought from a neighbor. You don't feel complete without an animal on the farm.

I had a cow, but it had red water: It was urinating blood. They were treating it, and it was not improving, so I had to sell that one off.

Then, the other cow, the big mother cow, was pregnant. But unfortunately, when I woke up one day, I found the animal had fallen on one of its limbs. When I tried to pull her up, she couldn't stand. Then, I realized that a bad person had come and hid out behind the barn and hit the cow. The bone was crushed, and there was swelling. So, we had to sell the injured cow to other people [for meat].

Now, I'm intending to get a new cow with a microloan from Mbale. I thought about using my savings instead, but I was a bit cautious. The cow would cost 2.5 million shillings [$747], and that's all of my savings and more. I said to myself, "What if these people try to steal my money?" If I borrow $50,000 [$14.84], then I have to give back $70,000 [$21], but I will still have money left in the bank and some for my other goal: to rebuild my shelter [barn].

My Favorite Foods Are Right Outside My Front Door

We also cook. I roast my grains on the previous evening, and then the next day, I prepare the grains. When the sun is too hot, that is the time for you to prepare lunch. Late afternoon, when it is cool and you have eaten, that's a good time to go about and visit the neighbors [as a CKW].

My favorite food is millet bread. It's nice for my diet, because the minerals help my bones and teeth, plus my digestive system. Millet has a lot of calcium and phosphorous. I also like the millet mixed with greens and amaranth.

For the amaranth, you crack the grain and then shred it into small pieces. You then boil or steam it and then mix it with other grains that have been pounded nice and fine. Then, you can make a stew to enjoy with your millet bread.

Most of the greens we use are local. You go to the market and trade for greens or cabbages. They are very common there. Also tomatoes and beets, either from our farm or from the trading center.

My Most Challenging Days with Work and Health

My most challenging period of my business was when my phone had some sort of a bug. It was the format. I went to teach the farmers, and I wanted to get proof from the phone, but I couldn't do it. Let's say if you want to type in an "A," it would just keep repeating. It would write so many. I could not get any information. But the good thing is, they took back that phone. They gave me this one here.

As far as life goes, my most challenging situation by far was in 1991. I had some fibroids. They became very painful, and I lost a lot of blood. I became anemic and had to be admitted to the hospital. At one point, I lost consciousness and went into a coma; I thought I was going to die.

When I was in the hospital, I realized that life is very important. I almost gave up on my health. I was very sick and had lost a lot of blood. It happened quickly: I became unconscious. I felt very close to death. But gradually, I improved.

From that time, I have just been thriving and growing my farm. I just keep enjoying life more every day.

Happiness Is When My Farmers Adopt New Practices

What makes me happy is when I call a meeting. Then, my farmers come. I try to advise them, and sometimes they adopt [new farming practices]. The moment when you teach something and it is adopted, you are very excited.

When I call a meeting with my farmers, I tell them, "Tomorrow, we're [covering these topics]." I don't force them to come. If there's not damage to check in the farmers' fields, we usually meet from 2–4:00 p.m., when it is cool. That still gives us time afterward to organize our cooking [for dinner]. Another social activity that we do is called "working together." We meet once a week, on Mondays, and clean different things around the community.

I can be teaching a person, and he literally doesn't believe me until I open the computer. Like, someone came here, and he wanted me to teach him about maximum growing. I taught, I taught, and I taught. He couldn't believe me. Then, I said, "Let's look at the computer." And all the information I had given him was right there. He was very impressed! [Laughs.]

So now, what makes me very happy is that, when I leave my farm, I am very alert. When I go out, I move with my head up, because I know I'm moving with the right information for my farmers.

District Chairman Calls Mary a Leader in Agriculture and the Community

Editor's note: While we're talking, a tall man in a dapper suit and hat strides confidently toward the white plastic chairs outside Mary's house, where we have perched to chat. His name is Mr. Eli Mujasi. He's the chairman of the district—and definitely someone you want to call "Mister."

A jovial man, he shouts instead of speaking and chuckles in between proclamations. Mr. Mujasi has heard that Mary has visitors from America, so he wants to mingle; it's as though we're celebrities on tour. He has a few notes to add about Mary that give a different point of view to add to her own.

Mr. Mujasi: I am also a farmer. I grow a lot of coffee and beans, also beautiful bananas! [Laughs.] I eat a minimum of two to four a day: three in the morning, and three in the evening.

I'm their leader. There are 450,000 people in my district. I come to check on all the people, to encourage them to continue being good.

Mary is very progressive! We use her to partner with farmers, going around with the CKW program. She's very good at that, because she has exemplified [what she teaches] with her banana farming.

In Uganda, mostly we are subsistence farmers. As you saw with these other farmers passing by, they have only hoes, instead of thinking of commercialization. With serious farming, he has to first bring a diversified type of production. If you are selling several different types of enterprises, you can easily sell some, go commercial, grow bigger.

The problem with the peasant farmer is that he's in a poverty trap. He wants to do more, but he doesn't have the means. We've been pressured by the government to start introducing tractors, but the farmers just refuse. They will not give up their hoes, which take them three weeks longer to dig.

But there he is: The poor man still traveling with a hoe is one of the reasons why many of our people stay stuck in subsistence farming. The government must come in and subsidize the farmers to give them the means to get out. Otherwise, he's just standing there with his hoe, praying for the Heavenly Father to give me rain for my crop so that I can get something.

The other problem is the people themselves. They don't want change. Unfortunately, often a poor person is also an ignorant person, and making him aware of the opportunities of development is so difficult. One, they're always steeped in drunkenness. How can you drink for eight hours? I mean, you can't! You will never develop.

And the most terrible part is that the men, they leave the poor ladies to labor. Though some of the ladies now accompany the men to drink. So, that is one of our problems: There is too much drinking, and that's made a number of our society lazy.

The other problem is the issue of ignorance. It's so bad that when we wanted to bring an irrigation system here—you can't believe it—the poor people refused! They literally refused. They said they wanted to farm the way their grandparents and great-grandparents did it. I tried to convince them, and they tried to cut me.

Mary: Seriously! They wanted to kill him.

Mr. Mujasi: Oh, yes. And I stood my ground. I said, "You can cut me if you want to. But I don't want to leave people who are poor." And luckily, their neighbors have agreed to accept irrigation in two nearby subcounties, so maybe we will use that example to tell them it will be good for them.

Mary is a leader. She's an agriculturalist. She's rare, in a productive sort of way. She didn't say, "I'm retired." Instead, she started this program. You can see that her thinking is different: The proof is in the bananas! Look at the size. Just the next neighbor over: His bunches are five times smaller than hers. Mary can be the chairman someday, too!

If I Were Rich, I Would Open a Training Farm

If the Lord put fifty million shillings into my account, I would still continue with the farming. People around here have neglected farming, but I tell you, farming is very good. People out there are starving; they don't need to be.

And then, I would open a farm where I could train farmers, and then, they would go out and train more farmers, all around. So you see, when you've got some money, it's better to do an activity on the ground. People will remember that Mary had this money, and I came back to help them.

And when I open this farm, I would be employing them. It would be a business where they would come and work instead of sitting. They would be active and also get money from it. If we can grow things on a wide scale, we'll be helping these people to get enough food, even if we are selling it [rather than giving it away]. Maybe we could get the government to help so that we can give out the raw materials to help them get started. I think that's better than a loan.

Money and Time: My Future Goals

I am just a very happy person. One reason is that [my coworkers at] Grameen feel like a very large family. The other reason is that God is great. Even though I do not have children, I have received these [adopted] children as my own. I'm very happy. [Laughs.]

If I were earning more money, I would first want to improve my house, so that it looks presentable to visitors. Right now, this house looks ramshackle! I want to furnish it, bring in more furniture, and put a roof on it. And then, I will build a veranda where you can sit in the evenings.

And in the summertime, I want to buy a cow. Then, I want to buy another piece of land so that I may expand my farm production.

If you come back to visit me in ten years, I am sure, if the Lord allows me to live up to that time, you'll find that I have rested. I'll be reaping what I have worked, what I have invested, what I have sown. My trees will be giving me money, as well as firewood. The cow is also going to give me money. The resources will just be pouring in, I am sure.

Now, I have technology, which is very useful. Knowledge is power. So, that makes me very happy. I'm appreciative of the road I've taken. Many people don't have the chances I'm getting. Knowledge has opened the door for me.

Arts
and
Culture

ten

ALBERTO

STAY-AT-HOME DAD AND ART TEACHER

Chicago, Illinois, United States

Editor's note: It's always the quiet ones . . . I'd met Alberto Alaniz several times over the years through my family's connection with "The Center" (Precious Blood Ministry of Reconciliation, pbmr.org) in Chicago's South Side. He works there part-time as an art teacher to young men in transition from gang life into school and employment, in an area where boys are born into gangs based on the block where they were born—no choice in the matter.

Because Alberto never had much to say, I overlooked him until his colleagues recommended him for this book, saying he was deeply respected by his students for having transcended gangland and incarceration. In an area where fathers are scarce, Alberto takes great pride in being a full-time, stay-at-home father. He's known for being able to instill confidence and coax talent from the most reticent students—and he's a damn good artist himself. His paintings reflect the extremes of violence and love that have shaped his sense of self, which is unflinching in a place plagued by gun violence and intergenerational poverty.[1]

Once he opened up and started talking, Alberto revealed layers of a fascinating man, who managed to extricate himself from his gang while in prison, chose sobriety over self-medication, and created a stable home on a meager salary that allows him the freedom to be the sort of father he never had. His mission in life is to be consistently present for his son and his students and to authentically embody his values of love and peace.

I'm a Teaching Artist and Stay-at-Home Dad

My name is Alberto Alaniz. I am thirty-six years old. I'm a teaching artist at The Center [Precious Blood Ministry of Reconciliation, pbmr.org] in Chicago, Illinois. I've had this job going on three years now. I work part-time, about fifteen hours a week.

Hopefully, we can increase those hours in the future. I'm paid by the hour and make roughly $300 per week. So, I don't splurge on things I don't need. [Laughs.] I just pay my bills and take care of our cars, and that's it. I don't go out. I don't drink. I don't smoke. I don't do any of those activities. I am also a stay-at-home dad.

My Parents Immigrated from Mexico to Chicago

I grew up in Chicago. My parents are immigrants from Mexico. There're six of us; I have four sisters and a younger brother.

I grew up in Little Village. Actually, when my parents first came to Chicago, they were in the Pilsen area, around 18th Street. Then, my father had a decent job, where he was able to save up enough money to buy a small house for us in Little Village.

My parents are not together no more. When they divorced, they sold the house, and they split the proceeds. I was probably around twenty years old then. But I was incarcerated since the age of sixteen. So, I really didn't see much of their interactions after the age of sixteen.

Arrested for Having the Wrong Facial Expression

When I was young, before I was incarcerated, I was stopped once for driving a moped without a license. The reason why they actually arrested me was because when the officer stopped me, he dropped my bike, and I got upset.

I didn't curse him out or anything like that. I just got upset. He dropped my bike, you know? And he started cursing at me, because he had the authority. He tried to swing at me. I guess I was making the wrong facial expression. He tried to punch me, and I ducked. So, he missed, and his partner, it was a woman officer, she saw him strike at me, and I ducked. It was just a reaction.

He tried to punch me again for a second time, and the same thing happened. I stepped to the side, and he didn't hit me. So, the lady officer grabbed him instead of me. She grabbed him out, because he was reaching for me, because he didn't have a chance to punch me. He knocked me on top of the bike, saying, "You think you're tough."

I'm like, "No." I said, "You're trying to hit me, you know?"

And then, the lady officer was like, "Let him go, let him go!" and a lady on a balcony of a house nearby started screaming, "Let him go!"

So, it was the lady officer and the other lady on the balcony that helped. If not, I think he would have done something a little more drastic. They put me in a cop car, and they arrested me for that. [Laughs.]

Incarcerated Since Age Sixteen

I was involved in a local street gang, the Latin Kings. I was hanging out with the fellas, and a guy shot at the rival gang members. The police picked up a lot of the teenagers in the area for a line-up. I was one of the ones that wouldn't speak. It wasn't in my mentality to so-called "tell." And I didn't see anything. I heard gunshots. But they wanted me to give some confession saying what happened, whether I knew the actual details or not.

That's pretty typical. It's been like that since as far back as I can remember.

We were four blocks away. But the police already know . . . They know the activity, the way gang members interact and associate in the neighborhoods.

So, let's say they hear gunshots, and there are some gangbanger-looking kids in the area. They'll pick all of them up, as many as they can, just to line them up, to see if they can catch somebody that was in the area or was involved in any way. That's what they do.

In this situation, the person who actually shot the rival gang member got caught with the gun and confessed to it. I couldn't afford a lawyer or anything like that throughout the trial and all that stuff. There wasn't even a trial, anyway. It was just court hearings, basically. The defendant tried to tell his attorney and tried to speak to the judge saying that I had nothing to do with it, but they had to go through a process to prove it.

I was first charged with murder, and then, it became intent to kill. What happened is the co-defendant had confessed to the crime. And so, any detail that was already in the paperwork in his confession involved me, basically saying what he did. And so, I couldn't fight it if he already confessed to the shooting, and then, the paperwork says that I was there with him, even though, if you look at the details, there's a lot of holes in it, a lot of lies, a lot of things that just don't match up.

At the time, I was tried as an adult, but he wasn't. I was sixteen. I think he was fifteen. So, I was going to the adult court. We were separated. For the first two or three court hearings, they had us together, but after that, we were going to court by ourselves.

Eventually, he confessed to the crime, and they gave him a plea bargain. They offered me a plea bargain as well. And the lawyers are telling you, "If you lose the case, you can get the maximum, ninety years or whatever," you know? At that age, it's very scary. You try to imagine yourself doing ninety years in prison. It's impossible.

Being Trained as a Latin King Gang Member

I was taught a lot of the secrets and details of the hierarchy, the way that gangs work, by an older Latin King member, who was already semi-retired. He lived a block away from me.

He would pass in front of me with a big fluffy white cat. And to me, that was a little odd that he would carry a cat with him. He would go to the local store and buy his cat his food and whatever he needed, and he would pass by.

He would see me right by my house, and, little by little, he'd talk to me. He was like a mentor, and he would tell me things that no fourteen, fifteen-year-old should be learning, like how each member is controlled by another leader, and what their role is, and what are they supposed to do. One of the things that he taught me was that the Latin Kings' foundation is supposed to be based on the Bible.

My Gang's Manifestos Are Based on the Bible

This is well known. The police have a lot of their documentation, manifestos and stuff. It's founded on the Bible, and it's meant to help the person, the family, and the community, but because of the leadership, it gets skewed. It changes, and the rival gang members force retaliation and reaction to violence or territories. It's really complicated. But if you read the manifesto of the Latin Kings, it tells you that we're supposed to pray to the Supreme God, which is the founder of life, God Almighty, the one that's in the Bible. And a lot of the writings and moral structures come directly from the Bible, almost word for word.

They're not supposed to do drugs that are synthetic, like cocaine and heroin, anything that's processed. Marijuana, if it's grown naturally, they can sell that. So, they try to use something that's natural supposedly. You know, marijuana's natural. God made it, you know? [Laughs.]

But the main thing my mentor was trying to teach me was for the gang not to control me in a way that I wasn't comfortable with. He was giving me this rainbow of how life is.

It wasn't just advice about gangs. He was teaching me like, for instance, how to respect your parents and go to school and study and take advantage of your studies. One of the things that sticks with me since he taught me was never, ever spit in front of a female, whether it's your mother or your sister or your girlfriend or whatever. Never spit in front of a woman. It was just stuff that should be common sense.

Supporting Myself Since Age Nine

My parents knew who my mentor was, but they didn't know about my involvement with the gang. I had a different point of view, a different mentality than other kids. Other kids wanted to join a gang to look cool, to dress, hang out, and stuff like that. Me, I wanted to have structure. I wanted something better for my family.

When I was nine years old, I started working at a local car wash. That's what my focus was, to work and be able to feed myself and clothe myself without having to burden my parents, asking them for money. So, I would go work at the car wash after school and make my money.

There was a little candy store a half-block away, and I would go there and have a little treat or whatever and play video games. My purpose was to be independent. Don't worry about having to wait for my parents to have money to buy my shoes or things like that.

And I would make enough money at the car wash to bring dinner home. I would go and order pizza or chicken or whatever and take it home for dinner. My father was still the one paying the bills. It's just the mind-frame I had.

It was self-service car wash. I'm sure it was illegal for me to be working there at nine. But the owner would see me clean up. I would put the hoses up and make sure everything was neat, the garbage cans. And for about a year or so, he wouldn't bother me. And then, after knowing me a while and seeing me there constantly, he would provide lunch every once in a while, on a weekend day.

And then, I suggested to him, why not do a drive-through? A drive-through car wash. He never thought about it, you know? So, the following year, he erected a drive-through car wash, and that's where I would work.

My Other Jobs: Walgreen's, Flowers, Flags, and Trucks

For other jobs, I would go to Walgreen's around like Halloween time. Kids would go in there and make a mess on the floor with candy and costumes and stuff. And I would ask the manager if I could help clean up.

I also worked at a flower shop. I would help them decorate and sell flowers. I would put together the flowers and go sell them on the street. I would sell a big bundle within an hour.

And around Parade Day [Mexican Independence Day, on September 16th], they would sell these little plastic Mexican flags on a stick to celebrate when Mexico became independent from France. This guy bought a big trunk full of flags and sticks. All he had to do was staple the flag to the stick, you know? And he didn't want to do it. So, I offered to do the assembly.

He paid maybe twenty cents for the whole thing, and he wanted fifty cents per flag. He put me in charge of selling them. I was selling them for a dollar, and I sold like 80 percent of them within a couple of hours. I was giving him the fifty cents for each flag, but he was still giving me part of that fifty cents. But he said, "You can sell them for whatever you want," and they were going for a dollar each.

I was probably like ten or eleven. There were some people who didn't want to buy flags, and I would give them a flag just so they'd have a flag.

I also worked for a trucking company. I would wash their trucks.

Living in Mexico at Age Fifteen

The year before I was incarcerated, on my own terms, I moved to Mexico, to Guanajuato, near Mexico City. That's where my folks are from. I was living with my grandparents at the time. My brothers lived there. I was fifteen. I loved it. I just loved the open space and the freedom.

I consider myself 100 percent Mexican and 100 percent American. It was amazing to live in a place where I could be myself, and nobody's judging me, nobody's looking at me, threatening me, telling me, "Oh, you have to do this. You have to do that."

My parents got permission through the courts and all that so I could stay down there. I just had to save up enough money to survive. I was planning to build a little house and buy little animals—dogs, a horse, a little pig, stuff like that. I was willing to raise animals and feed myself and those around me. I promised my cousins that I was going to build a swimming pool on a piece of land that my grandparents had.

I told my parents I wanted to come back [to Chicago] so I could work and save up some money. So, I came back in February. I was working, but in June, that's when I got arrested. I couldn't do anything else. I was incarcerated.

I got out of prison when I was thirty-one. I couldn't go back to Mexico at that point. I had to do parole for three years when I got out.

I Learned To Teach While Incarcerated

Then, when I was in the Juvenile Center, I had an art teacher position. They saw that I knew how to draw. So, I was able to help the teacher teach the students and guide them a little bit.

When I was incarcerated, I also got a job as a screen printer, printing T-shirts. I also was a janitor. There was a portion of the population that spoke only Spanish. They wanted to learn how to speak English and get their GED. I'm bilingual. So, I would teach them English.

When I was in prison, I took a couple of vocational training courses in culinary arts, automotive technology, small-business administration, and a little bit of construction. I was trying to learn as much as possible. I got my GED and my small-business administration certificate. I have certificates for automotive, basic and advanced, and for culinary arts and food service.

I Did Fifteen Years in Prison

I did fifteen years in prison. They gave me a thirty-year sentence. That was the least they could offer me for the crime. So, I accepted that as opposed to the ninety years that they said they were going to give me if I lost the case.

Most people don't see that, even though kids at that age have this streetwise mentality, they're not mature yet. They don't have an adult mature brain. I guess they just wanted a conviction, to get as many gang-bangers off the street as possible. I know it's a little strange to say, but I don't blame the court system for trying to get these criminals off the street. The only thing that I see is absolutely wrong is how they do it. I think if I had never been incarcerated, who knows where I would have been?

Leaving the Gang While Inside Prison

I got out in fifteen years instead of thirty, because, at the time, the laws allowed for a day-for-day good time. So, if I did a day without getting in trouble, I'd get a day off my sentence. So, my sentence ended up being reduced by 50 percent.

When I first went to prison, it wasn't easy. It was pretty difficult. But, again, my mentality was a little different than most people at my age at the time.

I had a tattoo of a crown that represented the Latin Kings. I didn't have it hiding under a sleeve. It was right there, right out front where everybody could see. That's the way I lived, you know?

When I was sentenced, I had to decide, do I want to spend the rest of my life or even get killed in prison, or do I want to do something with myself and change my path? I decided to break ties with the gang, because, to me, it didn't make sense that, on the street, in the free world, I was asked to fight a rival gang member . . . But when you're incarcerated, the gangs are all together. They eat meals together. Rival gang members in prison, they help each other. They laugh with each other.

I couldn't understand it. On the street, they wanted me to eliminate the enemy, but when I'm in prison, it's like we're friends? It didn't make sense.

So, I decided, if my own gang kills me for changing the way I live, I'm okay with that. So, I put a Mexican eagle (the one that's on our flag) over the Latin King crown tattoo.

I put the eagle on there to represent that, if I'm going to fight, stand for something, I'm going to stand for Mexico, for my country, for something that's greater that I can help, hopefully. And while I was incarcerated, I got permission to step away from the gang, because I spoke to the leaders, and they said I was right.

That doesn't happen too often. But I couldn't live any other way. I just couldn't. Whether I was in the street or in prison, the reality was too raw. I told the leaders in prison I'm not going to lose time watching my back in fear that you guys are going to come over here and stab me in the back.

I told them, "Right here, right now, you guys make the choice. I already got permission from the street. Make the choice. If you're going to kill me, do it right now. Don't be sneaky or anything like that. I'm telling you, do it now, if you're going to do it." And they said, you're right. They agreed with me. I got permission from both the leaders in prison and out in the street to step away.

I Became a Teacher and a Therapist

I don't have any fear for myself. The only fear I have is hurting my family, those I love, not beating them up or anything like that but just making the wrong choices and disappointing people. Even strangers, I help strangers out. I've done that since I was a kid.

So, I spent my time in prison helping people, teaching them how to read, how to draw, how to cope with themselves, their family and all. Technically, I was a therapist.

This one guy, he was probably like five years older than me. He was resentful, because his dad had abandoned him in Mexico. He left him there because he didn't want the son to get in trouble over here in the United States. So, he hated his dad for it. And his grandmother took care of him, and eventually, she saved up enough money to send him here. And then, he got in trouble.

Whenever I would talk to him about his dad, it's like his whole character would change. He had this anger built up inside him, and I would tell him, "You're still living with your dad's choice. The anger, you're keeping it alive inside of you, that anger."

I tried to get him to just let it go, don't hold on to it. You're killing yourself with the errors that your dad made.

Right before I was released, we talked about it. I didn't want to leave with him having this anger. I knew his point of view was changing. He would tell me that he spoke to his dad on the phone and stuff like that. So, he finally accepted that his dad made an error, and he forgave him. He was able to let that go. And I told him, it's not going to be easy, but it's necessary for you.

Strength, Faith, and Mental Discipline

I get my strength from my faith in God. He shows us so much patience and grace and love and peace and stillness, and we have to practice that, because it's not easy. It's not easy in our society.

I've never struggled with any mental health issues or addiction. I don't drink or smoke now, but I have in the past. I never let it control me, never. That wasn't a choice. I couldn't sit there and be addicted to something. I attribute it to my genes. I don't have an addictive personality. I also think it's my mental discipline. Smoking cigarettes, most people get addicted. Or people say if they stop drinking coffee for a day or two, they get migraines. For me, there's nothing I can't live without.

You Can't Hold on to Resentment

I try to make others comprehend or understand that I can't hold on to bitterness, anger, and frustration. I can't live with that. If I hold it in, then I'm not myself. I become this other person. I don't have the space for it.

So, just like I told my friend, forgive your father and then move on. Teach him how to be a son. This is how I want you to have been with me. I'm going to show you my love.

Life is complicated, but I'm not going to allow circumstances to make me live this long life of bitterness. It might be difficult for other people to understand, but to me, it's easy. If somebody can walk up to me right now and slap me in the face, I'm not going to react with violence. There's no point.

Life on the Outside, in a New World

I've been out for five years. That fifteen years seemed like an eternity. It seemed like so, so long, especially when I was halfway done with my time. Time would stand still.

Every day, I had to wake up saying, "I have this many days left." I had duties and tasks and people that I made friendships with. It was actually difficult for me to leave them behind, people that I really felt that they wanted something out of life like me.

When I was released, I was in a new world. I couldn't compare it to when I was fifteen or sixteen, when I was free. I was a different person. It was a different time. My family was different. I had nieces and nephews. I wouldn't say it was scary. I don't know how to explain it, but it was like walking into a jungle, and you don't have a map. [Laughs.] You've got to use all your senses at all times to figure things out.

Trying to Find Work with a Prison Record

When I was first released, my sister and my brother-in-law owned an irrigation company, and I helped them for a little bit. And then, I got a job at the Corner Bakery café, because I had experience with food handling. I had a food safety, sanitation, and managerial license. They hired me through somebody I knew that was working there. Submitting applications wasn't going to work for me, because on those forms, they asked if I was ever convicted.

Later, I switched to Panera Bread. When I started working there, I would do back of the house[2] duties. And then, because I drove and had a license and some of the people didn't have a reliable car or a license, they made me a delivery person. So, I did deliveries for them for a while.

Applying to Work at The Center

And then, from the screen-printing, the little pay that Father Kelly was able to give me, it was enough for me to not work at Panera. This just made more sense to me, and it was basically around the same pay. I decided just to work here.

I have two departments that Father Kelly kind of put me in charge of. One of them is screen-printing the T-shirts, and the other one is teaching art. That can vary from drawing to painting to pottery.

Right now, I have four students. We meet three days a week, Tuesdays and Thursdays from 4:30 to 7:30 and on Saturday from 11:00 a.m. to 3:00 p.m. It goes by so fast.

When my kids walk into the Art Center, we've already built a rapport when they walk in. They settle in for five, ten minutes. They get their paints and brushes. They have their music playing. Some kids put the headphones on. Most of the time, they focus. Then, 50 percent of the time, they're asking me, "What do I do next? What color do I mix in?" because they're just starting out. And I'm bouncing back and forth with each kid, trying to get them going on their project.

My Students Can Relate to What I've Been Through

And once they're at a point where their attention is shifting, we have a little break. We talk about what's going on in the neighborhood.

I think my experience in incarceration is a powerful component, because I can tell the kids what I've been through and what I've seen. Fifteen years is a long time for me to see the worst. I myself was never hurt or abused, but I saw things, and I heard about things. Fights, stabbings . . . A police officer wouldn't open a door for an inmate, and as soon as they allowed the inmate to come out, he took the broom from one of the janitors and beat the officer and tried to stab the officer with the broom, just because he wouldn't open the door for him.

People lose their minds in there. They're already over the edge with their mentality, and then, they go beyond that, because they're so frustrated with their own lives. The person that committed the crime I was convicted for, they say he committed suicide. I don't believe it. I believe it was somebody in prison that supposedly hung him. He was supposed to be in an area where it's impossible to commit suicide.

I don't think his death was gang-related. This prison is notorious for things like that. It could have been anything. But for him to have committed suicide, it's almost impossible. Even though he was the type of person that was devoted to his gang, he would never end his life like that.

So, I tell them little stories about before I was incarcerated and while I was incarcerated and things that should assist them in not falling into those pits that, that they can fall into if they continue to act the way they do or think the way they do.

And I tell them, "You may think that it's fun right now, because you're a teenager. You think it's fun, cool, this and that. But believe me," and I tell them, "and I beg you to listen, it is not fun. I see grown men crying to their wives or their mothers, crying. They need help. They need somebody to support them. They need money to be sent to them." I tell them, "It's not fun. It's not easy. It's not something you ever want to go through."

Talking and Painting

And some of the kids do go through it for a brief period, when they go to jail. They get arrested for something, and they're sitting in the holding cell. Then, they come back, and they say, "Man, it felt like I was in there for a month," and it was only a couple of hours. So, we talk about these things, and then, we go back to painting, or we'll do something else, clean the studio or whatever.

At my work at The Center, I also help Diana in her department, where she does restorative justice[3] and Project Repay.[4] Kids come to The Center because the Probation Department sends them. Project Repay is a program where—let's say a kid breaks into a car, and he gets caught. Instead of sending that kid to jail, the court allows the kid to come through The Center, to Project Repay. They do painting or some type of a craft, for example, a piece of furniture that they restore and decorate. That furniture or art is sold, and the proceeds go to the victim to help pay for the damages. It's a fraction of what they should be paying, but it's better than going to prison. They're going through this program mostly to get training for the experience that they should be doing something else with their time than getting in trouble.

The general public buys these pieces. They find out about it just through word of mouth, I believe. None of it is currently online. At the moment, Brother Juan is building up a website so we can be able to do an offering through an online store.

My Partner Is from a Rival Gang Across the Street

When I was released, I came into contact with an old friend from school, Jacqueline. We've known each other since sixth grade. We weren't dating, but we shared personal stuff, ideas and whatever. She knew where I came from and everything.

And then, I moved in with her. I had moved into my sister's house, but I didn't want to live with my sister for too long. So, I moved in with my Jacqueline. I was living in the rival gang's territory, because that's where her family lived. She has part ownership of the building with her mom. Her mother had a house across the street. We all got along.

My family was like, "Are you serious? They can see you, and they'll kill you." But I was confident enough to say that the way I looked, the way I dressed, the way I spoke, they were not interested in me.

I don't look like a typical gangbanger. I just look like an old guy, you know? [Laughs.] I don't wear flashy clothes. So, they don't look at people like me like, "Oh, this is a gangbanger. Let's try to start trouble with him." So, I pass by the gang members all the time. They look me in the face, and I look at them, and I say, "Hi," you know? No threat, nothing, just keep going.

Jacqueline is also Mexican-American. She is a nurse at a school. She is also the mother of my child, Alberto, who is now four years old. Although we're not officially married, I hope Jacqueline is my one and only for the rest of my life.

I think the commitment and the obligation is a little easier to have with the idea that you're free to make any choice you want. Some people get tired in this day and age. I'm a little more old-fashioned, and I told her, too, when we first started getting serious, "Look, I don't have much. I come from a bad background. I've got a lot of things to work on," and she was okay with it. A lot of things that she went through, I was also okay with that. We met in the middle.

Getting My Son Out of Gangland

She saw, too, that where she was living, there was a lot of violence, and here I come walking through it all like with no fears. She couldn't believe it. Most people would hide. It's not that I'm this superhero or anything like that. It's just faith, you know? I'm walking with faith.

But, with the birth of Alberto, I told Jacqueline that eventually we have to move, because I don't want my child to have anything to do with it—even just the sounds around here, listening to music at 2:00, 3:00 in the morning, and playing, gunshots, cars, things like that.

So, we got a blessing, and we were able to buy a house in Cicero, Illinois. It's like thirty minutes from here. It was a time where houses were super cheap. We searched for like a year or so, house to house to house, and our agent was very patient with us. He knew we didn't have a lot of money. He helped us out. And we found this little house, and we bought it and moved in. That's where we're at right now.

I don't want to take Jacqueline and Alberto down to Mexico. Ever since I was in prison, I've always had the hope and desire to move to Spain. So, that's going to be our major move, if she wants to tag along. [Laughs.] That's one thing I promised myself, if I'm able to, if God gives me the time and the ability to, is get to the point where I'm well off to own a piece of land in Spain, a house, and some horses.

My Best Moment Is When My Students
See What They Can Achieve

The sweetest moment at work is when a kid looks at me and is happy that they not only completed something, but they did something that they didn't believe they could achieve. Their facial expression is amazing. One kid said, "I can't believe I did something." Just that little phrase was like, it means so much that we're doing something here.

There is a huge range of talent among my students. They understand. Let's say one of the kids doesn't like art. I tell them that there're so many departments in the art world, whether it's advertising or curators and salesmen or just people scouting for art . . . preparing canvases and selling canvases, selling armatures [a framework around which a sculpture is made], opening up a little art supply store.

It doesn't have to be you have to paint. It can be, "I sell quality paint supplies," you know? And then, there's the framing business. They can provide quality frames to artists. So, I give them this idea that they're not stuck with just a brush stroke and some color. They have other options.

What's Sad Is What They Deal
with When They Leave the Studio

The thing that brings sadness to me is that when they're in our space, they're happy. They're playing, enjoying themselves. They feel safe and peaceful and accepted. But when they leave this building, they go back into that same environment where they have to put on this armor.

When I first started working here, just out of curiosity, I went past in the area, 1:00, 2:00, and 3:00 in the morning, and I would see these kids out there, riding their bicycles.

I wanted them to see me so that they'd know that I see you, I see what you're doing and where you're at. And when they see me out there at 3:00 in the morning just passing by, it makes them question, "Why is he passing through here? Why is he in this area?" and then, when they see me at work the next day, they see that I'm concerned, that I want to make sure they're safe.

Another way that I express to them my intention is that I tell them, I can go do something else in my life, but I want to be here to help. I'm not here to yell at you. I'm here to help.

It Offends Me When Kids Show Disrespect

I have never been harassed or abused in any way at work, but I've been indirectly disrespected. Sometimes, when the kids don't know who I am when they walk into the building, they comment on something, maybe not about me, just about The Center or something. It still offends me, if they talk about Father Kelly or something. It offends me that they would come into this space where we're offering them something, and they disrespect us.

Like one time, these kids were fighting, and Father Denny tried to stop them, and they hit him. That's when I jumped in. These kids had absolutely no respect for him. It got me so angry. I was telling them, "Are you serious? We're here to help, and you're over here doing this?"

We told them to get out. But we called them back. We're not here to take them out. We're here to show them, to teach them. So, we called them back in a [restorative justice] circle. We had a talk with them, like "Why did you get to that point?" and "How can we resolve it?"

They come around now without any incidents. If they feel that they have to get a little violent or to express themselves in a negative manner, they leave the building. They understand that this is a place where they should show respect. They need to come in here and respect not just the staff but also the other kids.

And they like being here. You can tell by their attitude. If they didn't like it, they wouldn't show up. Even though they're getting paid for it, they're being trained. They're not only learning art; they're learning how to get to work on time and be prepared, just the work ethic. They're learning art and drawing, and they're learning soft skills.

My Main Role in Life Is Fatherhood

When I'm not at The Center, I'm at home, raising my son. I would not allow somebody else to babysit my child until he's old enough to say, "This person didn't feed me. This person told me this." He needs to be able to communicate and say he's not being treated right, whether it's family or just a stranger, you know? We agreed to that before we decided to start a family.

Fatherhood: My main priority in life is raising my son. My teaching art is how I feed him. But if I had any other means, I'd probably be trying to sell paintings on the subway. That's what people tell me I'm good at. [Laughs.]

I'd Like to Teach People How to Be Productive

If I had all the money in the world, I would train people how to be productive. I would start a class to teach people what to do with their time, their life, and their careers.

In my point of view, a lot of the fault, whether people want to accept it or not, is in parenting. These kids are where they're at because of the parents, because of the situation and the way they raise their kids.

In poor communities, you see the parents struggling so much that a lot of them don't pay attention to the kid. They don't sit down with them to teach them how to read, how to write, how to interact, proper etiquette. They rely on the schools to teach the kid.

And the parent has to go and find means to feed their kid and clothe them and house them and so on and so forth. And so, they abandon their obligation to be a parent. I may be looking at it in a whole different light, but that's the way I see the major component of why these communities are the way they are.

Absent Fathers and Distracted Mothers

Although a lot of the families here are single mothers on public assistance, even though she is at home, her focus is somewhere else. But their sons are fiercely devoted to them. It's in their nature. When you have nothing to hold on to, you're going to hold on to whatever is closest to you.

Often, the mother is in a situation where she doesn't have a job, and she's not well educated, and nobody wants to hire her because of that. So, she's trying to figure out how she's going to pay her phone bill or her rent. If she's living with somebody else, then how does she get any money?

So, this child is stuck in the middle, but if I ask this child, "Do you want to go live with somebody else, another family member?" he would not let his mother out of his sight, no matter if he's starving. That's just the way they're raised.

I ask the kids, even, even people in prison, "Were you raised with your dad? What did he teach you?"

"Nothing, nothing," they say. "He was never there."

In some cases, they didn't even know their father. They had a stepfather that was in and out. Those that did have a father figure, the father was always mean, always stressed out and stuff.

I Want to Teach Patience and Love

Just recently, somebody asked me how the kids act in this neighborhood, and, if they misbehave, do I kick them out of the Arts Center?

I said, "No, it's quite the opposite to kicking them out. They need someone to be there to support them."

They need somebody to be in their corner, to show them that somebody understands and cares. If they do something drastic, then there has to be another form of discipline, but just because a kid misbehaves doesn't mean you send them away. It's got to be the opposite. You bring them closer. You try to understand why and teach them as much as you can.

It's important to find that place in life where you can be content with yourself and reflect that out to others. I think if a person shares that peace and that love and that understanding, then it will trickle down to others. It's important as a human being to possess that grace.

In the future, I hope my students and I will be able to teach and express to the younger kids patience and love and understanding, just life lessons in general.

If I can have that much of an influence on those that I'm teaching now and those that I'm affecting now, that they're able to pass that on, I think that would be success and a meaningful achievement that I have made in life.

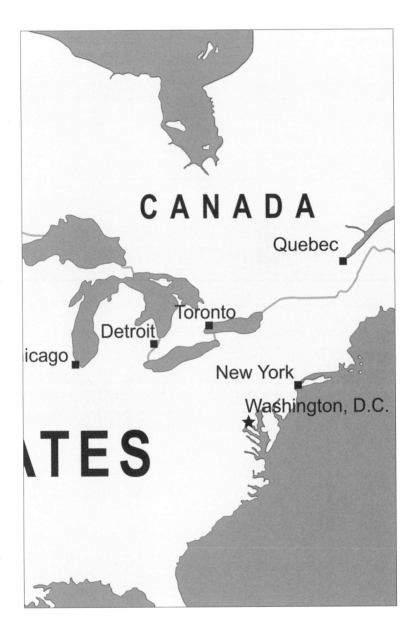

eleven

———

TANIA

DANCER

Toronto, Canada

Editor's note: Some of us never really go on vacation, even when we're on vacation. That's how it is for Tania Wong, owner of a dance studio near Toronto. She only takes a holiday when she exchanges performances for lodging, as she does for a resort in the Caribbean where we meet. I, too, am always on the job for this book series. Even before I see her perform, I am struck by her, and I know I have to get her story.

It's the way she moves—sort of like a cat—and the way her large eyes focus directly, with complete softness and openness, on everyone she passes. There's something about Tania that may be successful in the exterior world yet remains humble and shy. She's managed to live three decades on this planet without losing a pure, innocent trust in people.

"It makes her more attractive," says her friend Phil DuBois, who's traveling with her as a sort of unofficial business manager.

Given her warmth, youth, and physical beauty, a dancer like Tania may have been eaten alive by now, if not for this protective friend and champion. A professional recruiter[1] and amateur dancer, Phil met Tania when he took lessons at her studio, the Dance ConneXion.[2] They became good friends, and Phil began to help organize her business.

"Informally," he says, thrusting both hands forward and blushing just a bit, "I don't get paid or anything. She's obviously an exceptional dancer, but she focuses on her art, and her business could be a lot more successful. So, we just talk about how to make it more efficient and ideas for expanding different parts," he explains.

This tropical island (Turks and Caicos) feels pretty opposite from their home in cosmopolitan Toronto. The fourth most populous city in North America (after Mexico City, New York, and Los Angeles), Toronto throbs with 2.6 million city dwellers and serves as Canada's headquarters for business, finance, media, and the arts.

Phil joins our interview and ends up sharing so much valuable information about Tania (that he says she's too humble to reveal), that his comments remain sprinkled throughout her story, just the way the conversation naturally flows on this sweltering October day.

As Tania talks, her commitment to her art becomes clear on every level—mental, physical, and emotional. She works hard to eat well and hydrate, keep her body strong and limber, and focus her mind on new musical and choreography innovations to try. Her degree in computer science serves her well, as she manages her own website and balances an increasingly complex business. She's a perfectionist on every point, from social-media posts to choreography. Still, for Tania, the skill of the dance does not become art until one thing happens: "For me," she explains, "the biggest achievement is if someone can watch your show, like a three- or four-minute piece, and then, they're crying. It means that something you did, something in the music, something in your movement . . . touches their heart and makes them *feel*."

"Dance your dream"—that's her tagline. That night as we watch her dance[3] with her heart showing all over her face, we definitely feel that anything is possible.

If You Can, Teach

I'm thirty-four years old. I'm a professional dancer. I run a dance school/entertainment company, the Dance ConneXion, in Toronto, Canada. I teach group and private lessons in salsa, bachata, cha-cha, merengue, pretty much everything Latin, and adult ballet. *Bachata* is a dance from the Dominican Republic. There are two types of bachata: one is very romantic and sensual, and the other is fast paced, with more footwork.

I also have instructors who offer courses in ballroom dancing, Strip to Fit, belly dancing—whatever is hot at the time. The dance industry is very flexible.

For my classes, I charge $85 an hour. If students purchase multiple classes, packages, they receive discounts.

When I'm away, I have people subbing my classes—five people are subbing my classes right now. In the peak season, I have up to ten teachers, and when there's not so much happening (in the winter), then it might be just me and two other teachers. My assistant teachers do group lessons for me. Their rates depend on their experience, between $35–$140. It also depends on how big my classes are. If I cannot afford to pay the teacher, then I won't start the class.

Phil: The dance industry is extremely competitive. There are so many people who offer lessons, private or group or whatever, and they all discount their prices and offer huge group deals. It's very hard to make money. It's not as easy as maybe she makes it seem.

Tania: In addition, I have dance performance groups. Basically, I teach them routines, and they perform. We travel a lot. And I get invited as a guest artist to multiple venues. I have a few dance partners who live in different cities. We could go to what we call a dance *congress* [festival], a salsa congress, or a bachata congress. I would be the featured artist there. I would teach workshops and perform at night.

Dancing My Way Around the World

I love traveling, but right now, I'm traveling for my job. Like this two weeks in Turks, for me, it's a vacation. Other than that, dancing is my passion. Even when I'm off work, I like going to a dance club, and I still dance. It's my life. [Laughs.] And my guilty pleasures are coffee and wine. That's what I live on. [Laughs.] Coffee in the day, wine at night.

Just this year, I've been to Ottawa, Las Vegas, Washington, D.C., St. Louis, Detroit, and now here I am in Turks and Caicos. After this, I'm going to New York. I was supposed to be in Miami the week after, but I think I'm going to skip that one. I've also done a few Asia tours: Hong Kong, Malaysia, Thailand, Singapore, and Korea.

I love Asia, because it's not as developed, and the countries are so close to each other. So, when they have a big event, people from surrounding countries always fly in to see it.

I've performed for thousands of people at a time. In Toronto, I opened the show for Aventura,[4] one of the most popular bachata groups. I also performed at the premiere of a Bollywood film, which was cast with huge stars, at the Powerade Centre [arena]. They debuted the theme song of the movie, and my partner and I had to dance to it. I think about five thousand people attended that event. And from that, it was really funny, because I guess people in the Indian community knew me, and I ended up getting a lot of gigs there.

I always get stage fright. [Laughs.] I just try to breathe. I perform better under pressure, actually. I think it just makes me focus more; for example, backstage, I'll be concentrating on what I have to do, what I have to execute. Of course, it would be nice if I was relaxed, but that almost never happens, whether the show is small or big, because I'm a bit of a perfectionist. Even if I'm doing a small wedding gig where no one knows anything about dancing, I would be concerned that I'm perfect on everything. So, I'm always a little bit stressed; to me, it's the same show, big or small.

The Heart of the Dance

For me, dancing is a form of expressing myself. Let's say, if you listen to a bachata song, it's very romantic . . . Sometimes, you listen to a song, and it just hits your heart, like you feel something, right? So, when I dance, I want to be able to express what I feel in the music through my movement.

What I find is that *practicing* dancing, doing the right move, is not so hard if you put in the right [amount of] time, and you have the right coach, and you know, everyone can do it. To be honest, I think, given enough effort and commitment, you can do it.

So, the movement could be there. Anyone can do *that*. But in order to dance from the heart, that's a very different story. Sometimes, you see couples doing a very romantic, lyrical routine, flying around and doing stuff, and you just don't feel anything; that's because you see in their face that they are just doing the movement but not really feeling it. I mean, if you take dancing just as, "Okay, let's execute that move," then it's different. As I said, for me, dancing is all about feeling. It's from the heart.

I may not have the best legs in the world, but I'm expressing how I feel, and the audience can feel that. Honestly, my favorite performance to date was a show I did only once with a guy about two years ago. He choreographed it, and he was leaving town. I promised to do it with him just as a farewell gift to the dance community . . . I can't describe it. It's a very touching song. At the end of the show, quite a few guys came up to me and said, "You're not supposed to make people cry."

But that actually, for me, is the biggest achievement. If someone can watch your show, like a three- or four-minute piece, and then, they're crying, it means that something that you did, in the music and your movement, you portrayed something that reminds them of something, touches their heart, and makes them *feel*. That's, for me, the best accomplishment through dance.

I'm Never Really *Not* Working

I do group lessons, private lessons, and performance groups. The group lessons are very fixed in the schedule, whereas privates are all over the place. So, let's say I'm away for two weeks and I come back, I would be booked from morning to night for privates.

It really depends. The good thing about privates is that it's flexible. That's why, or at least one of the reasons why, they took the private. So, you need to be available for them. I've taught classes at midnight, just because that's the only thing I can fit in. And I've done classes at 7:00 or 8:00 a.m. the next morning, because that's just how it works.

Phil: That's probably only half of what she does. She has to plan for any future stuff, sales, marketing, and promotion. She's asked to be in shows. She's setting up other people's choreography. She's asked to consult on videos. The other stuff you've talked about too . . . weddings, there's a whole bunch more, and that's just the dancing part of it. She also does all of this administration herself.

Tania: [Laughs at herself a little.] I need to get some help. But it's really difficult for me to modularize my stuff, to actually hand it to people. Sometimes, it takes more time to kind of organize my thing and teach someone to do it. And then, half of the time, you don't trust other people to do your stuff, because it's not *you*. I mean, as he said, the business is so intensive; there're so many things involved.

I've done beauty pageant choreography. I do wedding first dance, bride-and-groom dance, father/daughter dance. I was in a music video; I was in a movie.[5]

There have also been plenty of challenges . . . well, I moved from a well-paid job with a very stable income to being a professional dancer. Running my own business, it's always up and down. It's not that I won't make the same [income] as before, but it's a lot harder, because it's all you. I have no help. I'm a one-man shop. I have all of these different things to attend to, and I have no vacation, because it's my own business, right? So, 24/7, I have to think about my business.

Let's say I hear a song here. I'll think, "Ah, that's a great song. I can use that for my next choreography." Like your head is always thinking about stuff. You're never really nine-to-five and then off from working—"Oh, I don't have to think about it."

It's stressful in that sense but a lot more rewarding at the same time, because this is all you, right? My schedule is ridiculous. When people get off work, nine-to-five, that's when I'm most busy, because that's when people come to take lessons. So, my weekends, my weeknights are pretty fully booked. On weekends, let's say for the past few months, all the weekends, I was out somewhere in a different country.

Blurred Lines between Teaching and Friendship

Phil: She also helps other people. Any time anyone needs emotional support or something, she'll be over there helping. She'll forego her administrative tasks if somebody says, "I need help." She will come and fix some part of their dance routine. She gives up a lot of her time for free.

Tania: I have about thirty or forty people in a dance team. There are teachers that are just out there with their students, and there's not a lot of interaction. For me, a lot of my students become my best friends. I'm a teacher, but at the same time, I'm also their friend. So, let's say one day this girl is upset and whatever. Then, I mean, I would go help her. It's kind of a different relationship.

Phil: People are drawn to her, because they see kindness, sympathy. She's very affectionate. She hugs people all the time. When people finish performances, she's the first one that runs up to her team and hugs everybody. Everybody wants to be around her, because everybody is like a child. They want affection. They like to feel wanted. She does a really good job about engaging the people that are in her circle.

To Be a Dancer, I Had to Defy My Family

I was born in Toronto, but I grew up in Hong Kong, where most of my family still lives. I have two sisters. We live on three different continents. The youngest sister is in London, England. My older sister is in Hong Kong. My mom travels around, and my dad is in Hong Kong. We're very international, let's just say.

I started ballet when I was six. But, since I was young, my mom has told me that there were three career choices for Asian kids: accountant, doctor, or lawyer. That's it. I didn't want to be a doctor, because I'm scared of blood. Accounting is kind of boring. So, for most of my early years, I wanted to be a lawyer. At that time on TV, they really glamorized being a lawyer, being in court and things like that.

In school, I was always the best in class. My mom was really strict in my upbringing. I had to study every day and memorize all of my textbooks. It's just the way she was. So, I always got first place. It was easy for me, because if you do the work, of course, you get the results. Then, for college, I went to the University of Waterloo, which is about an hour and a half from Toronto, and I studied computer science there.

As a kid, I had a lot of hobbies. I was involved in team sports. Before I had my dance school, I was a very competitive volleyball player. Once I had my school, that was another thing that I had to give up.

The Unpredictable Daily Life of a Dancing Business Owner

I now live in a brand-new condo in Toronto. I like it because it's very cozy, but it is also very modern and chic. It has all of this stainless steel in the kitchen and a nice marble countertop. The living room is really nice. Sometimes, I do my privates there. I have no furniture. I have mirrors on the wall so I can dance there. I don't need couches. I do solo stuff for fun. I like practicing moves, always. [Laughs.]

It's very hard to say what is a typical day, because it's different every day. But I basically wake up at around 9:00 or 10:00 a.m. I check my email, and I do my admin stuff for my school and my admin marketing. I prepare for my classes. I'll go through the list of privates and group lessons that I have that day and make sure that I have enough material, or I would get all of the material prepared for the day and drink my coffee.

Lots of coffee: That's how I get my energy.

When I'm not teaching, I'm on my computer, doing my business stuff, which I really should get to, but a lot of times, there're just too many classes going on. And I have privates during the day.

In the evening, I teach group lessons. Sometimes, I finish at midnight. I get to sleep pretty late. Let's say we have late rehearsals one day, and then, we finish at midnight. Then, I go have my dinner, and then, I'll get on my email again, and maybe do some stuff for the next day. By the time I go to sleep, it's about 3:00, 4:00 a.m.

When it's your own business, you don't really care what hours you're working. I love it. To me, it's not really work.

Phil: She'll post stuff, her business stuff, on her website at like 4:00 in the morning.

Tania: Yeah, he knows!

Phil: She loves what she does, and she's always thinking about what she has to do next.

Dealing with Drama and Harassment

It can be frustrating dealing with people. [Laughs.] When you run groups of dancers, there's a lot of drama. At the end of the day, you're the one who has to go clean up the mess. Because we work together so much, there's bound to be conflicts. Sometimes, people get really emotional, you know, they get into fights.

Phil: She refers to her dancers as her "kids." You can imagine the challenges that a mom has when the children are fighting or bickering with each other. She has forty to fifty kids, and when they start fighting with each other, when So-and-So doesn't like So-and-So, and it all lands in her lap, she has to solve all the problems. And just like with kids, if they don't get their own way, then they have temper tantrums, and they blame her for it.

She has to carry all the emotional baggage of all of these other people. There can be bad days like that, especially when people are stressing out about a performance or a competition. They can be very mean to her.

Tania: To be honest, I haven't really been abused or anything, but for group lessons, it's whoever comes in, right? But then, at the same time, I don't really have to have much body contact or personal interaction with them.

For private lessons, I meet the students, right? So, I have a good idea of how the person is and what he is like. And, if at any point in time, if I do not wish to continue teaching, I quit that student. But, luckily, that never really happened to me, anything kind of drastic. I've had people who stalked me, sent me messages and pictures, like a student who sent naked pictures of himself, and I had to straighten it out. I was lucky that, in that case, he was apologetic, and everything was cool after that.

I think, as a girl, you get hit on all the time anyway. So, I don't see it so much as my students hitting on me versus a regular guy hitting on me. It's just trickier for me if it's a student. But I haven't had really difficult situations.

Phil: Again, I disagree. I think it's blatant harassment. There was one situation about a month ago, one of her students basically asked her to go out, just as a friend type of thing and then started aggressively saying, "Why won't you go out with me? Why won't you give me a chance to be your boyfriend?" He actually made her very afraid.

She forgets all of these things. They happen. Every week, something like that happens. It's very bad that way. She maintains a very strong character about it, but she is harassed all the time. Some of it is very subtle harassment, but some of it is very blatant.

I think she just turns a blind eye to it, because she sees it as part of the job that she's going to be hit on by all of her male students.

Tania: He knows all my stories! [Laughs.]

Phil: All the time. And the dances, they're touch dances. So, the guys have their hands on her body all the time, and yes . . .

And then, there are the injuries. Dancing is a very physical activity, and she dances literally six, seven hours a day on her feet. Her feet take a beating. She always has a shoulder or a neck injury or something. She does tricks, flips, and splits. When you practice those, you're going to fall several times. So, she's always injured.

And as you get older, it's harder and harder. That's something that she didn't mention that's huge in what she does. They always talk about how singers can go on forever, but dancers have a very short shelf life.

Tania: I started ballet as a kid, and ballet is the most beautiful thing, but everything you do in ballet is against your natural body alignment. We always have to have our feet turned out, but your body's not used to doing that. Imagine twisting your body in ways that it's not naturally supposed to be.

So, for sure, I have knee injuries. You have to stand on your toes and dance and jump on them. Your feet are not designed that way. My feet and knees are obviously destroyed. But you talk to any professional ballerina, and they're going to tell you that this is worth it, because that's what they love.

And my personal life is pretty difficult, just trying to keep in touch with friends and family. If I have a love relationship, it's very challenging, unless my partner has the same schedule, which is very rare. But kids are not an issue. I've never really wanted kids.

The Healing Potential of the Tango

As for my "best" days, the superficial thing to say would be when I win competitions and things like that. But something else kind of sticks out in my head that is not necessarily a "day."

Basically, there was a lady, Marina, who had lost her husband. She was probably in her sixties, and she had been on antidepressants for a long time. Her daughter asked her to try something new, which turned out to be dancing. She had never danced with her husband, so it wouldn't remind her of him.

I started teaching her. She told me that she looked forward to my class all the time, that I always made her happy for the rest of the day because of my energy and everything. She told me that she was on an antidepressant, and she had started to lose her memory. She works at a day care center. She had begun to forget kids' names.

I introduced her to Argentine tango. She was very appreciative. At first, she didn't want to do it, because it's a partner dance with a guy. But I encouraged her, and I introduced her to an instructor. And the result: She's a very active dancer now in the tango community. She's off her medication. She's happy. I've seen her a few times. Every time I see her at a tango club, it makes me feel so good, because I helped someone.

My Vision: To Be the Best in the World — and to Change Lives with Dance

My vision is that I could set up the school so that people are not coming for me versus coming for the school; just to get everything running so that I don't have to be always tied to the school and can do other projects. I've also looked into doing more of the corporate and entertainment side versus doing mass group lessons.

My partner, Renaud,[6] and I have also started competing in world-level championships.[7] Last year, we were in the world championships in Hong Kong for bachata, and we came in third. Next week, we're in New York. We're going to be working with the world champion that is choreographing our next salsa routine, which we'll be competing for in February in Miami.

I would like to be a world champion sometime. I also want to be a more diverse dancer. There are some other projects that I'm working on that are still to be determined.

One thing I am working on, I don't know if I should say, because I've just scratched the surface of this so far: I'm also trying to see how I can use dance to change lives . . . In the case that I just mentioned, how I helped the lady overcome her depression: I think there's something there.

The Psychology of Dance

A lot of people come to dance because they have issues at home. Maybe it's a place for them to escape reality. I've had students who have relationship problems and people who lost their wives, and they've told me that the dancing and being involved in the community has helped them. It's almost like getting a new life.

I'd like to formalize that, look into the whole psychology and see how the two work together. I'd like to do something very concrete. "Okay, if someone has *this*, then *this* is the prescription for it." Right now, I need to gather all the cases I've worked on, just incidentally worked on, and put them into perspective.

Phil: For example, she was asked to tutor a fourteen-year-old girl from another country. This girl came over here for ten days. She had come from a broken family, and she suffered some pretty strong psychological ramifications from that.

Tania: My goal was to teach this girl to dance. But, as I said, I'm very close with my students. So, then when you become their friend, they start telling you stuff, and then, you just try your best to help them in whatever way you can.

In this particular case, the situation with her family had somehow made her feel very incompetent about herself. Dance really helped her with her confidence. You could see that the girl had a broken family, because, by day two, she was so attached to me. She was talking to me as if I was her mom, and everyone thought that she was my daughter, because everywhere we went, she was just hanging onto me.

I actually pushed her to do a performance in the big congress at the end of her ten-day stay. And during practice, she would miss a step, and she would run out crying. And then, she would say, "I don't want to do this any more," and I would have to talk to her. Sometimes, I had to be really strict, and sometimes, I had to be nice. Anyway, at the end of the day, she did an amazing job.

Phil: And she left a lot better than she came, psychologically. She wrote to Tania, "Thank you for helping me." It was very touching. They message each other every day now.

Tania: So, I think dancing actually can change a lot of things. It's not all just for fun. It is a life-changing thing.

238

twelve

MICHELE

ARTS CULTURAL-EXCHANGE OFFICER, STATE DEPARTMENT

Washington, D.C., United States

Editor's note: "Whatever you want to know, just ask," thirty-five-year-old Michele Peregrin says with a laugh that's surprisingly deep-throated, coming from such a petite person. "I'm happy to be as transparent as you like." This comment strikes me as quintessentially bureaucratic, but I'm hoping she'll reveal what it's really like to be a diplomat. After all, she had to get formal clearance[1] just to grant the interview for this chapter.

The only child of a software engineer and school administrator,[2] Michele cites both her parents as being her life's most unequivocally positive influences. They gave her the sense that she could do or be anything she desired. They may never have imagined, however, that she'd land in diplomacy at our nation's capital.

I've seen her "headquarters," inside the firewalls of the State Department, where you spend forty-five minutes getting in *after* you've been vetted. The cavernous building sits just a few blocks from the White House in the Foggy Bottom historic district of our nation's capital. Established in 1789 as the first executive department, the State Department employs nearly seventy thousand foreign- and civil-service employees to assist the Secretary of State with international diplomacy. Today, however, we're talking at her new home office in Santa Cruz, California.

Michele manages cross-cultural exchange programs in fifteen countries. She's passionate about using art—such genres as hip-hop music, digital art, mural arts, and dance—to connect cultures and transcend politics, prejudices, and even language.

"There's traditional diplomacy," Michele explains, "which entails governments talking to each other, high-level officials talking to high-level officials in another country, working out the affairs between those two nations. And then there's another section of diplomacy called *people-to-people diplomacy*, where it's happening more at the grassroots level." That's her domain.

Traveling periodically back to headquarters in D.C., Michele has "pioneered," as she puts it, the State Department's first West Coast–based telecommuting home office. She hopes to grow a State Department satellite office in the Bay Area. If that works out, she says, she could become a civil-service "lifer."

I Manage Cross-Cultural Exchange Programs in the Arts

My name is Michele Sharon Peregrin. I'm thirty-five. I was born and raised in Santa Cruz, California. I'm a program officer in the U.S. State Department.[3]

I manage cross-cultural exchange programs for the Bureau of Educational and Cultural Affairs, primarily in the arts. We create, fund, and oversee programs that send American artists abroad: dancers, musicians, and visual artists. We also have programs that bring international artists to the U.S.

Growing Up with a Balance of Back-East Conservatism and West-Coast Hippie-ness

I'm an only child. I grew up in a hippie town with parents who came from a more conservative upbringing "Back East," in upstate New York. I think they were, I don't want to say "sheltered," but they had limited exposure growing up. Maybe that was just a sign of the times. I mean, their parents lived through World War II, and they lived during the Cold War, and there was a whole mentality around the U.S. being the best country in the world and the safest place, and why would you want to go anywhere else?

But then, they started to broaden their own horizons and were really moved by the experiences they had. My dad had an MBA and an engineering degree and was working in corporate jobs. At one point, his company, GE [General Electric], sent them to Venezuela for over a year, and that was probably a pretty transformative experience for both of them. From there, they went to Italy and then Switzerland.

They came back with a much broader perspective. So, I think I had quite a bit of balance, thinking about both home and what was going on in the global community. I also feel like I grew up with [East-Coast/West-Coast] balance.

My Father Created a Virtual-Attorney Software Program

For the first ten years of their marriage, my dad was a businessman and the breadwinner. And then, he was laid off in the late 1980s.

He decided he wanted to try inventing something and establishing a company, which he worked on for the rest of his life. His background was in software engineering, and he designed a program that created cognitive 3-D mapping for the law. He was creating a virtual attorney and trying to democratize access to legal representation.

With this program, someone without much legal experience could go in and navigate all the U.S. legal code that's out there (which is massive) and get answers to their questions, without necessarily having to consult a lawyer. As you went through this map, it would ask you new questions about whatever situation you needed answers to.

It would say something like, "Well, was the [car] accident your fault or his fault?" and if you said, "Their fault," then it would bring up information relative to that scenario. And then, from there, it would say, "Okay, was this at night or during the day?"

It would pull from various legal documents about what was relevant for your case. I'm explaining it very simply. It was a lot more complicated than that, and really interesting. He worked on that for many, many years. He created a company and a foundation, but it never brought any income home. It never got off the ground in that way.

My Mom Became the Head of Household

So then, my parents' roles reversed. My mom had to assume most of the responsibility for providing financial support for the family. She worked within the local school system. She had a lot of different administrative roles, and she worked in special education for a while. She worked most recently in facilities management.

I inherited different traits from both of them. I balanced them out: I inherited grace from my mom. She's been a role model for being supportive and empathetic to others, and to always be mindful of how you may be coming across and to be gracious and accommodating and to be selfless. And from my dad, I learned the value of education, what's important in life, and what's important to stay focused on.

What My Parents Wanted for Their Only Child: Everything

My parents both wanted me to be well rounded and happy and to have a good quality of life—like all parents want for their kids.

What they wanted me to be definitely ranged. I have vague recollections of my dad saying, "You can grow up and be anything. You could be a U.S. ambassador!" [Laughs.] They had an only child, and she happened to be a girl, and my dad felt strongly that I shouldn't limit myself—that I should think broadly, both in terms of high-powered careers like an ambassadorship but then also outwardly facing.

Although my dad was an introvert, he saw that I was an extrovert. He encouraged me to get out in the world and see all that it has to offer. It's like, "Whatever interests you, find a career to pursue that." That may be just me latching on to something he said amongst a multitude of other things, because he also encouraged me to consider being a lawyer, and I never went down that road. My parents both talked about all of their different experiences, and that's one [diplomacy] that I most connected with.

I could probably spend a lot more time talking about my parents' influence on me. Being a very small unit in a big world, with just the two of them and me, they played a really big part in shaping who I was, and what I went on to do, and who I am today.

I Wanted to Be a Bartender

When I was growing up, I wanted to do many things. In third grade, I remember wanting to be a children's book author, and then, I thought about teaching.

At one point, when I was probably eleven or twelve, at the dinner table, I said that I wanted to be a bartender. I didn't even know what a bartender was. [Laughs.] I think I had seen an ad for *Cocktail*, the movie, on TV, and thought that that looked like a lot of fun. He [Tom Cruise] was with a lot of people, and everyone loved him.

That dream was short-lived. That's one my parents definitely shot down!

National Geographic Sparked My Wanderlust

In high school, I don't know that I had any real concrete ideas about my career. I just knew what I *didn't* want to do: medicine or engineering. I was interested in liberal arts and social sciences. I was always interested in archaeology. I oftentimes trace my career back to the fact that we got *National Geographic* every month for my entire life growing up. I would read the *Nat Geos* pretty much from cover to cover. That magazine really connected with something intrinsic in me. It taught me how big the world was and that I should go out and explore it. That's maybe the root of why I decided I wanted to study abroad when I was in college.

Being an only child, I was home a lot, reading. I don't want to sound like I wasn't out with friends, too. [Laughs.] I really was out with them every day after school. My parents had to push me to be home at 5:00 for dinner or to come home and do my homework. Despite liking to read and being on my own, I think I'm a fair amount extroverted. I also played classical piano for eleven years.

My First Job Was Painting Pottery at Petroglyph

My first real job was working at Petroglyph [a paint-your-own ceramics studio] in downtown Santa Cruz. I did that when I was eighteen as a summer high school job. I made about seven dollars an hour, a bit above minimum wage.

Another thing that was nice about my parents' upbringing of me was that they didn't require that I work. I'm sure people will have mixed reactions to that, but they always said, "Your number one priority is focusing on school right now, because you can work the rest of your life." In retrospect, I'm very grateful for that.

Public Schools All the Way Through

I went to public schools. I felt a certain responsibility to stay focused and do as best I could in school. I was very studious. I did all my homework on time.

That's what took up my time, and there was a twofold reason for that. One, I was self-motivated; it was just my inclination. I was fortunate to have a good group of school friends and good teachers. And then, of course, there was my parents' influence. So, I was motivated to succeed at school. It was a good environment for me.

I wanted to do the best I possibly could, because it would make my parents proud. And the better I could do, the less financial burden college would be. So, I went to University of California Los Angeles [UCLA] on a full-ride scholarship.

Landing a Scholarship to Study Abroad, Then Picking a Random Major

I was undeclared for the first two years at UCLA. I pushed that for as long as I could . . . The only thing I knew for sure was that I wanted to study abroad.

That was probably the beginning of my career path. I spent part of my sophomore year and my entire junior year overseas. I went to Italy and Spain, and then, I traveled a lot, anywhere else I could go, on breaks.

When I had to pick a major, I came across anthropology.[4] I didn't really know what that was, but I read this brief description that said, "The study of humankind." I said, "That's great. It's general. It sounds like my interest in all sorts of world cultures. So, I'm going to pick that."

Then, I worked briefly at the study-abroad office at UCLA. I started asking people about what they do as study-abroad counselors and directors of international student centers. They encouraged me to go to graduate school, which I already had in mind anyway.

In the process of searching for international affairs graduate programs, I came across a subspecialty called *international education*,[5] which was focused on two things—international exchange, which I had participated in, and international development, which was focused on education. I went to New York University [NYU]. There, I had to fund myself. I got an MA [master's in arts] in international education and really learned a lot about the field, not only academically but also practically.

From Study Abroad to International Exchange

My part-time job in the study-abroad office at UCLA set me on the career path that I'm still on. And then, in grad school, I worked for the exchange program that was implemented by NYU during the summers.

Then, I had a brief stint at the Institute of International Education, working on exchange programs; that was actually funded by my current bureau [at the U.S. State Department]. The director received an award to implement a program for international scholars to come to the U.S. and study American civilization, for an intensive program that was about six weeks each summer. In between my studies, that's what I worked on.

From there, my first solid forty-hour-a-week consistent job was the first role I had at the bureau, which was focused on scholars and students, language studies and academic studies. I worked with the alumni affairs office, which was expanding rapidly, to try and make sure that the relationships we had with the participants in these exchange programs didn't just end when they were done.

Working in Education and Cultural Affairs at the State Department

I've been doing my current job for about five years. I work at the Bureau of Educational and Cultural Affairs, one of the arms within the U.S. State Department.

The State Department is massive—I wouldn't quote me on this, but I think there are somewhere between sixty and eighty thousand employees worldwide. A big chunk of its work is by the U.S. embassies overseas, but then "headquarters" is back in D.C. There are bureaus that focus on topical things like refugees and migration, human trafficking, political affairs, and then, there are the regional foci in Latin America, Europe, Africa. My bureau is focused on public diplomacy.

There's traditional diplomacy, which entails governments talking to each other, high-level officials talking to high-level officials in another country, and they're working out the affairs between those two nations. And then there's another section of diplomacy called "people-to-people diplomacy," where it's happening more at the grassroots level. It's individuals talking to one another directly.

The Diplomatic Power of People Just Talking to Each Other about Life

The cultural-programs division is a small part in a much larger piece that's focused on people-to-people diplomacy and exchanges in different categories, for example, sending athletes, professionals, journalists, academics, scholars, or students abroad. The entire bureau's mission is focused on fostering mutual understanding between people in the U.S. and people abroad through these people-to-people exchanges.

For example, it's Americans meeting with high school students in Tanzania to talk about what life is really like in the States. The idea is that our individual citizens are as good as, if not better than, representatives of our country at giving a more accurate picture of our country to the rest of the world than what these people might get otherwise, either through the filter of their own governments or through Hollywood or other channels.

My sense is that, around the world, a lot of people like Americans as *people*, and whenever there are issues, it tends to be directed more at government or policy.

So, if you go to Kosovo,[6] the sentiment is very different than if you go to Pakistan.[7] I think it depends on how people get their information and how accurate that information is. Education is so instrumental in shaping people's understanding and experience and knowledge and perceptions. I really do believe the mission of the bureau: If we can just foster a more accurate understanding between one another, that's more likely to reduce conflict, should disagreements come up.

The Arts Unite People in Ways That Transcend Language

Working through all areas of education is important, but I think the arts are especially well equipped at reaching audiences that may not otherwise have access to, say, a language program or academic programs.

We can use the arts to reach non-elites, those that are disenfranchised, marginalized in their communities, and don't have access to high standards of education. The arts cross a lot of boundaries and barriers that might be there, like language barriers.

Using music and dance, we've sent artists to places where they don't speak the language and communities that don't speak English, yet they're able to have really powerful interactions through their art form. Art can foster a connection where there might otherwise be some challenges. By contrast, if you send a student to go do research at a university, they've got to speak the local language in order to get by, and they're only hitting that small segment of the population.

How We Find Participants in Our Programs

We reach people through our embassies. The public affairs sections within the embassies connect with all sorts of community groups and implementing partners who run our exchange programs.

So, it's not just me behind a desk trying to do everything for a particular exchange program. I'll work with a grantee organization, and oftentimes, they'll reach out to a local partner organization within a country. Those people have strong ties and networks within that country. Or we can connect with the embassy and ask whom they might refer. It's a multipronged approach.

For example, I could reach out to our U.S.-based partner and say, "Okay, we're going to do a project in, wherever, Indonesia."[8] My partner in this case could be Meridian International Center. It could be IIE, Institute of International Education. So, they may already have a connection. Or they might say, "We don't really know a lot of people in Indonesia. Let's just get online."

Our Arts Partners Are Amazingly Well-Networked

What's been amazing about working with arts organizations is to see how well networked they are. In the arts world, I've been very impressed with how it's all about whom you know.

I think this is because artists are moving around so much, and they work with so many different people and organizations. They don't have an office job with the same people day in and day out. So, they just have really complex, large, broad networks. Even if they didn't know an organization, say, in Indonesia, they might call up a museum in San Francisco and say, "Hey, I remember you guys hosted some Indonesian artist. Whom did you work with to get that done?" And so they fan out and do it that way.

It's great when things sync up. Sometimes, the embassy will say, "We recommend this local organization," and meanwhile, the partner in the U.S. says, "Hey, the Oakland Museum just recommended this organization," and they happen to be the same. The stars align, and that's whom we're going to work with.

Then, We Vet Them: Are They Innovative? Reliable?

We rely on the [local] embassy's experience on whether they think that organization is reliable. We would look at whether they have a past track record managing grants, like funding from the U.S. Embassy or other organizations.

But sometimes, it's a new organization, or a small one, or it's an individual who's participated in another exchange program and is really innovative and is starting something, and the U.S. Embassy has a great relationship with that particular individual who they think is going to carry most of the weight of the program. So, the embassies go out and do their own due diligence. They meet with them and talk them through what's expected. Some of it's a little trial and error, too.

Where We Work: Every Country in the World

We run programs in virtually every country in the world. Across the bureau, I believe we exchange about fifty thousand people each year. So, that's macro level.

Within my division, I oversee four exchange programs. I traditionally had a portfolio mostly in the visual arts, but I recently expanded it to also include music and dance. One's a multidisciplinary hip-hop exchange program that includes dance and music. Another is a mural-arts based program.

We also connect U.S. museums with museums overseas. They develop an exchange project that works with their local communities to address a topic of interest to them. And our American Arts Incubator program sends American visual artists overseas to work with local communities through workshops on creating public art that addresses some local issue and utilizes new media and technology to address those issues.

Projects within the Projects: Managing Artists from Afar

Within each exchange program, there are multiple projects. For instance, I oversee the hip-hop exchange program.[9] That's just one program with a U.S. partner, the University of North Carolina [UNC] Chapel Hill music department. As part of that program, we send groups of American artists overseas to conduct workshops.

It's a transformative experience. Hip-hop has a history of representing those who don't normally have a voice. It's a really great way to empower at-risk, underserved youth.

Where do they go? All over. This year, it's El Salvador, Honduras, Tanzania, Uganda, and Thailand.[10] We send four American artists together to each country. So, that's five projects within one program, and they're kind of spread out over the year. At any given time, I'd say I have probably twenty projects under my purview.

In terms of the visual arts and technology, we just sent an American artist, John Craig Freeman, to China. His background is in augmented reality. He's created all sorts of different public art projects—it's really cool. It's virtual artwork in public spaces—not physically building it there, but in a digital realm. He creates the artwork, and people can interact with installations to see what that artwork would look like there and alter it and play with it and do different things with it.

We Reach Out Beyond Traditional Diplomacy

We select countries based on need. We place a high priority in reaching other audiences there that are maybe not being reached through traditional diplomacy. That's a high priority in terms of our relationship with that country. Also, where is the program going to fit well? Where is it going to have the most impact?

So, some of our tech-based programs, we may not send to Africa as much, for instance, because there's connectivity challenges there. We weigh all of those things and then put in the call for artists to apply for where those countries are, and then, they submit an application[11] and say, "I'm interested in this because of this topic."

The Hardest Places to Work Are Where We Need to Be

The hardest places to work are anywhere we don't have great official relationships and where there's a lot of skepticism of Americans. Those places are always a challenge, but they're also where there's the greatest need.

Venezuela[12] would be an example. Cuba[13]—it used to be that we really couldn't do anything there, and now, we're doing so much. It's transitioned so quickly. Pakistan, Afghanistan, those kinds of places.

Cooperative Agreements and Grants Provide Structure for Our Relationships

There are about twelve of us working on arts-based exchanges. I used to oversee our interns, but now, I supervise relationships with the partners outside. We stay very involved in the program. We'll issue what we call a "cooperative agreement," which most people think of as a grant, but it's kind of technical in that [with a grant] you turn over the money, and you let them go do what they said they would do. A cooperative agreement, rather, means that we're jointly implementing this program.

The length of these relationships varies anywhere from five days to a year. Some of our programs support people pursuing doctoral studies, say, for five or six years—for example, the Fulbright Program is a well-known example that's under my department.

Usually a cooperative agreement runs about twenty-four to forty-eight months. So, they have a long lead time. And I'm in touch with them on a weekly if not daily basis, talking about key milestones, such as announcing the call for applications, selecting the countries, choosing the artists, or conducting orientations. Then, there's the actual execution of the projects. Often, if the partner organization has performed well, and we think the program is meeting its goals and objectives, we'll renew it for another year.

We have twenty projects going on at any given time but only four principal partner relationships. But other relationships trickle down from there. I work with the American Alliance of Museums, UNC Chapel Hill, ZERO1, and Meridian International. And then, there are all sorts of other stakeholders involved, the embassies in each country, and the local partner organizations. However, I only have to oversee and really nurture in the long-term those four immediate relationships.

Ways I Nurture Our Artists from a Distance

I provide guidance, especially with new relationships, about all the different stakeholders that are involved and who needs to be consulted. Small arts organizations will get an award from us, and they won't have any idea how to work with the U.S. Embassy, and they won't understand the relationship between us and them. So, we spend time explaining who needs to weigh in at what point and then actually facilitating that communication.

We also provide technical expertise on how to submit reports, questions about visas, and what's allowed in terms of the budget. I'm usually their first point of contact for questions about that sort of stuff, and I can answer them most of the time.

My Budget Is Around $6.6 Million

I oversee a budget of $2,238,000, but that's for one fiscal year. Right now, I have this times two and am working on the third. So, currently, I'm overseeing $4.4 million but also working on the next cycle. Technically, one of these cycles will close as the other one starts. There's a bit of overlap, so at any given time, I have actually more like $6.6 million coming and going. Of the fifty thousand people reached through my division, I probably see about 135 to 150 exchange participants.

In this job, I can't say I make six figures,[14] but it's a very good living for the field. In international education, there are four main sectors: NGOs [nonprofits], which primarily rely on either private donations or grants from foundations and government and have the least financial security. There's the government, which is much more stable and can provide me a comfortable living. There's higher education, like study-abroad offices at universities, and foundations, which have their own issues: They can't spend too much on administrative costs and on salaries for their staffs.

A lot of people come to my bureau after spending ten, fifteen years working for one of our partner institutions—for example, a nonprofit doing the work on the frontlines. They're coming in with quite a bit of experience. I was definitely on the young end when I came in. I feel very fortunate that I was able to leapfrog in some ways.

Our health benefits are good. Everyone thinks the government has these amazing benefits, but they're pretty standard. It used to be that there were pensions. Those have been significantly whittled down. My generation and the generation after me won't have much to lean on.

The State Department: Both Civil and Foreign Service

The State Department has two corps of employees. One is the Civil Service staff, which is domestically based, in which you're hired because of your expertise in a certain genre. And then, there's the Foreign Service, which are the people who rotate around the world, working at U.S. embassies abroad.

They both carry their pros and their cons. I think the Foreign Service set of benefits is very different than Civil Service, because these people are sacrificing permanency somewhere in order to serve our country. So, if they serve in an area that's in conflict, they can get hardship pay. They can get relief for their student loans. I think it's right that what they get would be a lot more interesting than what I get as a Civil Servant.

Background Checks and Security Clearances

Before working here, we had to go through an extensive background check. I don't know exactly what diplomatic security is or is not looking for, because they don't really share much. They just make you fill out a ton of paperwork. They're looking for anything out of the ordinary, where they would question your allegiance or your ability to safely and successfully perform the job, whatever that is.

You have to document your entire life in the ten years leading up to when you're applying for the job. For instance, I had to write down the address of my apartment where I lived for the ten weeks I was studying abroad in Italy. I didn't have that anywhere, because all my mail was sent either to my permanent address here or to the school. It took a lot of digging—at one point, I remember I was looking at Google Earth to find the street address on the building itself.

My office in D.C. is a pretty standard cubicle-like space with some offices. It's a very secure building. We're right across from the main State Department building. You have to have a badge, and you go through a card reader, where you punch in a PIN. Even our interns have to go through this security clearance process in order to access the building. You go through the door; there's kind of a maze of hallways, and then, you hit the land of cubes, and that's also a maze.

When communicating with partners across the U.S. and around the world, we talk mostly by email and phone, and occasionally in person. We can't do any sort of videoconferencing from within the building. On occasion, I will work from home in order to be able to use those tools.

What a Day in the State Department Looks Like

A typical day really varies. My standard day is checking email, making sure nothing has exploded overnight, and catching up on any correspondence. From there, it just depends on what sort of projects I have. I may be doing a lot of reading, drafting, responding to requests from senior leadership for background on a program. It really varies, but it's mostly an office job.

My job is outwardly focused: The majority of my day is communicating with my [international] partners. And the person sitting across from me is doing the same thing. We don't have a reason to talk to each other much, other than compare notes. "Hey, I have this situation over here with this partner, this exchange participant. Have you ever encountered that?" We share best practices and challenges and things. But we're not working together much.

The highlights are when we're building toward one of these program milestones that I mentioned, where we bring program artists together for an orientation and actually get to meet with them. We'll do different workshops; sometimes, we'll bring in outside experts to talk about conflict resolution or a nonprofit that's doing work in their area to talk about sustainability.

We're a Very Vertical Organization

We're a very vertical organization. We try to communicate what we're doing up to our senior leadership, and we hope they'll share it with the right audiences, whether it be on the Hill or through the press and social media. We have a great social media presence on Facebook, Twitter, Flickr, and that sort of stuff. A lot of people follow us, like people who are interested in international exchange, students, public diplomacy practitioners, scholars, and artists. It's a pretty big range.

I generally work a forty-hour week. Occasionally, there'll be weekend events or these program milestones, but it's a pretty normal workweek.

My colleagues around my bureau are so dedicated and passionate about the work. They believe in the power of exchange programs and people to really make the world a better place. It sounds kind of cheesy, but I think that's why they come to work every day.

We hope that, if a foundation of trust and understanding is there, we can avoid a lot of conflicts. And I just think it's important for people and American taxpayers to know how seriously we take their responsibility as being stewards of these federal programs.

My Best Days: When We Get to Meet the Artists in-Person

My best days are when we get to bring everybody together, to talk in-person with the people that we've been doing so much with behind the scenes. Those are moments where we feel like the program we've envisioned and drafted, that we've done a ton of paperwork to pull together, is now real. It's come to fruition; it's actually *happening*. And we get to meet people from all over the world.

When I started working on a program in the hip-hop exchange about a year ago, I was pretty stoked to go to the orientation for that. We brought twenty-five American hip-hop artists from all over the country together to prepare them for the workshops they were about to do overseas. They were such dynamic, interesting people. And then, it's also really nice to see when they go have their own experiences in places like Uganda or Thailand and all the positive feedback we get back from them. That's really rewarding.

What the Arts Have to Teach Us about Diplomacy

I think the arts have a lot to teach about diplomacy. Everyone can have a voice. Art is a tool for everyone to be able to weigh in on matters that impact their lives. That's something that government and people in influential positions should really pay attention to and take into account. Those that are decision makers and policy makers can learn from it.

As we saw with the Arab Spring,[15] people can use the arts and all sorts of different platforms to voice frustration or voice their hopes and dreams or voice what they want the future of their country to be, what they're not happy with, and what they want instead. Art is an accessible tool that young people and old people all around the world can use to communicate with.

What's Challenging: Keeping Americans Safe Abroad

I wouldn't say there are too many bad days. The most nerve-wracking part of the job is making sure that everyone is safe. We take every measure possible to ensure that everyone is safe, but there are some things that are just outside of our control.

The responsibility largely falls on our embassies overseas to make sure that appropriate security measures are in place. They have what are called *regional security officers* at each embassy who brief the exchange participants about what neighborhoods are safe, what neighborhoods aren't safe, whether they can walk around late at night or not. A lot of it's just common sense; for example, don't carry a fancy new camera.

A lot of the rules and guidance are the same if you were going to New York or San Francisco as a tourist, but there are places where it's challenging, because the electricity may go out at night, or it's hard to get hot running water.

We put them in places that can be trying, and so we ask them to be very flexible. On occasion, someone's fallen ill. We've had to get them back to the States to make sure they got appropriate medical attention. Or some sort of crime—that's always what's on my mind and, knock on wood, I have had very, very few incidences, but when they do come up, your heart just drops. You're just stressed, trying to figure out what to do.

My Husband, My Home, and My Cat "Marbles"

I live in Santa Cruz, California, with my husband, Joe, and our cat, Marbles. My husband is forty. He grew up on Long Island, New York, and was pretty much East Coast-based his whole life up until this year, when he moved here with me. We met in the end of 2006, at a bar on the Upper East Side. [Laughs.] And then, we dated for seven years and then got married. We've been married for two years.

Joe works for Wells Fargo Bank in co-branded credit cards. He's taught me a lot professionally, because he already had a successful tenured career in the workforce before I was even starting out. I got guidance from him on things that seem basic now, but I really had no clue about early on. It's like, if you have a problem with someone, try to address it directly—don't ever go to the person above them. Don't go around them.

Things like that were really, really helpful. He's taught me internal diplomacy. [Laughs.] We do a lot of that, for sure. So, that's been good.

Joe is a very focused man. He's very generous and kind and loves me to pieces. So, I can't ask for more. I feel like I've seen him really grow as a person since we've been together. Since we started dating, we started to travel and go outside the country. And now, he's just totally exploded in terms of his interests and his openness to going, pushing his boundaries, improving himself, and trying new things. I really respect that.

My Hobbies Are Traveling and Dancing

In my current life, I don't have hobbies. I think my hobby is traveling, but the reality of having to work doesn't allow me to travel as much as I would like. And I love to dance. I learned how to swing dance in high school, and I still like dancing in general. I always want to get into projects such as scrapbooking, but I never actually do it.

If I had to list the most interesting places I've traveled to, I'd include those with unique religious history and amazing archaeological sites . . . I found Turkey just fascinating. It sits at the crossroads of Europe and Asia, and you can really see that in the architecture. Up until that point, I'd been through most of Western Europe and Central and South America, which are mostly Christian-based societies. What else? I love Croatia. The Mediterranean is beautiful. Spain is also fascinating because of the changeovers through history. I love to explore religions, temples, cultures, and architecture.

What's Next: Seeing Our Programs on the Ground, in Person

I'm lucky to feel really connected to our mission and what I do. I mean, I *really* believe in it. That's what keeps me going, day in and day out. The most rewarding part is getting to interact with the people benefiting from our work. When I get those positive, meaty stories back—about how this exchange changed my life, or I've gone on to start my own nonprofit, and

I'm now reaching twenty young girls a week in afterschool programs or in the arts, whatever it might be—getting those anecdotal stories of impact is always really rewarding.

Going forward, I would love to get some more international experience and see more of these activities actually taking place abroad.

In the future, one goal is for Joe and me to start a family in the next three to five years. We were in New York, then we were long distance between D.C. and New York, and then, he joined me in D.C. And now, we're feeling pretty settled in California, but with him working out of the city [San Francisco] and me being here, that's kind of in flux. So, that's something that we want to work on.

I'd also love to move into a role that had more managerial responsibility, and that might be in higher education. I'd like to start a West Coast-based office for my bureau. We have an office in New York, a very small office, but 90 percent of what takes place within the bureau is in D.C.

I'm a little bit of a pioneer right now with being out here and trying to make this work. My dream of dreams would be to make that a more sustainable situation and potentially start a small division that handles West Coast activities and affairs. In which case, I could be a lifer. It's possible. There are lots of them in my bureau.

Activism
and
Diplomacy

thirteen

JUNIOR

ENVIRONMENTAL ACTIVIST

Naoma, West Virginia, United States

Editor's note: Junior Walk,[1] the son and grandson of coal-miners, has watched his relatives die in coalmines or emerge stricken with black lung, choking for air and struggling to survive on disability in an area plagued with poverty and depopulation, with boarded-up windows and a thick layer of coal dust over all. He says his home has become "toxic and poisonous" and "the coal industry has murdered my friends, family, and neighbors."

He believes their true legacy is not coalmining but self-sufficiency and "living off the land"—hunting, farming, and gathering medicinal and edible foods.

His role models are local activists—his mentors, the late Judy Bonds, who founded Coal River Mountain Watch, and Larry Gibson, who started the Keeper of the Mountain Foundation. His passion for protesting comes from a deep love of the mountains, his family, and Appalachian culture.

When I meet Junior, he's wearing what he calls his "standard anarchist uniform" of camo pants and hiking boots, along with his mountain-man's bushy beard and flannel shirt. He speaks softly yet with certainty about a career so controversial that he's been disowned by family and friends and threatened with stones and bullets.

"It isn't only the right thing," he says. "It's my *duty* to stop these corporations from destroying the place I come from and poisoning my people for another day, by any means necessary, even if that means sacrificing my personal safety and freedom."

My Job: To Preserve Our True Mountain Culture

My name is Junior Ray Walk, and I'm twenty-five years old. I'm the volunteer and outreach coordinator of Coal River Mountain Watch [crmw.net] in Naoma, West Virginia.

I'm not just an environmentalist; I'm an activist, too. There's a lot to do in the community. We try to preserve the culture of self-sufficiency that we have around here.

Legacy of Farming and Hunting

Coal has always been a boom-and-bust industry. Whenever there were hard times, people had to get by. They grew gardens and hunted in the fall, dug medicinal roots out of the woods, and pretty much lived off of the land.

Before the coal industry ever came into this area, people were subsistence farmers. Not very many, if any, Native Americans actually lived here. Most lived in the Kanawha River Valley. You'll find a lot of places where people were buried or artifacts or things like that. But Coal River Valley, where I live, was primarily used for hunting.

White Europeans Settled Here, and It's Still 99% White

The first people that settled and lived here long-term were the first European settlers. Now, we're definitely like 99 percent white people here.

There were a lot more people of color who lived here back in the 1970s–1980s, but they were generally poor. So, they lived where it didn't cost that much, up in the head of a holler² somewhere, the farthest point back that you can get to without owning an ATV.

When large-scale mining operations started popping up in the area, who do you think were the first people pushed out? It was the people of color. I really don't know where they went. I would assume they went to the same places that anybody else goes whenever they leave: either Ohio or North Carolina.

Who Owns Our Land? Not Us . . .

Ninety-five percent of the entire landmass of Raleigh County, West Virginia, and 98 percent of the entire landmass of Boone County, West Virginia, are owned by large corporate interests outside of the state, some of them outside of the country.

Rowland Land Company owns Coal River Mountain. We're used here as a resource colony, just like anywhere else in the world. The coal that's come from here fueled the Industrial Revolution, and it's fueled modern America up to today, and we haven't gotten so much as a pat on the back for it.

Mountaintop Removal Affects More Than Mountaintops

When people talk about mountaintop removal,[3] and they throw out numbers like "five hundred mountains destroyed in Appalachia," that's not quite right. We're not talking about just one peak, like in the Alps or whatever. It's a range of peaks and valleys, vast swathes of pristine forest land that end up just totally decimated. It's like two thousand, three thousand acres—sometimes even larger areas.

We Live Right Below the Destruction

You can't really see [the destruction] that well from the valley. Everybody lives in the valley. But if you get up on another ridgeline, specifically on Coal River Mountain, and look around you, it's pretty much everywhere.

This is the last intact mountain in the entire watershed, the last mountain they haven't totally mined out yet. But it's permitted to be strip-mined. If that happens, it will be every single one of our mountains gone. There won't be any wilderness left.

Coalmining Is Breaking Our Backs

Even if they totally stopped mountaintop removal and strip-mining and just went back to underground coalmining, I would not be in favor of it.

I just don't agree with the fact that you send thirty, forty men into an underground coalmine to break their backs and kill themselves sixty hours a week, twelve hours a day, every single time they go to work. They kill themselves either outright in a mine explosion, or a rock fall, or later on by black lung and other coal-related illnesses.

And there's somebody sitting up on Wall Street who's never had a callous on their hands, ain't never worked a day in their life, never seen West Virginia, and they're making millions upon millions of dollars off of the sweat and blood and labor of those people working in that mine, people who don't have hardly nothing to show for it.

"Anything for Us Without Us Is Against Us"

Our miners get a percentage of a percentage of a percentage of what that coal is worth. I personally have had enough of that. That goes for *any* [energy] industry that would come in here, wind farms or anything else. If it's not totally controlled by the local population, and if the local people here aren't getting full profits, I wouldn't be for that, either.

I believe it was a Black Panther saying back in the sixties and seventies that stated, "Anything for us without us is against us."

West Virginians Are Strong and Resilient

Unfortunately, it's come down to preservation of the environment, local culture, and the health of the people who live here, versus jobs in the mines.

The way I look at it, you can always make money doing *something*. You don't need to be begging for that paycheck from the coal company.

What really needs to be done here is a concerted effort to retrain people who have spent their lives working in the coal industry to do something else, *anything* else. West Virginians are really strong. You put them to work in a factory; they can do anything you ask them to do.

Banjos, Bluegrass, Hunting, and Stories

Here, in West Virginia, you hear banjos all of the time. It's the Appalachian thing, banjos and fiddles, bluegrass and old-time music.

As far as food, we've got lots of deer, turkey, bear—pretty much anything that has legs and runs in the woods, we'll eat it, except for possum. Don't eat a possum. Take my word for it. Just don't do it. It's gross. It tastes like grease.

And ramps[4] are a really big thing. It's like a wild leek or onion that comes up in the springtime and grows everywhere around here. There are big ramp dinners[5] every spring at different churches all along the river. Also mushrooms, wild harvested mushrooms, chanterelles or morels, *chicken of the woods*, what we call "Molly Moochers."[6]

But I think what ties all of that together, our food and our music and our stories and everything else, is this intense feeling of trying to be as self-reliant as possible, living off of the land, and not living beyond your means.

My Office Is in an Old General Store

Right now, I'm sitting in the Coal River Mountain Watch office in Naoma, West Virginia. We just did a big fundraiser and bought this building. It was an old general store. It's a beautiful two-story brick building, built in 1912.

About eighty people live here. There's a post office directly across a two-lane blacktop highway that runs through the middle of the town, and a bunch of houses. Maybe thirty yards down the road from us, there's an auto repair shop. That's about it.

My Appalachian Ancestry

On my mom's side, my relatives have been here since the mid-1800s, when my forebears moved up from Kentucky. As far as my dad's side, I haven't been able to trace that back very far. They don't have anything to do with us, really.

I was adopted [by my stepfather] when I was a kid. That's a little bit complicated. My mom is my birth mother, but she got a divorce from my biological father when I was like a year old. Then, he had partial custody.

My biological father was a Pentecostal preacher. I used to have to go to his house every other weekend. When I was about eight, the situation with my real father was not very good, to say the least. He was a pretty violent person and not a good man to be around as a small child. All he gave me was somebody who showed me how *not* to be. So then, my dad adopted me. He was my stepfather, and now I just call him Dad.

Growing Up Right Next-Door to a Coal Slurry

I grew up around ten miles down the road from here, in a little town called Eunice. Fewer than fifty people live there.

I have a little sister, Natasha. She's twenty-two. She goes to community college in the big town nearby, Beckley ("big" means big enough to have a Walmart and a movie theatre). It's about an hour away. She's still living with my parents, and she's getting married to a coalminer. She agrees with the vast majority of what I have to say about the situation here, even though she couldn't publicly come out and say it, for fear of her fiancé losing his job.

I went to school from kindergarten until sixth grade at Marsh Fork Elementary, which is situated about three hundred yards from a coal prep plant[7] and a coal slurry dam.[8] That's where coal's taken after it's mined (whether it's surface mined or underground mined), and it's put through a series of different chemical washes and screens. The idea is to get all the material out of the coal that's not supposed to be burned in a power plant and sent into the atmosphere per the Clean Air Act regulations.

After they load the coal onto the trains and it goes on down the line, what's left here is what's called coal slurry or coal sludge. It's this thick, viscous, muddy material that is all of the chemicals that they used to wash the coal. They'll dispose of this material in one of two ways: put it into old abandoned underground coalmines or put it into these huge earthen dams, the impoundments, which is essentially just rock and dirt piled up at the face of a valley, and they'll backfill the whole thing with slurry.

The dam behind Marsh Fork Elementary School holds back 2.3 billion gallons of this toxic waste. The biggest one on Coal River, which is actually the largest earthen dam in the Western hemisphere, is the Brushy Fork coal slurry impoundment, and that holds back 7.8 billion gallons of coal sludge. That's less than a mile above mine and my parents, and my grandparents' homes.

Precarious Slurry Dams Can, and Have, Given Way

It's held back with material from the mine site from mountaintop removal mining: rock and dirt, just stacked up and compressed right there at the face of a valley. And these dams have fell before.

I mean, you look at Buffalo Creek, West Virginia, in 1972. That was a coal-slurry dam, just like these ones we're talking about. The only difference is, at the time, they didn't have the technology to make them so huge, and they didn't produce quite as much coal slurry. So, that one held back three million gallons, and when it broke, it killed over a hundred people.

My mother had just been born then, in 1972. She doesn't remember that event. My grandparents talk to me about it, though. They had family down that way. They went and helped out with the cleanup and stuff from that.

My Teacher Used to Threaten That Our Noise Would Break the Dam

When I was in fifth grade, when we'd get like loud in class or whatever, my teacher would slam his fist down on his desk and say, "If you all kids don't shut up, that dam up there is going to bust and wash you all away."

I had no idea what he was talking about, at the time. I knew the prep plant was over there, but I didn't realize there was a huge lake of coal sludge right behind it.

Learning about Coalmining from My Grandpa

Growing up, I talked to my grandpa all the time. He was a union coalminer. He tried to impart to me at a young age that the coal company is not your friend, not to be trusted. I think that has a lot to do with my current opinions. He was involved in a lot of strikes in the mid-1980s, when Massey Energy came and bought up all the coalmines and told all the workers, "Either you're not union anymore or you don't have a job."

Today, there are about 30,000 coal workers directly employed by the coal industry in the entire state of West Virginia. There're only a handful of active coalminers that are still in the union, and the majority of them are retired.

Growing Up, No Electricity = No Video Games

Then, my family lived up in Horse Creek, at the head of a holler. We only lived there for about six months.

We didn't have any power, no running water. You had to go outside to use the restroom, and we had a hand-pumped well. We had a lot of chickens and animals, goats, a horse. I hated it so bad, and I really wanted to have electricity so I could play my video games. But now, looking back on that time, I really miss living that way.

We Ended Up Living in a Coal Camp

Then, we moved down to Eunice, to a small coal-camp house. *Coal camp*[9] is a general term for housing built by coal companies for workers in the early 1900s. They had to live in the company house, and they were getting paid company money that could only be spent at the company store, and they could get kicked out of their house at any time.

Our house now has vinyl siding on it, but when it was originally built, it was all wood siding and wood shingles. There's a lot of mismatched wood, like crazy boards, braces, and stuff that just should be totally different. They built a second bedroom onto it. It's just a tiny little house with a wood stove. It's in pretty rough condition; the plumbing and wiring are atrocious. Not the nicest house in the world, but it's a roof. I'm thankful to my parents for providing me with it; that was as much as they could do.

That's where I live at now, too. I bought a place right next to my parents and my grandparents.

The Water from Our Taps Was Blood Red

Shortly after we moved there, the water started coming out of our taps blood red, smelling disgusting. Later, I learned that was from coal slurry getting into our well water.

They were doing an underground injection permit on the ridgeline above my parents' house and also had a surface mine active on top of it. So, they were setting off blasts, and that cracked the aquifer and let the slurry seep through to our wells.

Our water was nasty for about seven years. Eventually, our town got municipal water put in. There was a lawsuit against Massey Energy, and they had to pay to put the waterline through. I'm not sure how much it cost, but I guarantee it wasn't anywhere near the value of a life.

Wanting to Get Out of Coal Country

During my senior year, I realized I really wanted to get out of this area. I didn't want to be a coalminer. So, I applied to a bunch of colleges, got into a few of them, and then quickly learned that you need a LOT of money to go to college.

I was pretty much up a creek. I was the first person in my family to graduate high school, let alone have any idea how to go about applying for financial aid or scholarships or anything of that nature.

So, I was stuck here. I couldn't afford to go to college. There were guidance counselors at school, but the kids down at this end of the river, unless they had exceptional grades, they didn't have no attention paid to them. And I was a really awkward kid. I felt funny about walking in there and asking for help in the first place.

I was just a teenager. Honestly, up until I got involved with this activism, I was pretty shy. I wouldn't really go into restaurants or anything like that. But after I started speaking publicly about my experiences in the coal industry, I realized what I have to say could be important, and possibly I could have a hand in making an actual change here. I figured it was worth it to stop being awkward [laughs] as much as possible.

Options: Coalmining, Enlisting, or Selling Drugs

As a young person, I was presented with only a handful of options. Either I could go to the military or go to work for the coal company or sell drugs—mostly prescription drugs, opiates. That's the big thing around here. That was about it, then. And that's about all there is here today.

I took what I thought was the lesser of those three evils, and I went to work for the Elk Run coal prep plant, the same plant my dad worked at.

I did general maintenance, cutting the grass or welding on equipment, fixing scoop buckets, stuff that you don't need a lot of technical knowledge for. Some days, I'd be walking along the belt line. Other days, they had me in the basement of the plant, waist-deep in coal sludge, the same coal sludge that tainted my water as a kid.

I only worked at the coal prep company for about seven months. I was seventeen. My dad was having bad health problems at that time. I knew that working in that environment was what caused it. I knew if I kept working that job, I would have health problems, too. It was fairly obvious.

From Flipping Burgers to Sitting Security

So, I quit that job and tried minimum wage work for a while. I flipped a lot of burgers and worked in retail at the dollar store. Then, a friend of the family offered me a position as a security guard on a strip mine.

I figured sitting on my butt for twelve hours a day making money, I could handle that kind of work. So, I jumped all over it.

But within the first week, I felt like I had blood on my hands from getting paid to do that. I watched those machines tearing that mountain up, and I knew the people who lived below that ridgeline were going through the same things I went through when I was a little kid. It made me feel miserable, and I knew I had to do something about it.

Blood on My Hands

So, that's when I came to Coal River Mountain Watch. Judy Bonds, one of the people who helped to start this organization in 1998, was in the office when I came in. I'd known her ever since I was a little kid, because she used to work at the gas station with my grandma.

I asked her what I could do to help. She started having me write for the Coal River Mountain Watch newsletter anonymously, so I wouldn't get fired [from my security job]. I didn't have to worry about backlash or anything like that.

My Computer Wired to the Power Pole

So, that's what I started doing. It was actually kind of funny. I didn't have a laptop at the time; I couldn't afford one. So, I'd take my desktop computer and put it in the passenger seat of my car, and drive it to work with me, and run an extension cord out to the power box on the power pole, and write articles for the Coal River Mountain Watch newsletter on that while sitting there getting paid as a [coalmine] security guard.

In December, Judy offered me a position on staff for Coal River Mountain Watch. I knew if I took that job, it would mean a lot of changes in my life. A lot of my extended family won't speak to me anymore, and if they do, oftentimes they won't have nothing nice to say, to say the least.

I Got Kicked Out of the House to Save My Dad's Job

And my parents had to kick me out of their home—not because they disagreed with my position at all.

Keep in mind: They lived with that same crappy water that I did, all those years. And to be fair, I was nineteen. It was probably about time for me to leave the nest anyway. But still, they had to do it. It was forced upon them. They knew if I was doing the things that I do now and living under their roof, my dad would have lost his job in a heartbeat.

I don't think that's right. It's just a good example of how the coal industry can control people's lives. It's definitely calmed down a fair bit now, but at that time, there was a lot of heated debate about how we tried to shut down the coal industry. People were real upset, to the point where they'd make threats and do very threatening things.

Brake Lines Cut, Guns Pulled on Me

I used to have a truck, but I had my brake lines cut on it. I've had people throw rocks and bottles at my house. I had an apartment in Whitesville where somebody tried to kick the doors in. I've had guns pulled on me at the gas station. They'll be in their vehicle and point it out the window and be like, "I'm coming for you" kind of thing. And then, they'll just drive off.

I've never called the police. They wouldn't have come. For the cops to come down to Coal River, they would have to drive like an hour. They're not going to come out for something like that.

I know for a fact, there was a gas station robbed about five years ago, and they called the cops after the robbers left. And the cops were like, "Well, are they still there?" The lady was like, "No," and he was like, "Well, call us if they come back."

So, if they would have shown up, it would have been about two hours after I called them, and they would have beaten me up with a nightstick.

Beginning to Gain Allies

But there've been more people allied with us over the past couple of years, especially as the coal industry has hit really dire economic times.

People are opening their eyes and realizing that we need to find another way [to earn a living] around here. Honestly, our most hardened supporters have been old union underground coalminers who *hate* strip mining. They're *all* about what we do.

Learning to Be a Spokesperson for My Cause

So, I started work at the Coal River Mountain Watch in 2010. At first, I was just the office manager, making sure the printers all had paper and the computers were working right, that sort of thing. But I fairly quickly transitioned into doing outreach and speaking to groups of college students, Quaker groups, our volunteers, or what have you, telling them about the history of the area and what's going on here now.

Most of the questions the college students ask are fairly similar, because they're just learning about these problems: questions about physically how does it work to blow up a mountain, the culture and history here, and dynamics in the community.

Sometimes, I get really dumb questions like, "Oh, why don't you all just move?" like a snarky college kid will do. Then, I get pretty in-depth on the poverty issues here and the fact that, even if people wanted to leave, they couldn't. Also, culturally, this is home. People wouldn't want to go. They wouldn't want to move to the city and live in an apartment when they can live here.

We hold summer camps, bringing in young kids and college students and teaching them about the issues here. We sleep in tents. There's also a spring break and a fall summit.

Lobbying in the State and National Capitol

When I first started working here, I fell pretty quickly into doing lobbying work, both in Charleston, West Virginia [the state capital], and in Washington, D.C.

We've lobbied Congresspeople and Senators. It's like speaking to a brick wall. Whenever you're lobbying and trying to pass something, you're operating under the assumption that those people up there actually care about poor people . . . and they don't.

So, you're just spinning your wheels. I got burnt out on that pretty quick.

My Typical Day at the Office

We currently have three full-time staff members and two volunteers. My hours vary. If we have groups in, I could be working upwards of fifty hours a week. But then, we have slow weeks when I will only work thirty or thirty-five hours. I feel like it balances out.

I come up here to the office at nine o'clock in the morning. Usually Debbie, one of the directors of the organization, is over there at her desk, and Peggy's at her desk. She's our office manager, doing what I used to do. She's a great local organizer, too. She knows a lot of the people around here.

I check emails for a while, drink some coffee. If we have a group in or if there's yard work that needs done . . . There's a cemetery out back here that we also try to keep cut. I am the young guy, so if there's anything heavy that needs moved or any holes that need dug, they always ask me to help out with that. I'm the go-to guy.

There really isn't any average day though.

What I Earn as Director

This is the best paying job I've ever had, and I am eternally grateful for it. I get paid on salary for a forty-hour workweek, and I receive a check for

$950 every two weeks. They used to offer health, dental, and life insurance, but we fell on some fairly rough financial times a couple years back.

In 2013, they laid me off for about six months. I kept volunteering, though. I was brought back on staff about six months later. I was part-time for a while, but now I'm back onto full-time. But we still don't really have the budget to offer any kind of benefits package right now. So, I try really hard not to get sick.

Doing All We Can to Save Our Mountains

We've done about everything we can think of to stop [the mountaintop removal], from lawsuits to keeping on the DEP [Department of Environmental Protection], which is our state regulatory agency, to making sure that any violations that happen are getting reported and that the company is going to have to pay for those violations.

We get local people out to public hearings, so they can state their opposition to the mining. And we've done direct-action work up on the mountain, blocking roads, doing tree-sits, and locking people to equipment, so they can't mine up there.

Getting Arrested for Protesting

I've been arrested a couple of times. The first time was in 2011; I was involved in a tree-sit on Coal River Mountain. I helped get all the equipment up there. Then, I walked up to the edge of the mine site, waiting for security, and told security state police where the tree-sit was, so they knew that they wouldn't be able to blast right in that immediate area anymore. So, I was taken to jail for that.

And then, in 2013, five of us blocked a road to the Alpha Natural Resources corporate headquarters in Bristol, Virginia. It was perfect, because there's a two-lane road, and corporate headquarters is the only thing on that road.

There's a tiny bridge there, and we just chained ourselves right across it. A couple people had their arms in giant barrels full of concrete. They had a five-hundred-gallon water container and then a metal cage around that. We took one of those and drilled a big hole in either side, put PVC pipe through, and sewed it up, and then proceeded to fill the entire thing with coal slurry—and that's what I had my arm locked into. So, when they cut into it to get us out, they spilled the coal slurry everywhere.

I've spent roughly about two weeks in jail. Jail here in West Virginia actually wasn't that awful bad. It wasn't super crowded or anything. I mean, obviously, it was still jail. So, it was bad on that point, but as far as jails go, it was okay.

My Fiancée Worked at Kmart

My fiancée, Dani, lives with me now. For ten years up in Pennsylvania, she worked at Kmart. We met on top of Kayford Mountain at a music festival of mostly bluegrass and old time music.

We hit it off pretty quickly, because she did a lot of work, where she's from in northeastern Pennsylvania, against the natural gas industry. There were a lot of similarities in our work, and we enjoyed the same things. So, I talked her into moving here and marrying me. Now, she's taking a few months off before she finds another job, mostly trying to get the house in order.

A year ago, I bought a place right next to my parents and my grandparents, a little coal-camp house that needs a lot of work, on about an acre of land.

I bought it from a guy my dad used to work with. Actually, I didn't buy it outright. I'm doing rent-to-own. Overall, it's going to be twenty-five grand. I was sued by Alpha Natural Resource, the company who bought Massey out. I could never get a loan, so I'm pretty thankful I can do the rent-to-own thing.

My fiancée has a car, and I've been borrowing it. It's a Honda Civic, a 2012. I've got a couple of motorcycles, but they're sitting in my yard and don't work at the moment. They're 1983 Yamaha Viragos, 750s. Two of them are just parts bikes.

My Grandfather Inspired Me to Propose

I asked my grandfather about marrying Dani. My grandparents are the one relationship I can point to in my entire life that is actually really good. They really are in love with each other. So, that's whom I go to for advice.

I went to my grandpa, and I asked him, "What do you think?"

And he said, "Could you imagine yourself living without her?" and that got me. I was like, "No."

"All right. Done deal."

I'm Getting Married at My Office

She knew I was going to propose, so I had her pick out the ring. It's a sapphire. We have not set a specific date. But it will probably be next spring.

We're going to have two ceremonies, one here and one up there [in Pennsylvania]. I think the other one we're actually going to do here at the office. There's a fair bit of property out back. We're just going to do it out there.

My Parents Work in the Mines and at the Gas Station

My mom's forty-three and my dad's fifty. My dad worked for fifteen years at the Elk Run prep plant in Sylvester and just got laid off about two years ago.

Soon after that, he was diagnosed with Parkinson's. So, they're having kind of a rough time right now. Mom's worked a couple of gas station jobs and at the dollar store, but that's about it. Right now, she's mostly trying to take care of my dad. They're just trying to get on disability.

Their financial situation is pretty rough. Between me and my grandparents and my sister's fiancé, we've been trying to make sure that they're doing okay. My grandparents help a lot, a whole lot more than we're able to.

My Grandparents Get By on Pension and Ginseng

My grandfather was an underground coalminer for twenty years. He retired with a full union pension. He also gets military benefits, because he was in the Vietnam War. My grandma is the same as my mom, working a couple of gas station and retail jobs here and there but mostly just taking care of my grandpa.

My grandparents also make a little extra money by digging ginseng[10] or other medicinal roots. I'm not sure who taught my grandpa what to dig up, but my grandpa is who taught everybody else! [Laughs.]

There's what we call yellow root, which is what most people refer to as goldenseal, bloodroot, blue and black cohosh, and a couple more.

We don't actually use the medicinal herbs; we just sell them. Last year, me and a friend of mine dug a fair bit of ginseng. He took it all up to New York City and sold it all to a Chinese restaurant at a much better price than what you can get around here.

We could make a lot of money if we could do a New York run a couple of times a year. The thing is, you're not allowed to start digging ginseng until September 1. The berries on the plant need time to form and fall off and take root, to grow a new plant. Also, with all of these giant surface mines that we have around here, some of them take up two and three thousand acres of prime ginseng habitat.

Relatives Have Died from Black Lung

I've had a lot of extended family get sick and die of black lung. Whenever you work in an underground coalmine, you're breathing in coal dust the whole time you're down there, and that gets into your lung tissue.

It's a situation similar to silicosis, for people who dig tunnels. They'll get a lot of silica dust in their lungs and develop silicosis where they can't breathe.

And a number, my grandfather included, are struggling with black lung right now. It feels like asthma. That's what I get from watching my grandfather struggle—it's like he's having an asthma attack when he can't catch a breath.

Video Games, Books, and Movies

I dreamed of being Spiderman when I grew up.

These days, I play video games—when I have the time. I really like RPGs [Role-Playing Games]. I like Skyrim and Fallout. Another hobby is driving my ATV. If you're doing anything back in the woods, you're going to need one.

I like to read, mostly political books and anarchist philosophy, such as Emma Goldman. For fun, I read fantasy and science fiction: *Lord of the Rings, The Hobbit*. I like *Harry Potter* a lot. I also like Isaac Asimov. And I watch old movies and superhero movies: the classics, like the original three *Star Wars* films, and cheesy old action movies, too, like Schwarzenegger in *Predator*.

If I Could Buy Coal River Mountain . . .

If I had all the money I could ever need, I'd buy Coal River Mountain outright from the landholding companies. I'm sure if you wave enough of a dollar figure in front of their faces, they'll jump for it.

I would make sure that it would never, ever be mined, ever. Maybe this could be a place for impoverished people and people working for human rights, where people fighting in their communities can come and get trainings. It could just be a spot in the woods where people go and pitch a tent—but where people can come together and share skills and stories and learn from each other.

No Kids for Me, Never

I don't plan on propagating. No kids, ever. There's been a number of health studies done, one of which showed vastly higher instances of birth defects in children who were born here, whose mothers lived in an area where mountaintop removal was happening while they were pregnant—that's where I live. So, that's a big part of it.

And there are too many people in the world as it is. Our planet can't sustain this many humans. Adoption would not be out of the question down the road. But as far as bringing another person into the world—I don't want to say it's "irresponsible," but for me, morally, I couldn't justify it.

If You See Something Wrong, Do What You Can to Make It Right

I guess my philosophy of life would be, if you see something wrong, do what you can to make it right.

When people ask me, "What do you envision the economic future for Appalachia to be?" I really don't know. I'm more of a problem kind of a guy. I'll stand up and say, "There's a problem over here." I don't necessarily know the solutions.

At least with the economic viability in this area, I don't think it's my responsibility to come up with the solutions. It's not my fault that a strip miner can't make his truck payment because the strip mine got shut down, you know? I'm just happy that people aren't going to be dying now.

Oppression Anywhere Is Oppression Everywhere

I have great respect for people who come from impoverished or ethnic communities who stand up and fight for themselves.

I look up to those people a whole lot—people in the African American community, who've been fighting hard the whole time they've been on this continent for freedom, and people in the Native American community, who have resisted colonization to the best of their efforts for the past however many hundreds of years. The immigrant population we have in this country, as well as queer people, have been beaten down by the powers that be for as long as they've been here.

It's a different situation for sure here in Appalachia, but there are certain similarities. Oppression anywhere is oppression everywhere, whether it's here in Appalachia or if it's in ghettos in New York City or Los Angeles or queer kids getting beat up. There're connections to be made. I have great respect for pretty much anybody who stands up and speaks truth to power.

This work is something I really believe in. If not, then I wouldn't put up with all the flak I get for doing it. Honestly, even if I didn't get paid at all to do this work, I would still do it, because I feel like it needs to be done, you know, whether it's me or somebody else. Somebody needs to be doing this stuff.

fourteen

GREG

MIDEAST PEACE DIPLOMAT

New York, New York, United States

Editor's note: I grew up hearing that the Jewish diaspora finally reclaimed their homeland in Israel in 1948,[1] after millennia spent in exile that culminated in gruesome persecution and genocide during the World War II Holocaust.[2] But I wondered: If the new state of Israel was rightfully reclaimed, why did decades of Mideast conflict[3] ensue?

This question also confronted Greg Khalil, the son of an archaeologist and a theologian, when, in his early twenties, he visited his father's relatives in Palestine for the first time. Although he was born and raised in San Diego, California, much of his extended family still lives in Beit Sahour, a predominantly Palestinian-Christian town near Bethlehem.

"Here were all these people who looked like me, had the same aller-gies, the same sense of humor," Greg reflects. "Yet I could work hard and get an education, while they were living in incredible injustice." Greg wanted Israel, somehow, peacefully to coexist with Palestine. He wanted to become part of a solution no one had yet been able to define.

Greg went on to Yale Law School and became an advisor[4] to Pales-tinian leaders on peace negotiations with Israel. A self-professed "proud liberal," Greg realized that peace depended on not just Middle Easterners working across nationality but also Americans working across the aisle. He teamed up with his friend Todd Deatherage, an evangelical Christian from Arkansas and a former Republican chief of staff. Together, they launched the Telos Group,[5] a nonprofit organization that leads Holy Land tours and educates Americans on how to advocate for peace back home. For him, diplomacy must begin at the level of interpersonal relationships and extend from informed citizens up through political networks—not the other way around.

When he's home in the U.S., Greg lives in both New York City and San Diego and spends time at the Telos office in Washington, D.C., as well as flying around the country to build networks of powerful peace-makers. Also, maybe ten times per year, he leads tours through Jerusa-lem, Ramallah, Tel Aviv, and Bethlehem. For vacation, his favorite city is Paris.

"I'm a vagabond." Greg laughs. "I'm always on the road. That's where I feel comfortable." He's learned to carry a huge suitcase with "every-thing from business suits to a yoga mat" wherever he goes.

He's a man who prefers to shine a spotlight on everyone else rather than to step into it himself. As much as Greg wants to facilitate the power of others, the next pages are dedicated to his own.

My Purpose in Life Is My Company, "Telos"

My name is Greg Khalil. I'm forty-one years old. I live primarily in New York. I'm the president of the Telos Group. *Telos* means "purpose or objective" in Greek; it's the purpose to which all efforts are directed. Our purpose is security, dignity, and freedom for all Israelis and all Palestinians.

Our organization builds social movements in America around the Middle East. My job relates to managing the organization, building relationships and movements, resourcing a lot of other leaders . . . everything from fund-raising to programming implementation.

But my primary responsibility is a little unusual: It's about connecting people together. That's the bread-and-butter of what I do: getting to know people and expanding their worlds through relationship.

Building Peace by Seeing All Sides of a Conflict

There's a great Harvard conflict-resolution expert named William Ury, who wrote a book called *The Third Side*—a short, simple idea[6] that there are at least three sides to every conflict, not two. So, say a husband and a wife are battling. You might typically think it's husband versus wife, but there's also the community around that particular conflict, which has a role to play in that conflict.

It's a little simplistic, but the same is true in global conflict. You know, Israel-Palestine feels half a world away: It's not. We've imported that conflict into our own culture. So, that necessarily implicates us. We *do* play a role there, and we have a responsibility to play a better role.

We're based in Washington, D.C., although we pretty much have a virtual office. We have another office in Jerusalem. Our goal is to build a movement of pro-Israeli, pro-Palestinian, pro-peace American activists to change our culture here at home, to have impact on the ground there, and also ultimately to change U.S. policy.

We're a very, very small organization with just five full-time staff. We work with some outside service providers. In the last five years, we've done sixty trips for Americans to the Mideast and thirty-five trips of Israelis and Palestinians to America.

We Build Networks by Educating Leaders

We equip leaders with relationships, knowledge, and skills. One key way is by taking people over on trips. These are not advocacy trips. We want a leader, first and foremost, to fall in love with both Israel and Palestine and, second, to have a sense of complexity of the issue.

A lot of times in the modern world, we just want to drill everything down to two words—*this* or *that*. That's just not reality. We want people to connect, to see the complexity, and to develop relationships with people of goodwill on all sides of a conflict.

For us, the trip is just the beginning. When people get home, we work with them and their communities to dive deeper into that educational process and invest with some of the folks they met. We connect trip alumnae with each other.

We have a Telos conference each year, by invite only. Almost everyone has been on at least one trip with Telos. So, that enables us to weave together a community of people stretching [ideologically from] far left and far right, really devout faith-believers to people who are secular. They've all shared this transformational life experience.

When you sit down in the room with somebody who's gone through something that's completely rocked their world and tested and pushed their assumptions—just like you—it means there's a level of trust that wouldn't exist otherwise. It transcends your political beliefs.

Strategic Counseling for Impactful Action

We assume we're not going to change something systemic by doing just a few one-off actions that feel good. You've actually got to build something to scale. How do you effect change if you're a religious leader with twenty-five thousand people in your church or if you're a major business leader? How do we bring this out to your particular community, so we can build something that's sustained for the long term and that actually deals with the magnitude of the problem?

We advise you on how to talk to your member of Congress or take five hundred people from your [business or church] community to see the conflict on the ground . . . Our trip alumni have invested on both sides of the Green Line that divides Israel and Palestine, some for-profit, some nonprofit. They know what's going on. They know how to take specific action. That's the difference between just doing stuff that feels good and doing stuff that has an impact.

We're Actually Funding the Mideast Conflict

Palestine has the highest number of NGOs [nonprofits] per capita in the world. There's a lot of money going into the Palestinian territory. Israel is also one of the big nodes of philanthropy in the world.

The Mideast conflict, in my view, is very good at attracting goodwill and using it in the service of sustaining the conflict. If you go over there and your heart breaks for a community, that's wonderful; I mean, if you're human and you see injustice and suffering and you *don't* feel something, there's a problem.

But if the response is just sort of a knee-jerk reaction of like, "I'm going to give these people money," that doesn't necessarily help. In many instances, what happens is that money helps entrench this system. It reinforces this conflict that uses that goodwill to relieve somebody else from accountability.

Giving Starving Farmers Sacks of Flour from Kansas

Let me give you a tangible example. There's a small Palestinian village in the West Bank called Wadi Fukin, near the border with Israel. It's a couple-of-thousand-years-old community of farmers. They'd been farming their land for generation after generation. One day, I was visiting this community with the head of a major international aid agency. We went down to speak to some villagers.

Wadi Fukin happens to be right underneath an Israeli settlement that is expanding over the village and dumping raw sewage on the farmland. The farmers can't even access a lot of their farmland, so they're unable to take care of themselves. To feed their families, they've gone on international food aid. They literally get sacks of flour from taxpayers in Kansas. That's not a joke. This happens all over the West Bank. Here's the punch line: Those folks are getting sacks of flour to feed their families so they don't die.

They don't want sacks of flour. They want to do what they know how to do and what they've been doing for generations, which is simply to farm their land. The problem is that these people aren't victims of a natural disaster; they're victims of a political problem, and there needs to be a political decision to end this systemic issue.

Taxpayers in Kansas shouldn't be giving sacks of flour to people in Palestine. What we should be doing is adopting a policy that strongly supports Israel and its right to security and self-defense—and the same thing for Palestinians as well. If that were our foreign policy, those farmers would be farming their land, and we wouldn't have anything to do with subsidizing a family getting a sack of flour.

We Wouldn't Support Settlements If We Knew the Truth

Settlements also wouldn't be happening if we knew the truth about them. It would be criminal to imagine [the opposite situation] a rule that Jewish people couldn't live in the West Bank. That's wrong.

But it's also criminal to say that anybody can come in and confiscate land, put the local population under military control, basically put them into prisons, not allow them use of their resources or to move between their own communities, to go into Israel, or even to have basic human rights. Settlements are highly problematic. They're causing a lot of the suffering in the West Bank that we are spending hundreds of millions of dollars on trying to alleviate.

Americans Are Part of the Middle-East Problem

America is not responsible for the conflict, but our posture toward Israel and Palestine definitely influences that. The world is becoming a less safe place, not solely because of but in part because of our connection to this conflict. We send billions of dollars there every single year. We just increased our military aid packages to Israel by more than a billion dollars. I'm not saying that that's a bad thing. Israel is our ally . . . It's not a question of whether we are involved. We *are* involved, to their detriment and to ours.

We need to start being part of the solution. At Telos, we're trying to make sure that we're involved in a better way and to look out for American interests, as well as Israeli and Palestinian interests.

I think there are these entrenched camps who really love Israel and who are all about protecting Israel, even if they don't know a lot about what's happening on the ground, and the same is true on the other side with pro-Palestine people. It's caused a lot of division, both in our political system in D.C. and throughout America.

Many Americans are religious and care about "the Holy Land." They may have some connection to the place based on where they worship on weekends. But most people don't know the difference between Palestine and Pakistan. They don't know where Israel is on the map. They don't know that the world's first Christian community actually is in the Holy Land, where Jesus walked. So, your average person may not have any factual knowledge, but many people do have an interest.

Jerusalem Used to Be a Paradigm of Tolerance

Before this modern conflict began around the turn of the twentieth century, most of the Middle East was under control of the Turkish Ottoman Empire—not a harbinger of human rights advocates by any stretch of the imagination. However, for four hundred years, it was relatively stable. Meanwhile, Europe experienced war after war after war.

Today, Jerusalem is seen as a paradigm of intractable conflict, and yet for much of its history, it wasn't. It was actually the opposite: a place where religions and cultures intersected and didn't necessarily all love each other but found a way to get along.

The problem today is a sort of calcification of extremist trends among a variety of different religions around the world and even, in some instances, among atheists. But particularly among the Abrahamic faiths (Christianity, Islam, Judaism), there are some extreme trends that promote violence and view the world as either/or, us versus them.

Those trends are increasingly laying claim to what happens in Jerusalem, and that's dangerous for global security right now. What happens to Jerusalem certainly doesn't stay in Jerusalem. It reverberates throughout the entire Middle East and, in fact, much of the world.

Being Both Pro-Israel *and* Pro-Palestine

We believe every human being is created equal. I think that's sacrosanct for anyone who's involved with our work. We want to empower leaders and help them build a movement that's meaningfully pro-Israeli and pro-Palestinian.

Who's Greg Khalil? I'm nobody. What I can do is I can help folks who have privilege and influence to connect to what's happening on the ground and to see that how we talk about it in this culture is not only wrong but harmful—to see that we're implicated. We're part of this mess, but we don't need to be. We can help write a better story that values every human being there.

Born and Raised in San Diego, California

My childhood was amazing. I was born in 1974 and raised in San Diego. My mom was born in Boston to Danish immigrants. She was an archaeologist specializing in Ancient Greek history. My dad's Palestinian, from a town near Bethlehem; he was a religious studies professor who specialized in Patristics [early Christianity]. He taught at San Diego State University [SDSU]. I also have a brother, Alex. He's five and a half years older than me.

My parents are both phenomenally brilliant and kind people. So, I think that made a really huge difference.

My dad dropped out of school in seventh grade, but he went on in his late twenties, not only to make it to the States but also to earn his PhD at the University of Chicago. My mom was the first in her family to go to college. By twenty-four she was fluent in seven languages and had a PhD from the University of Pennsylvania. This was a time when women couldn't even go to most of the Ivy League schools, yet she was teaching at the number one school in the world for her field, the University of Chicago. That's where they met.

Shortly after I was born, my mom developed a whole host of autoimmune disorders and other diseases that slowly stole her mobility. By the time I was six, she was on crutches. She was in incredible pain every day. She was deformed. I knew my mom was in incredible pain, and I could see what was happening to her, but I didn't know anything different, because that started happening before I had memory. My brother has memories of my mom as being strong, and I don't. That was difficult for all of us.

Living in a Castle in Syria, on an Archaeological Dig

When I was six, my dad won a Fulbright to study early Christianity. The first Christian kingdom before Antioch was in modern-day Southern Syria. It was called the Case Kingdom. Through time, it had sunk and disappeared. My parents both got a job digging it out, to find the first Christian community on the planet.

Because of her health issues, my mom had taken a pause from her career as an archaeologist, but she decided to help my dad with the excavation. So, we went to southern Syria.

We drove all across the lower 48 [states of the United States], put our truck on a ship, drove all across Europe, went up to Denmark to visit my mom's family, and then drove to Greece. Then, we put our truck on a ship and went over to Syria. We lived in Damascus, in one of the best-kept Crusader castles in the world. It was amazing.

Under Siege in Syria

We were in Syria during the last uprising. The first day we arrived in Damascus, we registered at my new school, the American School. After we left, there was a suicide bomber who drove up right across the street. We'd just missed the bomb.

We were in Hama a couple of days after the Syrian regime had finished massacring twenty-five thousand people there. Then, Israel invaded Southern Lebanon,[7] and there was all this horrible stuff happening in Damascus.

We had friends who were also in Damascus on a Fulbright; on our last day there, I was at the American School, and my dad came and got us. We were running in the streets. There were all these planes flying, and there weren't any cars on the street. You heard distant sounds of bombs and whatnot. It wasn't anything like being in Lebanon or Beirut, but there was stuff happening in Damascus that wasn't being reported.

We went, not to our house, because we had a higher-level apartment, but to our friends' place. They had a basement apartment, and we thought it would be safer to stay with them. We were on the couch, just sitting there. I remember this feeling of dread that, "Oh, my gosh, my parents can't protect me. They're scared, too." So, that was kind of a big moment in maturation, an end of innocence.

San Diego Felt Like Another World

When I got home, my world was different. I felt like I'd lived on the moon, in an ancient castle. Syria was really the cradle of civilization, where some of the most beautiful and pristine archaeological sites in the world were, many of which had been destroyed or severely damaged.

But we'd also been there during the time of the last uprising against Bashar al-Assad's father. There was violence and death and unpredictability.

Then, my mom went from being able to walk in extreme pain with her crutches to being confined to a wheelchair, with no hopes of ever having her career again. Progressively, after we got home from Syria, my dad had to do all the cooking and the cleaning, and he had his career on top of that. It was really hard on everyone. Life became very different.

Finding Solace in Music, Where Everything Made Sense

For me, I found solace through music. Music was a world where everything made sense. My mom was a serious flutist. It wasn't her profession, but she premiered a concerto with the Athens Symphony Orchestra. She performed, and she was good.

I had an aptitude and a love for music from before I could use words. I wanted to be a violinist; I started playing when I was six. Everything in music is beautiful—particularly, for me, classical music. Music can make you feel sad, or want to cry, or feel rambunctious. Music can be violent, but then, it has an aesthetic. It's a contained world, a world where you can experience and play. You can safely engage things that are dark.

The music I listen to completely depends on my mood. I like silly pop music, which can be restorative and energizing. Some of the most meaningful music to me is by Bach, particularly some of the slow movements like sonatas and partitas for solo violin or the cello suites. There's something incredibly deep and profound about his music that's completely restorative for me.

I Almost Became a Concert Violinist

I graduated from the University of California at Los Angeles (UCLA) with a degree in music and violin performance and another in French literature. I was a professional violinist. I was playing and performing quite a bit.

However, I was having trouble controlling a couple of my fingers. I was twenty-one. They did all of these tests, and finally, this diagnosis came back that I had *focal dystonia,*[8] a genetic neurological disorder that affects muscle movement. I had the gene and all the symptoms and history, and there was no treatment for it. I had to quit music.

I had other interests, but music was something that I absolutely loved, and now it was clear that that wasn't going to happen. I could still play a bit, but I couldn't perform in public anymore.

What to Do with My Life, Now That My Plans Were Shot?

I had to figure out what I was going to do with my life. First, I got a job at the airport in San Diego at the commuter terminal slinging bags because I thought I'd get free flights, but I never got any time off to be able to use the flight benefits. It sounds like a great idea until you realize, "Oh, I make $6.75 an hour, and I work fifty hours a week, and I don't know when I'm going to get a day off for like six months."

Then, I planned a trip to go and spend some time with my family. I had this big family out in the West Bank [Palestine] that I communicated with my whole life, most of whom I'd never met. I'd never been there, and I didn't speak a word of Arabic.

My First Trip to Palestine and Israel Completely Blew Me Away

I went over there and was just completely blown away. Here were all these people (I have about a hundred first cousins) who looked like me, had the same allergies, the same sense of humor.

I had pretty much every opportunity I wanted. My family's not wealthy, but I'd already learned, if you work hard, you can do a lot. And not only did I work hard, but I had a good education. I had a good network. I could do stuff.

And here were these people just like me, who in many instances were much more disciplined and diligent and creative and smarter and had nothing and lived in this incredible context of injustice that I could not reconcile. It didn't look like anything I saw on the news.

What you see on the news is like, "Israel good, Palestinians evil, bad." I knew more because I had family there, but I still had received that narrative. It's not that Israelis are bad and Palestinians are great, either.

It's just not that simple. The situation on the ground was so different from what I'd expected. I felt that America was a huge part of the problem. It was my country that was doing this to my family. Had I been born differently, I would be on the receiving end of this. I felt like, I can't *not* do something about this.

An Israeli Lawyer Got Me Thinking about the Power of Law

There was a professor of religious studies who was Israeli and Jewish, a friend of my dad's, who took me all over Israel. My family couldn't really travel around Israel. So this professor took me to a bunch of legal conferences. I'd always been obsessed with philosophy and legal theory.

I had previously thought of the corporate or legal world as being very staid and not creative, but I realized, "Wow, this is really fascinating.

Law school doesn't mean that I'm going to go push paper in a big corporate firm or work on closing deals. There's something else here: I could actually gain some expertise and use it for good."

I returned to the States, to New York. I got a job at a law firm as a paralegal, applied to law schools, and got into Yale. I was like, "This is a perfect place for me." It was a transition point.

My Inspiration for Telos: Two Friends with Opposite Views

Prior to law school, I had worked for four years on the [Israel-Palestine] negotiating team and lived in Ramallah. It was a really dark experience for me. I never wanted to have anything to do with this issue again, yet I still felt this incredible sense of responsibility.

Then, I was in D.C. President Bush had just finished hosting the Annapolis conference, which was intended to restart the Mideast peace process.

I don't want to name their names, but I was making the rounds with a lot of my friends, and in the same night, I was with two opposite types. I saw one friend who at the time was the most significant pro-life powerbroker in D.C.; President Bush had credited him with winning the first election by bringing out the conservative vote. He talked to me about this life-changing experience he'd recently had in the Middle East.

Fifteen minutes later, I was talking to a national/international religious leader, a super liberal guy who had been officiating at gay weddings back when that topic was totally taboo. He really pushed that issue forward. These folks *hated* each other in public, but I had really strong personal friendships with them.

That was my moment. I thought, "How is it possible that these two men who hate each other, who think that the other isn't even truly Christian, have the same feeling about the Middle East?"

I said, "Hey, I need you guys just to trust me on this one. I know you both, and actually you have something in common. Can you guys get together for lunch?" So they got together, and they both said, "I'm not going to change my politics on this or that, but you're on to something. I want to continue this conversation."

That was when I had the idea for Telos. That was the moment when I realized, "Oh, my gosh, if these two people can talk, I know literally two thousand other people, I'm not exaggerating, who should also talk. There's something here."

Going into Debt to Make My Dream Come True

I just started introducing people together. It was a very natural thing for me to do, to take my network and leverage that into something. I started thinking strategically about creating a community far left to far right, Democrat to Republican, liberal to conservative, all of these good people who want to do something different.

I know it sounds a little arrogant, but I really believed that. I spent all my savings and went $65,000 into credit-card debt, going around all over the States and Europe on my own dime for more than a year, to launch Telos.

I reconnected with my friend Todd Deatherage. I consider myself liberal in terms of American domestic politics, proudly liberal. However, Todd was chief of staff for policy planning at the State Department under Condoleezza Rice in charge of Israel-Palestine, chief of staff to a Republican senator from Arkansas for ten years, and an evangelical Republican. He's at the total opposite end of the spectrum from me.

But he, too, felt so personally convicted as an American, a conservative, and an evangelical. He'd had the same idea that we need to get American leaders out on the ground. It's not to turn them against Israel; it's rather to be truly pro-Israel. The only way to do that is to ensure that Palestinians have a future, too.

I told Todd about my crazy idea, and I shared my business plan with him. Much to my surprise, he said, "I want to work with you on this." He has a wife and four kids. I was just a thirty-three-year-old kid.

My Best Day Was When We Got Our First Grant

My best day with Telos was when we were just starting up. It was on my birthday, July 25th. I got some of the most amazing calls and coincidences in the space of one day.

We'd put in our application for nonprofit status with the IRS. We got the approval on my birthday and got our first major grant of $476,000, which was like nothing I'd ever seen before. We hadn't even applied for this thing. Some people called us for advice on the issue, and we provided them advice, and they'd say, "Can you please send an application?"

I said, "Oh, how do we do that?" I wasn't expecting a grant. I was completely broke. That day was like everything coming together in one moment—like the universe telling me that this was meant to happen.

By that fateful day in July, it had been fourteen months we'd gone without a paycheck. I was spending incredible amounts on debt payments. Now, I had a paycheck for a few months. It was small, but it was just enough to live on.

My Worst Week Was on My First Vacation in Years

The darkest moment for me was with an employee, when I was on my first vacation in years. I hate saying this, but it's true: I made a very bad hire. This person knew that I was going to be on vacation and was being passive-aggressive. They [he or she] wanted to make me work on my vacation.

So, I ended up just working at this hotel in Paris, which is my favorite city, where I have a lot of community and friends. I was there for a week, and I was stuck in my hotel the whole time, doing stuff for this employee. I didn't know how to hire or fire at this point.

Also that week, I got a notice about an article that came out right when I was in that low moment. I was in a nadir. This well-known journalist (that we paid to come on a conservative leaders' trip) published a cover story in a major publication that was the most extreme, dare I say, *bigoted*, thing.

I know he'd had a completely different experience than what he wrote. I saw exactly what he experienced and what he felt. I saw what he said to certain people. Then, he came out with this really nasty, nasty piece. It was very clear that he was not being honest. That just set me off. It unlocked something in me at that moment when I was on my first vacation in my favorite city, and I couldn't do anything about it. That week sucked.

We Intentionally Go into Dark Places to Experience Racism

We intentionally go into dark places. We're not meeting with people that we agree with. And, quite frankly, there are a lot of racist people in the communities that I work with in America, and there are a lot of racist people that I introduce folks to on the ground [in the Mideast]. Part of my job is to sit there and to take it. It feels like a dagger through my heart every time, but it's not my job to let people know that. My job is to give them a platform to engage and hear and listen and wrestle with things. Sometimes, that feels like injury, but that's injury I willingly take.

It also happens at the airport and other places where, when I show up, I'm taken aside and held, sometimes for hours, simply because of my last name. Sometimes, I'm treated in ways that I think are inhumane and wrong. That's ironic, because I know so many people in Israel (including Israel's leaders), and I may be very critical of some of their policies, but I'm working for the benefit of everyone there, and I don't think anyone could legitimately say otherwise.

I'd say that, as a species, we are all racist. Everybody is a little bit racist in some sense. I don't want to give a pass to anyone. We're social beings. So, we create our little tribes, right? We look for ways to differentiate.

It's important to recognize the emotional logic of racism. One reason it's hard to combat racism is because it's so hard to see it. It's not like, "Oh, I think that black people are this" or "Muslims are that," you know, blah, blah, blah. People don't think about it that way. They think, "I'm a good person. A racist is a bad person. Therefore, I'm not a racist."

I want people to start seeing it differently. "Oh, my gosh, I thought you were one of them, but you know what? You're one of us, too. We're actually more connected than we realize." That's absolutely critical if humanity wants to survive the next few decades.

Another thing that feels injurious sometimes (perhaps I'm being a little too frank, but it's true) is that a lot of people we work with are incredibly privileged, and they expect a lot. Sometimes, I'm actually personally subsidizing some of these trips, and some of the people that we work with—I don't fault them, because I know that when you get into a position of leadership, you just always have people doing stuff for you—but . . .

Sometimes people just expect that somehow their bag gets to their room, and all sorts of their emotional and physical needs get met. People expect me to be the diplomatic expert and facilitate a relationship with some super-influential person whom they couldn't get access to on their own, and then they want me to be their servant as well, and sometimes that feels like crap, and I just bite my lip.

Being Multicultural Is a Blessing and a Curse

I guess in some sense I've experienced racism from a few angles. I pass for so many things that I get it from all sides. It's a blessing, and it's a curse. I can go to many countries around the world and have people think that I'm from there, which is great, yet when people assume you're something you're not, they'll often open up in ways that reveal their biases and prejudices. So, it's really instructive.

Wherever I Am, I Start My Day with Meditation and Eggs

The most important thing for me is my morning routine. It's my sacred space. My evening routine is less so, but wherever I am in the world, I do the same thing every single morning, and it makes me feel grounded and energetic. It gives me a sense of purpose throughout the day.

I wake up, and I do prayer/meditation to get centered. I come from an Orthodox Christian background. I very much connect to that narrative and that worldview.

Then, I exercise. I do hygiene. Then, I have a really, really big breakfast. I love breakfast. [Laughs.] For example, I'll sauté a ton of fresh veggies and then add a couple of eggs. So, it's kind of like a reverse omelet, emphasis on the vegetables. I love fresh veggies and coffee, very strong coffee, and lots of water.

After that, I look at my rotating to-do list and decide on my top two priorities for the day, the things that I *have* to get done. Sometimes, when I'm on a trip, stuff gets out of hand, and so I just put it on the list. After the trip, I go back and reassess the list.

The way I deal with a lot of messages coming in is that I get my inbox down to zero, and I do that by just delete, delete, delete, and then, if there's something that I can respond to, I do. Otherwise, I look at it later and then categorize. That helps me not have energy around something, if I can just park it somewhere. So, that's my little system.

My Typical Week Involves Travel

My typical week involves travel. I'm up in the air. I travel to the Middle East with a delegation maybe about eight to ten times a year. Or I travel among our network, primarily back in the States. When I'm on the road, I work from my iPhone and my laptop. There's a lot of different kinds of tasks I have to do, but I'm really, really good at doing them mobile-ly.

I'll often debate with myself, "Okay, I need a hotel here, because I don't have a friend to stay with," or "I really need to go on this trip, but it's hard to rationalize that to use this money." So, I'll use my travel miles. I usually travel between 160,000 to 200,000 miles a year. Then, I also take a vacation once a year, and I'll usually get a free ticket to Europe with all those [frequent-flier] miles.

What I Earn and How We Fund the Business

I make $150,000 a year. My salary level was set by the board when we founded. I don't do what I do to make money. Also, I haven't been making that much, even though I've been approved at that level, for the full six years we've been in business.

Our salaries come mainly from fund-raising, just like our other overhead expenses. On some trips, we inflate the costs, but often, we subsidize. Our largest single source of revenue is from the trips. I think that's pretty cool for a nonprofit, but we don't do enough profit-generating trips to fund our organizational overhead. We still have to fund-raise for all the other work that we do.

Our vision is to build a large-scale movement, since our model [of travel] is in incredible demand. We're possibly going to split off a for-profit arm, and the rationale there is twofold. One, it would allow us to take investment, which would help us scale more quickly, and, two, it's actually very much in line with our mission.

Money, Money, Money, Money

If I had an unlimited amount of money, I'd be doing the same thing but with a better, more efficient team. We'd be putting a lot more attention on the trip follow-up. It's so much easier for us to sell the trips [than the diplomacy and leadership we want to create after members return home]. That's not why we do what we do. What matters is what happens after the trip.

But if I had ten million dollars today, we would be a sustainable institution, scaled all around the U.S. within three years—not just working in five communities but in thirty to forty, which to me is a significant tipping point. We could resource our leaders, facilitate significant conversations within their party networks and political structures, and influence political campaigns and the national conversation. We'd have films made.

Scaling Our Model into a Worldwide Approach to Peace

I see Telos going into exciting places. I don't know if we will reach a two-state solution at some point or if there'll be some other solution to the Israeli-Palestinian conflict. That's something I can't predict.

In ten years, I won't be working on staff at Telos. I'd love to be associated with it, but I want to build a robust organization that's not connected to my personality. The pro/pro/pro movement will become just a default way to engage, because it's so obvious and so necessary. Our model of engagement will be applied to other conflicts around the world and in our own community, deeply engaging in issues, and building human networks designed to transform conflict.

I'm a Vagabond Who Carries My Home in My Suitcase

My dad's my closest family to me. My mom died a year ago. My brother lives in San Diego. He has a lab at the University of California at San Diego [UCSD]. He's a musicologist, but he also works in neuroscience. He studies the way that the brain processes time and develops interventions to deal with cognitive disorders like ADHD.

I'm single. I'm not in a relationship. I don't have children or pets. I can't even keep plants alive! [Laughs.]

But I do have a really strong group of friends around the world. I travel a lot, but I go to all the same places all the time. So, I have community in a variety of different places. My personal friends, we get together a lot, at least once a year, in a different part of the world. It's like family. So, I have a strong sort of network through my personal life.

I have a really big suitcase. I have everything in that from business suits to swimsuits to a yoga mat, a foam roller. I can do anything anywhere—and that's my home in a way. I do have these places that are home. But I call myself a vagabond, because I feel comfortable on the road.

Unless the World Ends, the Israeli-Palestinian Conflict *Will* End

My vision for the world extends in time far beyond the Israeli-Palestine conflict: All human conflict ends. Things that seem so intractable do end. For example, if you were in Europe in 1943, you'd say, "Oh, my God, we've been fighting for hundreds and hundreds of years. We're just going to be fighting until the end of days."

Unless the world ends, Israel-Palestine *will* end. It takes serious intention, and it takes serious long-term work.

Even if it's solved today, however, we'll be living with the consequences for many generations. That's a fact. But I think we can get to a different place, where we see Israel-Palestine more like Northern Ireland or South Africa, places that are still troubled but are modeling something different that nobody ever thought would happen.

As dark as this current moment is, I think within a decade we will get there.

Look, I'm not a pacifist. I'm an idealist in the sense that I believe things can be better—not on their own but when there's intention behind it and people really work hard to see the world as it is. I believe in realpolitik:

That's the right approach. A lot of people will say that folks like me are naive. I think *they're* naive, believing, for example, that keeping two million people in Gaza for generation after generation is going to end in a good result. That's only going to end in more conflict.

You Can't Keep Two Million People Trapped in Gaza

Gaza was once a highly educated population. It has one of the most beautiful beaches in the Mediterranean. It has an incredibly rich history. For hundreds of years, Gaza was a center of intellectual learning.

It wasn't a conflict zone until the birth of this modern conflict, around 1948 when Israel was established. There was an influx of refugees from what became Israel into the Gaza strip. So, the population of Gaza literally tripled in just the period of a few months, this tiny, tiny little area, and those people never went home.

Israel removed all of their settlements from Gaza. The border's closed between Gaza and Israel and Egypt. And now, people want to put Gaza out of sight, out of mind. You can't. There are almost two million people there. By 2020, there will be four hundred thousand more. The majority of the people in Gaza right now are under the age of eighteen. They don't have regular clean water or electricity. They know what the rest of the world looks like, and they can't leave.

They're cut off from the rest of the world. Obviously, there've been some extremist movements that have taken root there that have launched terrorist attacks against Israel. The problem is, those people aren't going anywhere. Imagining a scenario in which two million people are going to disappear is actually delusional. And to imagine a scenario in which they somehow fall in love with the country that periodically engages in war with them and the rest of the time denies access to basic goods is also delusional.

Nothing can justify terrorism or violence against civilians, no matter who's committing the crime. That situation will necessarily keep getting worse and worse unless there is something done to address the needs of the people on the ground in Gaza, as well as the needs of Israelis on the other side.

There's Something Worse Than Al-Qaeda and ISIS Out There

There's something worse than ISIS out there. People think talking about the potential of better scenarios is naive; I think that's crazy. Each and every person on this planet has influence. The question is not whether we do but how we use it.

I worked on the disengagement when Israel removed its settlements and its permanent military bases from the Gaza strip but tightened the control around the Gaza strip. I will tell you, at that time, Jack Straw, the foreign secretary of Britain; Tony Blair, the prime minister of Britain; Condoleezza Rice, U.S. secretary of state; President George W. Bush; James Wolfensohn, the head of the quartet responsible for managing and negotiating the Gaza withdrawal—every single one said that if Gaza was closed off from the rest of the world, there would be extreme political crisis and humanitarian crisis.

Everything that we're seeing today was predicted. My simple point is that it's naive to think that, if we allow certain realities to exist, that there won't be massive conflict, that things like ISIS won't replace the boogie men of Al-Qaeda.

My #1 Skill: Relationship Development

I'm good at relationship development, connecting with people, and more importantly, connecting people together. That's something, for whatever reason, I love doing it, and I don't even have to think about it. I think I'm good in a leadership position, working with my board and managing high-level folks. I have very strong relationships there.

My weakness is that I can really inspire people, but I'm probably not the best day-to-day manager of people. I've grown considerably, but it's not something that comes naturally. And I sometimes still take things personally. That's a place that I'm trying to get to, but I'm not there yet. Sometimes, people think I'm being harsh, when I don't see it: That's just a red flag that I need to listen a little bit more carefully.

I can be the vision guy, the big-picture guy, like motivating the trips. I'm not the operations person; it doesn't come naturally to me. As for the financial stuff, I'm good at coming up with business plans and schemes, but I don't have a background in business. That's a gap that I have.

Trying To Live Up to My Parents' Example

Both of my parents had brilliant, extraordinary life trajectories and yet became some of the most humble, kind people you could imagine. They've been through hell multiple times in their lives and are still just amazing. Their legacy is an example that I've felt has weighed on me, because I don't think I can live up to it.

I've also been blessed to be around a lot of amazing people in the world, through my work. I don't think I'll get there, but I hope so. [Laughs.]

Life is about relationship. Many people will say that, but they don't appreciate the depth of it. Whether it's this building we're sitting in right now or a car, a business, technology, or anything in the world that exists that impacts human beings, it all starts with an idea and becomes reality because of human relationship. Connecting people is at once the simplest thing that you can do and the most radical, if you want to change the world.

Postscript from My Piano:
Miracles for Me and the Mideast[9]

My left hand is now being healed by a phenomenal team of doctors at Mount Sinai Hospital in NYC, who enrolled me in their research study. It feels like some kind of miracle is happening. Nearly twenty years ago, my body revolted against me and stole the one thing that then brought me the most joy in life: making music.

That loss set me on a new and completely different life path, reconnecting with my Palestinian extended family, eventually becoming a lawyer and social entrepreneur, committing to do my part promoting fundamental rights for all peoples in Israel/Palestine.

Now, it looks as though I might be able to play again. While I'll never go back full time to music again, it's more than a little thrilling to imagine a life that might again be filled with it. Fingers weak but crossed!

The day of my last round of injections happened to be on Orthodox Christmas, just after the winter solstice, when at the year's darkest moment light begins again to pry an ever-wider gap between shadow and storm.

Today, in a dark and cold season of birth and rebirth, I feel like so much is coming full circle. Even the long-overdue transformations with which I consume myself in the Middle East—even as darkness grips ever tighter there now . . . so much feels possible now, because it is.

fifteen

MICKEY

FRINGE DIPLOMAT

Tel Aviv, Israel

Editor's note: "It's Mickey," he grins. "Like Mickey Mouse."

Wearing his signature all-black uniform—black jacket slung over black T-shirt and pants—he looks like a Secret Service agent, but he claims not to be packing heat. Michael "Mickey" Bergman may look affable, but this former captain of the planet's most baleful army, the Israel Defense Force,[1] has killed more people than he can count.

These days, Mickey works on the other side of conflict resolution: He runs a consulting agency he calls "Fringe Diplomacy" out of the Aspen Institute.[2] His international diplomacy is not for the faint of heart: rescuing American hostages, assisting democratic elections in volatile countries, and raising private-sector investments for countries in need.

He utilizes the old-school force of personal relationships and convening power to rally people and resources.

He's a funny, shy man who blushes as easily as he smiles. He will bend your ear with tales and ply you with photographs on his mobile phone of his wife, Robin, and their little girl, Noa. He's a complete badass who's completely understated.

You don't really find out, until you dig a little, just how worldly he is. He holds three passports: Israeli, British, and American. Or how smart he is: He sailed through degrees in international relations at the University of California Los Angeles (UCLA) and Georgetown University, where he now teaches a high-level graduate course at their School of Foreign Policy.

He speaks Hebrew and English and a little Nigerian and Arabic. "In which language do you dream?" I ask him. "English," he replies. That makes sense: The three most important women in his life—his mom from England, his wife from California, and his daughter from Washington, D.C.—are all native-English speakers. He resides in Washington, D.C., but he works from Africa to Asia and calls long international flights his "vacations."

His bio[3] lists more jobs than this chapter can cover, including co-leading tours[4] for religious, political, and philanthropic leaders from the U.S. to the Middle East—that's how I meet Mickey. (See Mickey's friend and coworker, Telos Group cofounder Greg Khalil, in Chapter 14.)

This chapter hails from Tel Aviv, where Mickey grew up, where his extended family members still live, and where we splice together his interview in several interrupted portions, on bus rides, in a hotel lobby, and two idyllic hours sitting on the sand of downtown Tel Aviv's stunning Bograshov Beach. If only all my work could be conducted from such scenic places . . .

Why I Call It "Fringe Diplomacy"

My name is Mickey Bergman. I'm thirty-nine years old. I am the founder and director of Fringe Diplomacy. What I do is a little complicated . . .

I work in fringe diplomacy. "Fringe" is my word for it, picked up from the TV show *Fringe*. I'd been doing this for about ten years but never had a name for it until then. It kind of kicked in; it helps to frame and explain what I do.

"Fringe diplomacy" is the space beyond what governments are able to do amongst themselves in international relations. It relies heavily on the assumption that people—individuals, companies, NGOs, artists, and academia—all have very similar interests in making this world more peaceful, stable, and prosperous. And at times, there are things we can do as private citizens that governments cannot do.

We create a layer of personal relationships between people that manifests either in business-to-business or people-to-people partnerships. That trust helps mitigate risk when it comes to crisis—economic, societal, or political.

Real Diplomacy—Not Just the Photo Ops

We joke that this field works in the neglected dimension of official diplomacy. We don't need to do the photo ops. It's not procedures. There's no game or dance to be played. It's just real people meeting, talking about common interests, and advancing specific projects and programs.

The way I look at it, there are two types of activities when it comes to fringe diplomacy: engagement design and intervention. Intervention is when President Bill Clinton flies to North Korea and brings back Laura Ling, the jailed journalist [in 2009]. I wasn't there on that one. Or when Governor Richardson, whom I often work with on those types of things, is able to help the release of the Al Jazeera journalists[5] [in 2015] from Egypt.

Everybody loves intervention, because it's quick, tangible, and sexy. It gets all the news, immediately. But very few people recognize that in order to have successful intervention, you need to build that engagement for years before the event.

Not every engagement will end up in intervention. You can't predict the future, and intervention is not the objective of this work: We focus a lot of time on the engagement design to make sure that it adds positive value to society or the environment. And we won't do engagement that will abuse any resources.

I Grew Up Just North of Tel Aviv

I was born in Tel Aviv and spent most of my early life in a small city a little bit north of here. In my immediate family, I had a mother and father and a brother.

In my extended family, I had an uncle on my dad's side and an uncle on my mother's side. Three of my grandparents were dead before I was born. So, I only ever met one grandmother from my father's side.

We Were Israeli Jews: Secular but Not Religious

I grew up in a household that was very anti-religious, despite the fact that we're Jewish. One doesn't trump the other. Judaism is more than a religion.[6] It's considered to be almost like a family. Some people are traditional and see themselves as religious, and others are secular. They're still Jewish. I was one of them.

If you're secular and you live in Israel, you still live according to the Jewish calendar. You learn the values, lessons, and history. You don't necessarily believe in God and practice any of the religious rituals, but you're still considered Jewish. If you look around, everybody else is Jewish, all around you.

It's not purely *nationality*, because there's a link between Jews that live in Israel and Jews outside of Israel. If it were purely nationality, that link would not be sustained. So, the bond there is a *cultural* religious one. With Judaism, the identity started with religion, but there hadn't been a Jewish state or a common place for ten thousand years, up to 1948. During the diaspora, the Jewish people were spread around the world, for centuries. They never had a national narrative.

If you look at Germany, even just prior to World War II, you had religious orthodox Jews and secular Jews. And yet they were all bound together, not only by definition of the people who tried to kill them but also by their own definition. It's like a family. You have crazy cousins, but they're still your cousins.

My Childhood in Israel and Nigeria

When I was growing up, my father was a land surveyor. My mother was an English teacher for many, many years and then moved into marketing for a large English textbooks publisher in Israel. She wrote an English textbook for seventh grade, and then, she kind of got roped into that work.

We were never rich. At some point when I was a little boy, we had to move to Nigeria for three years, because my dad couldn't find work here. There is an Israeli company called Solel Boneh, a construction company that operates a lot in Africa with big, big projects in Nigeria. That was the time of building the capital city of Abuja and all of the country's infrastructure. This experience of being abroad was fantastic for me. The years that I lived in Nigeria as a child were very, very happy.

When I was growing up, I knew two languages, Hebrew and English. I didn't really learn Yoruba in Nigeria. It's kind of a broken English mixed with the local language, but I could never really speak it well. And then, I tried to study Arabic when I was in high school. I can read it very slowly. Vocabulary doesn't exist, though, for me. So, I can't really speak it or understand it.

When I was eight, we came back to Israel. We were able to buy an apartment, mainly with the money that my father was able to make in Nigeria.

My Parents Expected Top Grades, but I'm a Slow Reader

My parents had a fundamental value and really high expectation for me to excel in school. I probably took part in that because my brother was less of a good student.

Say, if I would get only 90 percent on an exam, I would be very nervous to go back home to tell my parents . . . unless it were an exam in Bible [studies], and then, my father would say, "Don't ever come back to me with such a high grade in Bible." [Laughs.]

That competitiveness, the need to perform, probably came from my parents. There was that little bit of tension, but other than that, I lived a very happy childhood.

Physics, biology, and chemistry were my focus areas in high school. These subjects came easily to me. Math also made sense to me. But I'm a horrible reader. I'm very slow. Preparing for my history exams was my best time for naps. I would fall asleep with the book on my face; I still do! My wife will attest to that. I'm such a slow reader, and it just feels so good to fall asleep with a book. [Laughs.]

Becoming a High School Activist and Leading My First Strike

In high school, my life started taking a turn. My principal and my physical education teacher both encouraged a lot of activism in the class. I had been a very shy, quiet person. Then, I went into the student council. I know that sounds really dorky. But going from high school council, to regional student council, then the national student council exposed me to a lot of activism.

I have a funny story, my version of teenage rebellion. In Israel, teacher strikes are very common. The teacher union tries to improve salaries, which have not been that great. When I was in high school, those strikes occurred all the time, and one of the agreements between the Ministry of Education and the Teachers Association was, "You get back to work.

You'll get your increase, but you'll have to supplement for the days that you have been on the strike."

And so, they decided to supplement one strike on a holiday, during a period in which Israeli students are supposed to study for their big exams at the end of high school. The student council said, "Enough of everybody fighting on our back. We lose in the teacher strike, and then, we lose again when they're demanded to bring back those missed days."

So, we tried to influence that. The Ministry of Education was not taking us seriously. So, we said, "Well, like teacher, like student. We're going to go on a strike."

I was seventeen at the time. Nobody believed us. My high school was small, probably about four hundred people. At this point, I was head of the national student council. It was really quick to network through the other student councils.

This wasn't online: We barely even had computers at the time, and there was no Internet really. Yet we had 85 percent compliance on this one. People just didn't show up to school.

Now, given, it's not that hard to get high school students not to show up to school, but it sent a statement. It was exciting just to see the impact. It was troublemaking, maybe; noncompliant, maybe. Personally, I'm not by nature one that jumps out in front. I know it sounds weird for most people who know me now.

Now, I have no fear of going public and speaking, but that was something that was learned, not natural. I found this was a way to communicate "out of my shell." It allowed me to see how you move people, how you influence things, how you find different levers. That's something I figured out retroactively.

Becoming an Officer in the Israel Defense Force

At eighteen, I joined the army [Israel Defense Force]. It's mandatory. You have to join the army for three years. You start exams for it in twelfth grade to determine where you're going to be positioned. I went for the pilot course, to join the air force. That was my first entry to the military. I did that for about eight months, until I was dropped.

I was dropped before the [training for the] fighter jets, during the Piper lessons. It's a two-year course. Four hundred cadets begin the course, and only twenty actually graduate. So, most people get dropped.

I'm always proud to say that it wasn't because of my flying skills. Rather, it was because of my level of performance on commanding. To be honest, I was only eighteen years old. I was a kid. I was not ready to command anybody, and in the pilot course, six months into it, you actually start commanding the next class while you're just a cadet yourself in basic training. I had a hard time handling that.

Captain of Special Ops Unit in South Lebanon

So, I served in the IDF for six years altogether. I was discharged at the rank of captain, the commander of a special ops unit. My assignment was between 1994 and 2000. I spent most of that time inside South Lebanon, in the eastern portion in a place called Marjayoun,[7] which is a beautiful city and castle. We had to work and develop a relationship with the local community.

Formally, I was an artillery officer, assigned to special units. My job would be to practice with them and make all of our plans, and then, I would go with them on the special operations. If things went wrong, I would move into action to bring support fire that allows for evacuation and things like that.

I Have Killed People—It's Hard to Say How Many

I have killed people . . . it's hard to say how many. I don't think very many. It's hard to make a direct assessment of that, because the way we say it in the profession of the artillery is that, even though we carry a gun, our biggest weapon is the radio.

With the power of the radio, we order the bombardments of places. The air force and artillery units work together using this as a statistics weapon. It could be that a gust of wind changes the location from where you aim to where it hits. Especially in highly populated places, you need somebody to be able to direct it, to make sure that you maximize what you're trying to achieve and minimize the risk for others.

I Had Five Pieces of Shrapnel in Me and Didn't Know It

I've lost good friends in combat, and I've been injured in combat. I got shrapnel in my elbow. Most of it went into my radio, which I was wearing on my back. That was lucky. In that day, radios were big machines.

That was a very specific four-hour combat. It was really bad in terms of our unit. The doctor and I ended up being the only officers who were still intact. I didn't know I was injured until three days after. When you land back, you have this routine where everybody strips off their clothes and checks each other to see, because, from the adrenaline rush, you don't know if you got hit or not.

We instructed everybody else to do it, but we didn't do it ourselves. Three days later, we were in our debriefing. Back then it was [Defense Minister Ehud] Barak, and I was standing there and explaining why I did what I did and so forth. We used a lot of support fire in that operation. The doctor called me in the middle of the briefing. He said, "Come over here. Show me your hand."

At that point, my elbow was completely swollen. "You have scratches everywhere," he told me. They did an X-ray, and they counted five foreign objects in my elbow. So, that was my injury. It wasn't serious. It took me down for about six months and put me out of commission, because my liver was—hmm, I'm losing my English now—infected. I became a little bit yellow for a few months.

Meeting My American Wife While on Sabbatical

In your sixth year in the military, after you earn the rank of a captain, you're eligible to have a flight abroad or a trip abroad for service. It was a great experience altogether in terms of my self-development. You mature very quickly, for better or worse.

Most of the troops go to Poland to see the [Nazi Holocaust] camps. Because of my student-council activity in high school, I was offered another option, to go to California for a month to participate in this Jewish summer camp for young adults. I looked at it this way, "Yeah, a week in Poland or a month in California." My decision was a little easy. [Laughs.]

Meeting My Wife and Chasing Her Down the Aisle

The love of my life's name is Robin, and she is currently my wife. [Laughs.] I met her in 1999. I moved to L.A. in 2001. We got married in 2002. That's the timeline. She was born and raised in New York, but she spent eight years in California. She graduated from USC [University of Southern California], but she worked at the Hillel at UCLA [University of California Los Angeles].

So, I stayed in America because of chasing a girl there . . . and it was a successful chase. I got the girl!

I got into USC, and I got really excited until I saw the price tag. I realized I couldn't afford it. So, I went to UCLA instead and studied international relations. Robin was working at UCLA at Hillel, but she's a USC alum. So, we're a mixed marriage, apparently. I didn't know that. And just saying that in this chapter is going to hurt me badly back at home! [Laughs.]

Being an Old College Student at UCLA and Georgetown

My undergrad experience at UCLA was not great but not at the fault of the university. At that point, I was twenty-five years old, and I was running through undergrad with eighteen-year-olds that were in a very different place in life than where I was.

I wasn't there for the party. I was there to catch up with the rest of the world as fast as possible, because I missed out on six years of getting my degrees as a result of my military service. That's how I felt. I went directly from undergrad to my graduate degree, also in international relations.

Later, when I applied to Georgetown, I applied for a fellowship called the Wexner Graduate Fellowship that encourages leadership of young Jews. Not only did I get this Jewish scholarship, but they paid for my master's at Georgetown, which is a Jesuit [Catholic] school.

I Landed My Dream Job in Mideast Policy in D.C.

Six months before graduation, I was in complete panic. I figured, "Who the hell is going to pay me to do something that I want to do anyway?" I was applying on paper to any job that I could—the U.N., the World Bank, different organizations, but my paperwork just didn't get me anywhere. I had about fifty informational interviews but never a job interview. I was getting nervous.

Then, somebody told me, "Obviously, your paperwork doesn't work for you. Don't rely on paperwork. Just rely on people. Go and start talking to people that you interned with or who know you based on your work."

And that's what I did. During graduate school, I was interning at the Washington Institute for Middle East Policy. Through that work, I met [Arab-Israeli diplomat] Rob Malley and a woman named [diplomatic advisor] Sara Ehrman. She now works at another tiny NGO called the Center for Middle East Peace [centerpeace.org]. I did some joint work with them on mapping as an intern. This was the initial days of GIS, of electronic mapping, focused on the Israeli-Palestine conflict. Back then, it had just surfaced as a technology around the world.

Sara said, "What do you mean? You don't have a job yet?" That was basically a week before graduation.

I said, "No, I don't," and she said, "Okay. Get me your resume," and she took my resume, and she took a blank piece of paper, and she handwrote this, "Get this guy a job!" with an exclamation point. She started faxing it—yes, *faxing* it, in 2005, to everybody that she knew, all her friends, and that fax landed on Rob Malley's desk at the same exact time that Rob got an email from President Clinton about launching the Clinton Global Initiative (CGI).

This is something that I constantly tell my students when they are worried about jobs. I say, "Look, getting a job is about getting the resume to the right place at the right time, and the more places it gets, the more times it hits, the bigger chances you have in somebody picking up on it."

Working for the Clinton Global Initiative (CGI)

When I graduated with my master's in international relations, I was lucky enough that my first job was with the Clinton Global Initiative (CGI). I joined literally the first day that President Clinton launched it. He asked Rob Malley to be his chair for religious and ethnic conflict, and he told him to bring a deputy, and Rob asked me if I would take that job.

Of course, I said "yes" in a second. It was a dream come true to work with the former president on this new initiative.

I found myself on the initial team that designed the inaugural conference and worked out the kinks of it. Then, we implemented the first conference. What happened to me personally, having grown up in Israel and focused all of my life on the Israeli–Arab and Israeli–Palestine conflict, was that my eyes opened. I realized that the world is actually bigger than that—and fascinating.

And the second thing I've learned through this is what Bill Clinton did with this conference. Through the lens of action, he brought the private sector together with the public sector. It was the first time I was truly exposed to what power that brings. So, my life took a little bit of a turn as a result of that, and I found my passion for diplomacy.

How I Became a Lifelong Consultant

I decided early on to be a consultant. After the inaugural meeting of the CGI, I was given two options: to work full time, mainly to build up a nascent commitment department, which we knew was going to become the heart of the work, or to continue to do the religious and ethnic conflict as a part-time consultant.

I picked the second option. It was the first of many decisions I've made that rejected full-time employment. I felt like going full time, moving to New York and working for this emerging new initiative, would put me inside an office, working on Excel sheets. I didn't want to do that. I wanted to stay current. I wanted substance.

So, I picked the latter, and I started picking up other contracts to supplement it. At first, I took everything that people would give me, because when you try to go independent that way, you freak out that you won't have enough money to support your family.

I never advertised. It was just from word of mouth. The CGI did me a huge service, because when people see you at a meeting like that and you're running things, it creates an image of you as somebody people would want to hire.

Initially, I thought that my consultancy life would be advising diplomatic issues. Rather, very quickly I found out that what people needed were project implementers. There were many, many ideas running around, lots of seed-funding for those ideas, and very few people who were able to take an idea and actually turn it into a plan.

Working for Nelson Mandela, Jimmy Carter, Kofi Annan, and Aung San Suu Kyi

Then, I was hired by The Elders,[8] the group created by Nelson Mandela that included President Jimmy Carter and Kofi Annan and about twelve or thirteen former world leaders.

Aung San Suu Kyi was an Elder too, but back then, she was under house arrest. So, she couldn't really participate, but they included her symbolically. Their idea was that they were all former world leaders with a lot of political capital and could help in different areas. I was hired by them to help them both on Sudan and the Middle East.

Helping the Aspen Institute Create a U.S.–Palestinian Venture-Capital Fund

My next project happened during Condoleezza Rice's last year of tenure as secretary of state. She approached Walter Isaacson from the Aspen Institute and said, "We're in the middle of renewed peace attempts between the Israelis and the Palestinians . . . The political negotiations will be handled by the White House, and the security accommodations will be handled by the DOD [Department of Defense], but for the economic development, we need the U.S. private sector to step in."

I was invited by the Aspen Institute to put that into a reality. Together with Toni Verstandig, I built up the U.S.–Palestinian Partnership,[9] with a steering committee of American private-sector leaders.

We conducted meetings to identify the gaps and bottlenecks within the Palestinian economy that needed to be addressed. Out of that came a lot of failed projects and some really significant successes, one of which is Sadara Ventures,[10] a venture-capital fund focused on Palestinian early-stage technology companies.

Technology was something that was identified very quickly as a sector of potential growth in Palestine, especially since there's such a R&D [research and development] hub right across the border in Israel. We helped with fund-raising, brought investors in, raised about twenty-five million dollars to start it, and then spun it off. It's a for-profit project, and they're doing very well. They've invested in several companies that are creating a lot of jobs, and four more venture funds now follow that model.

Hillary Clinton Expanded It to Eleven Countries

When the administration shifted at the U.S. State Department— Condoleezza Rice left, and Hillary Clinton came in—we went into a period in which everything was frozen, because it's a new secretary of state and a new party. Hillary Clinton approached the Aspen Institute and said, "What you did with the U.S.–Palestinian Partnership, we should do that better and bigger. And we'll call it Partners for a New Beginning."

Initially, it was supposed to be five countries. It grew up very quickly to be eleven different countries. The State Department provided some seed funding to get it started, but most of the funding comes from the American private sector.

When we started, we insisted that we learn from our mistakes. Early on, we had a structural failure in that we rushed to the American businesspeople first. I've learned since, when you do engagement, unless it's locally owned and locally driven, you will not get traction.

Now, we first study every single country that we go to. We have a local chapter of private-sector partners that help identify what are the top three priorities for their country and how to approach them.

These projects take very different shapes and forms. In Palestine, there was a focus on technology and youth; for example, we supported an education NGO [nonprofit] in Nablus, Tomorrow's Youth Organization [TYO, tomorrowsyouth.org]. In Turkey, it was the integration of women into the local economy. What the Turks want to focus on is different than the Tunisians, the Moroccans, or the Jordanians. There are some trends that are across the board—water, tech, and youth are themes almost everywhere. That's a great opportunity, because you can then cluster together a bunch of private-sector actors (e.g., multinationals) that you can rally on all of these.

As for corporate partners, the first company that stood up to support and to take leadership was the Coca-Cola Company. Both financially and in terms of developing the idea, Cisco was huge when John Chambers was the chairman there. Intel, Hilton, Morgan Stanley—they've all stepped into this. These are the big hitters that formed the steering committee that helped us drive this forward.

Still a Consultant, Ten Years Later

Ten years into it, I still work as a consultant for the CGI. Recently, I've focused mainly on the CGI University [CGIU] on issues around peace and human rights. It's a renewable annual contract. Every year, we have a team of about ten different young professionals [collaborate] on specific themes like poverty alleviation, climate change, global health, and education.

For the Aspen Institute, I run the Global Alliances program. I wanted to expand it from the Middle East and take that model elsewhere. So, we established "Global Alliances." They won't let me call it "Fringe," [laughs] but everybody knows that it's Fringe [Diplomacy]. So, I do a lot of private-sector engagements through my role in Aspen.

Doing Rescue Missions with "The Secretary of Thugs"

I also work with the former governor of New Mexico, Bill Richardson, at the Richardson Center for Global Engagement (again, another bombastic name for a center). He wanted to focus on private diplomacy and to be able to do interventions. He has a rare talent and skill for connecting with people that others can't connect with.

When Governor Richardson was his secretary of energy and ambassador, Bill Clinton used to call him "the Secretary of Thugs." President Clinton would send him to all sorts of places that others wouldn't be willing to go and meet, and he would get results.

I've been working informally with Governor Richardson since 2007, formally since 2011—meaning that, for four years, I did it without getting paid, because he was still in office, and there was no center. We were just doing special-ops projects on the side. In 2011, we were able to establish the center, and I actually started getting paid.

My Most Dangerous Mission, to Khartoum

The most dangerous mission was probably one of my first Fringe missions with Governor Richardson, to Sudan. We went to Khartoum to try and negotiate a unilateral cease-fire. That was January 2007. We went there to get President Bashir out of a cease-fire declaration for ninety days—to allow the rebel groups to do a conference to be able to unite politically—so they could actually bring a group in to negotiate.

It was the most dangerous to me personally, because that's before I was even an American citizen. I was then an Israeli/British citizen. I was a captain in the reserves of the Israeli Defense Forces, which was at war with Sudan, and here I was in Khartoum sitting with President Bashir.

I first met the governor basically half an hour before we took off on that mission. I told him, if the Sudanese decide that this delegation is not a positive one, things could go *really* wrong, and they could go wrong really fast for me. The governor responded with a silly smile.

He said, "Mickey, do you know what I'm famous for?"

I'm like, "What is that?"

"I get people out of jail. So, worst comes to worst, you sit in a Sudanese jail for a few months. Think what that will do for your career."

After he said that, I knew I *had* to go with him, but I was actually very fearful. It was a very small delegation. I traveled there with a Palestinian-American friend who used to be a member of the Palestinian negotiation team. We didn't know that we were going to be together on this mission until we ran into each other at the airport. I asked him if he wouldn't mind us sharing a room at the Hilton in Khartoum, because I was just certain that somebody would knock in the middle of the night and take me away.

My friend's response was even funnier. He said, "Mickey, are you kidding me? They hate me more than they hate you. They'll take me first."

Working in North Korea in "Soft Engagement"

What we do in North Korea is soft engagement. The governor and I have been involved in this for years.

We do human-deterrent intervention, supplying food for orphanages and wheelchairs for people, kids with disabilities. Currently, we're working on providing seeds and trees to try and help replant trees that have been lost over the years. I'm becoming an expert in how to plant trees! The goal is to stop floods, help the irrigation, and help food supplies. All of these projects are not just out in space: They're related to some objectives that we're trying to get together with the North Koreans.

At times, it's Americans that are detained in North Korea, and at times, it's being able to credibly go there and help reduce tensions that we've seen growing worse, lately.

I have not met [President] Kim Jong-un, not yet. But I was in Pyong-yang once, soon after he came into office. Pyongyang is surprisingly modern looking. We were there in January, which is considered to be the "small" winter. It was –20 degrees. There was no heat anywhere. Ice covered the whole place.

North Korea is a fascinating place. I spent my time trying to understand North Koreans' identity, why they see the world in the way they do, and how they see it, in order to be able to predict how they'll behave and act in different scenarios.

We were very, very aware that our hosts designed our trip. We only saw things that they wanted us to see. However, every now and then, we got some spontaneous diversion, such as a trip on the local subway that included a blackout. So, we were able to spontaneously engage a little bit.

Otherwise, everybody and everything that we saw was a part of the North Korean elite, either members of the military or the party. We were never given access to see anybody in the camps or anything like that.

When you encounter the people "outside" (the people who are not the ones who handle you), they don't pay attention to you at all. We walked in the subway there, and everyday people would be walking all around us. Obviously, we were the only foreigners there. But they didn't even look at us.

At first, I thought maybe it's out of fear, and then, I learned it's actually not fear. It's a very strong notion of how this needs to be a highly productive society, which means that looking to the side or paying attention to any distraction is less productive. So, they don't do it.

But being who we are [obvious foreigners], if we get into their face and we say "hi," they light up. Then, you realize that North Koreans or South Koreans, they're the same people. They're the same families. This gives you a lot of hope. On that individual level, they are warm. They're friendly. But, of course, they see the world very, very differently than the way we do, and therefore, they react very differently.

People like to say they're irrational. I would argue that they are very, very rational but just see things very differently.

All the Different Hats I Wear at Work

I have to manage all my different hats. In terms of the Aspen Institute, people think it's a think tank, but you don't get your budget from this organization. There are about thirty different policy programs at Aspen, and each of them is responsible for its own fund-raising. More than that, we pay Aspen Institute an overhead.

It's great on many levels. You can look at it almost as a social incubator. As long as your idea fits within the mission and vision of Aspen— values-based leadership—and you're able to make it sustainable financially, you can do it.

When I come to Walter [Isaacson] and I say something like, "Oh, yeah, next week, you might see in the news that I'm traveling to North Korea with Eric Schmidt [founder of Alphabet and Google] and Governor Richardson," he looks at me, and it's like, "That's fantastic! How do we get Aspen involved?"

So, when I reached out to him on [our recent mission to] Cuba, he said, "Oh, yeah, I'm in." I get that great support from Aspen. The same goes with Governor Richardson. He's all about the intervention. He loves working on getting Americans out of very bad situations. He loves going to North Korea and being able to defuse tensions with the South at moments of pique.

He has thirty years' worth of public service in which he's accumulated a lot of political capital. For example, the Richardson Center in Myanmar is now a very, very known project, because we've done political training of over three thousand people. We've brought in delegations of investors. If things go wrong in Myanmar, I can assure you that I can get Governor Richardson there to meet the president, and the head of the opposition, Aung San Suu Kyi, the key players, within a day . . . They trust us, because we've been responding to what they've asked us to do through the years. We've helped them lead up to this moment, and that builds a lot of capital to use for good things.

Four Jobs and Counting . . .

There are a few other projects I work on as well. For me, it's been finding all of these jobs, then firing some clients over time. What happens is, you get overwhelmed, and you also get your confidence that you've found your niche, so you settle in on a few that are really meaningful. To me, these are the jobs or contracts that give me enough autonomy and flexibility to advance this concept of Fringe forward.

In many cases, there's overlap between them, which allows me to leverage the advantages of all. Aspen is a known brand. That helps me with my "convening power." Governor Richardson helps if I need a contact somewhere, to do the initial outreach. People will respond. And then, it's up to me to build it up on a personal level.

Local Consultants Are Cheaper, Nimbler, and More Skilled

In this work, you need to be nimble and flexible. I'm actually pretty proud of my business modality, which I learned when we built the Partners for a New Beginning and the Middle East Program in Aspen. Fourteen full-time employees is a top-heavy organization. It's really tough. You find yourself chasing fund-raising all day long, and you never catch up. You don't actually fund-raise for the future.

So, when I started the Global Alliances program, I changed the modality. I said, "We have delegations to Myanmar. We have delegations to Bhutan, delegations to Cuba, to Tanzania, to Colombia. There's no single individual that can help you in all of them."

So, instead of hiring one full-time person, I get contractor consultants with specific skills for each of those locations. The number of people I'm currently managing fluctuates significantly. Sometimes, they reside there, or they're from there. Sometimes, they're Americans that I've worked with over the years that I trust. But hiring locals whenever possible cuts the overhead costs of the program in a significant way, and I lead by example, because I'm not an employee either. I am a contractor myself.

In a Good Year, I Make Almost a Quarter Million

The Richardson Center has active programs in Myanmar, North Korea, Cuba, the Middle East, and Africa. We're running an operational budget of $250,000 a year, which is tiny, relative to the activity that goes on. For the Global Alliance program (i.e. Fringe-Aspen), the annual budget is $63,000, which is nothing. I wish it would be bigger just so that I could take a bigger salary out of it.

In a good year, I make about $240,000; in a lean year, $180,000. Sometimes, I need to supplement my income with contracts that are less Fringe-y.

I'm trying to build the revenue stream for Fringe. I take an annual salary from Aspen of only $35,000 for this, which is way under market value, but I do it because I believe in what I do. From the Richardson Center, I get paid $120,000 a year. So right there you have a base of $155,000. Then, you look at the different consultancies, the Clinton Global Initiative, if it comes in, the teaching at Georgetown, which is a little bit, and, every now and then, there's a little consultancy that I take on to supplement my income.

And I Teach at Georgetown University

I currently teach in the same program that I graduated from, international relations at Georgetown University, which is a great source of pride for me. You definitely do not do that for the salary, because you barely get paid anything. I'm an adjunct professor, and I teach one course a year. The course is called, "Engaging Change: Middle East and North Africa." It's a second-year class.

The Fringe-y part of it is that we focus this class on giving the students the opportunity to try and understand the world—in this case, the Middle East and North Africa, from the perspective of the local community, not U.S. foreign policy but quite the opposite. How do different factions and groups there view the Middle East itself and U.S. policy toward it?

I Get a Guy from Hamas to Talk with My Students

We cannot fly a speaker from [the Palestinian terrorist group] Hamas to class. They won't be allowed in the United States; it's problematic. But we can Skype. So, we have videoconference sessions every year with a Hamas member.

The person we typically use is somebody who I believe grew up in Syria, but he currently resides in Europe. He's online all the time. Language-wise, it's easy; he speaks very good English. He grew up with Khaled Mashal, the leader of Hamas.

One of the great things about it is, he's not afraid. He's not ashamed. He is very, very confident in his worldview and his stand. So, even when he talks to American students, he's not masking it to make it nice so that the American public would like it. No. He talks . . . and for me being Israeli, sometimes it's really hard to sit there and listen to things that he says.

But because it's remote, the students are not afraid either. These are *real* conversations, and nobody gets to any agreement on them. The point is not to reach an agreement. The point is to dig deeper, to ask why, to understand what is his viewpoint.

After a class like that, I believe students have a better understanding of why Hamas is like that. They don't agree with it. They don't adopt it, and they definitely do not legitimize it, but when they get into a position when they need to deal with that, they can predict what and why Hamas will do, how they'll react. We try to get them authentic messages that they wouldn't be able to hear otherwise. Some of these students will become foreign-service officers. They go from this course out into the world.

Citizen of Three Countries — Which Passport Do I Use?

I hold three passports: Israeli from birth, British because my mother was born there, and American because of my marriage to Robin. We currently reside in Washington, D.C.

When I travel, I use my American passport unless I'm not allowed to. So when I come to Israel, by law, I have to use the Israeli one to enter. But, other than that, I just use American—and British, I just have it on the side.

Changing My Views about the Use of Force

It wasn't because I regretted what I was doing in the army, but I did have a very clear sense that use of force in the long term never works. In the short term, it [military force] might be necessary here and there.

Since then, I've been reducing even that [idea] significantly. I'm currently—I wouldn't say a pacifist—but as close as you can get to that, because I see the devastation that violence causes in the long term. Even the short-term cost, if you pay by trying to avoid it, is still worthwhile. But then again, if somebody has a gun to your head, you need to do something about it.

I don't carry. I refuse to carry weapons anymore, anywhere. Everything in the private sector, development, stuff like that, I never, ever, ever touch arms or anything like that.

When It Comes to Engagement, I'm a Fundamentalist

This might not be politically correct, but I'm a fundamentalist when it comes to engagement. That means I actually believe in engaging and talking with somebody; but exchanging ideas doesn't mean that I legitimize the person. It doesn't mean that I agree with what they say or even believe what I hear.

It means that you actually are able to get better information, articulate more authentically what it is that you are trying to convey, hear from them, and understand better what the motivation is, what the logic behind somebody's behavior is. And my claim is that not only does it create more flexibility in finding different solutions, but it also allows you to predict how somebody will behave.

I resist the notion that everybody we don't agree with is irrational. "Oh, the Iranians are irrational. We can't deal with them. The North Koreans are irrational." I have never met in my lifetime somebody who was irrational.

I'll take it to the extreme: Suicide bombers are rational people. They just have a very different way of calculating and looking at the world, and unless you try to get into their shoes and understand what it is, it will be really hard to get anything positive from that engagement.

So, as I say, I'm a fundamentalist when it comes to engagement, and that's a big part of the power of Fringe.

Working toward Mideast Peace with the Telos Group

I also work with the Telos Group, which was founded by two good friends, Greg Khalil and Todd Deatherage. When they shared with me their vision, I was a little skeptical, because they're targeting the most difficult (in my perspective) segment of the American population, trying to get them to see the Israeli-Palestinian conflict in a more nuanced way.

What Telos has been able to do is penetrate that segment that didn't used to look at the conflict through the lens of universal human rights. That's really impactful and something that a lot of other organizations, well-funded organizations, have not been able to do. So, to me, Telos is a long-term project, because it takes a long time to get to critical mass in this, but it's absolutely worthwhile.

Another project that I've done over the years was to help the establishment of J Street (jstreet.org/about) with Jeremy Ben-Ami. I've consulted there, especially on their operation of Israel and how to talk and communicate with the Israeli community.

Learning Diplomacy from My Baby Girl

Our daughter, Noa, came into our life twenty-one months ago. We worked on her adoption for about four and a half years. Then, one Friday afternoon, we got a phone call. I was just back from Colombia. Robin was on the New Jersey Turnpike on her way to see a friend. They said, "Hey, the baby girl has been born. She can be yours, if you say yes, and if you do say yes, you need to collect her in three days."

She was born in Baltimore. That's not a far drive. We collected her in Maryland, where the agency was, nineteen days after she was born.

So, we had a very, very short pregnancy. [Laughs.] Some people have said, "Oh, my God, how did you do it?" It was like, "Are you kidding me?" It's so much better than a nine- or ten-months pregnancy, because we only had seventy-two hours to panic. She's a gift to us. We could not have asked for anything better than this little baby.

Noa constantly says "thank you" to everybody and everything. We didn't teach her to do this. We don't know where she picked it up. It's this sweet little "thank you," and you see what that creates in people, that tiny little gesture. It lights them up. People then talk to us. She says, "Thank you," and immediately, we're in the middle of a conversation with that person.

I don't think I've fully appreciated the power of that. It's not just about saying "thank you"; it's about that tiny little show of acknowledgment, respect, just that smile and nicety that opens so many doors into other communications. In essence, that's a lot of what we do [in my work].

Too Much Time on the Road, Away from Family

I claim that I have shrunk my travels since we adopted our little baby girl. My wife will laugh at that. She says I travel a lot. I probably travel internationally an average of once a month. I try to make those trips not more than eight days. When you travel to Myanmar, it's hard to contain this, but I do it in eight days. Cuba, it's usually six days. North Korea, the time on the ground was only four and a half days, which is the time it takes you to travel there and back—it's probably about eight days all around.

On these travels, flying is the only time that I actually have rest. There's no Internet connection. There's no phone connection. Nobody can reach you. People feed you, and you can watch movies. So, it's kind of a vacation. I'm very thankful that, when I travel on Richardson Center, I am able to travel business class, which is very helpful.

When I travel on Aspen, because of my own lean budget, I travel economy, but it's not easy if you're expected to land and perform. You can't fly for twenty-four hours in economy and suddenly show up in a meeting with a head of state and perform. So, it's tough, but at the end of the day, when you only take a $35,000 salary, you'd rather not spend $8,000 on a ticket. So, these are all calculations that go into it.

How I Unwind: Sitting on a Beach or Playing Soccer

Where I live, in Washington, D.C., I don't have a beach. But if I can sit by the beach, listen to the waves, see people, I get recharged. I'm horrible at things like meditation and yoga. I can't quiet my mind enough to focus on breathing or whatever.

There is one activity that I do that absolutely makes me focus on one thing: playing soccer, because when I'm on the field, to me, that's all I care about. We play every week. We have a group in Georgetown that's made up of all sorts of administration people, embassy people, anybody who's not just purely American . . . because it's not as big a sport in the United States as in other countries.

At home, when I don't travel, my commitment with Robin is to get home by 5:00 p.m. every day, or almost every day. Then, I can spend time with Noa. She goes to sleep at 7:30. That's when I get my second wind of work, and typically what I do, I sit on my couch with my computer, typing along, having basically silly comedies on TV, because if you need something mind-numbing, there you go.

The shows change. Lately, it's been *Modern Family*, which constantly has reruns. Most of the episodes, I already know by heart. If Robin is still up and she says, "Oh, this is a good one, you should stay for that one," I'll watch it, but I don't need to really watch it. Robin laughs. At night, it used to be that I would come home, and I would start talking, talking, talking, and she would just put her hand on my mouth like, "Enough. Shut up."

My Role Models: The First Prime Minister of Israel and Our Former Rabbi

My first role model was probably David Ben-Gurion, the first prime minister of Israel, just because of everything he had to put together, the balancing, the way he declared the State of Israel, and what he intended with it. Growing up, he was my hero. Since then, I've learned more of the narrative, and so there's some cracks in that image.

I have the tendency to collect mentors: for example, Congressman Dennis Ross, who helped me a lot. He got me the internship at the Washington Institute. Also, Rob Malley, he's one of those people who you just look at the way he analyzes things. He's the one I started teaching with. My high school principal, who got me all into this activism, whom I'm still in touch with more than twenty years later . . .

And there's the rabbi who married Robin and me, who was also my boss in California. He's much more than a rabbi: He's a humanitarian leader. He embodies everything that to me is positive about Judaism and someone that I connect with on values. Through him I started realizing a part of Judaism that I actually can relate to—it's not about the divine; it's about the values and about the way you conduct yourself in your life.

I Want to Do Fringe Diplomacy for the Rest of My Life

I have this picture collection. It may be unprofessional, but I make sure to take advantage of opportunities and people that I meet to take pictures, because you have a lot of moments of doubt. Sometimes, you're on a high, "Oh, my God, I'm doing so great," but every now and again, it's like, "What the hell am I doing?"

So, there are pictures of different amazing people and places that I can show you in my phone: being with [former Vice President Joseph] Biden or [Governor] Richardson, giving a press conference in Hilton Khartoum, being with [Chair of Alphabet/Google] Eric Schmidt in Pyongyang, hanging out in the Palace. Then, when things don't go your way and you're frustrated, and you're very hard with yourself, you remember these moments and say, "Okay, I'm still doing okay."

If I had all the money and time in the world, I would—and I say this honestly—do Fringe for the rest of my life. I have found my thing. I am happy doing this. I cannot retire. If I could do Fringe, not worry about income from it and be able to spend a significant segment of my time anywhere on a beach, that would be my dream. I hope it will be my legacy.

NOTE TO READER

Dear Reader:

Books have the power to share our most intimate stories. I hope you've felt the vulnerability of these fifteen narrators and maybe even seen some of yourself in their experiences.

I believe that—in a world that can feel chaotic, divisive, and lonely these days—our shared experience of work unites us. Everyone has a job! We all share struggles to land that coveted role or manage a nasty boss or irritating coworker. Conversely, we experience the best days of our lives on the job, form lasting friendships, and derive our sense of purpose from the work we do. Every job matters, from cleaning toilets to designing the first commercial spaceship. It takes all of us working as a system to maintain society and evolve humanity.

When we share the stories of our jobs, often we end up—as these narrators have done—revealing much more about our early life experiences, family influence, trauma and triumphs, hopes and dreams. The story of "my job" turns into the story of my life . . .

I wrote *My Job* Books 1 and 2 for three reasons:

1. **To share voices** and stories of our innovative narrators, many of whom have overcome huge obstacles and made heroic contributions to our world;

2. **To raise funds** to create more jobs in places of poverty and unemployment in the U.S. and abroad (100 percent of author proceeds and reader donations go to nonprofit job-creation programs); and

3. **To create community**, connecting readers to narrators and
   each other, getting acquainted with people in cultures and jobs
   vastly different from our own and discovering what's unique yet
   universal.

Your opinion matters! Please **share your feedback** about this book by:

- Posting a review on Amazon (amazon.com/Suzanne-Skees/e/
  B001KHC32K) or our Facebook page (facebook.com/
  myjobstories)
- Sending me a note via email with ideas for improvement
  or people you know with fascinating job-stories:
  Suzanne@myjobstories.org

And **join our community** by:

- Sharing your "job story" on our Facebook page (facebook.com/
  myjobstories)—even just a brief description with a photograph
- Sharing the *My Job* series with your family and friends, book
  group or class, coworkers, or boss
- Signing up for updates and short stories, as well as contests and
  giveaways, on our blog, Job Talk (myjobstories.org/job-talk)
- Donating directly to create a job: (skees.org/project_category/
  job-creation)

It takes a community to make a book the best it can be, so I really hope
you'll be in touch with your ideas for improvement and future editions of
the *My Job* series. With your input, I'm ready to get to work.

Suzanne Skees
Central Coast, California
2019

WHAT'S YOUR JOB STORY?

REFLECTION QUESTIONS

Chapter 1

Mike Kenward recalls his childhood in London, England, as one full of laughter, love, and happiness but lacking in financial security and a father. He has set his career path in direct opposition to that of his wealthy workaholic father in the United States. Has there been anyone in your life who's modeled for you what you do not wish to devote your time and effort toward in your own career? Also, Mike purports that gambling has beneficial impacts for many people and that everyone has addictions (his is peanut butter-and-jam sandwiches). Do you believe that "addictions" ever can positively enhance one's productivity and health?

Chapter 2

Kevin Zazo directly credits his trauma at age five in Puerto Cortés, Honduras, witnessing his father murdering his mother, with his current desire to care for as many people as possible through nursing. He doesn't regret the pain of losing his mother, or anything else he's been through, because it's made him who he is today. Can you track your own life story to find places where suffering and loss have shaped who you've become? Did your experience influence your choice of your current livelihood or future career goal?

Chapter 3

Sandra López made a series of clear decisions that led her away from organized religion and the machismo culture of her upbringing in Ciudad Vieja, Guatemala, and toward education and freedom. Her experience of giving birth sparked her desire to become a midwife, and now she believes that the circumstances of our birth set the stage for health and peace throughout our lives. How might the way you were born, your birth order (if you have siblings) and family dynamics, and the presence or absence of healthcare and home resources impact your current level of stress or serenity? If you have given birth or assisted a birth, did your life change, as Sandra says that hers did when she decided to have "Juansie"?

Chapter 4

Nadine Niyitegeka sees herself as proof that any girl can become whatever she dreams. She recalls being very shy and quiet, struggling to learn English to apply for college in Kigali, Rwanda, and evolving into the confident public speaker and admissions counselor she is today. Do you believe that everyone has the ability to become a leader? What does *leadership* really mean? Describe three pivotal people in your own life: someone who convinced you that you had it in you to follow your dreams, someone whom you see as a leader you would like to emulate, and the type of leader you'd like to become in your own family, church, community, or workplace.

Chapter 5

Kelly Kang exemplifies the contradiction she laments about Korean culture: The relentless pursuit of academic success pushed onto young students has equipped her with the skills to teach, yet it also saddens her to witness how exhausted and stressed her students are as they muddle through afterschool tutoring until 10 p.m. Kelly wishes they had more free time to play sports, learn music, and pursue extracurricular activities.

Yet in South Korea, 93 percent of students graduate from high school on time, and they rank among the highest in the world on global standardized tests. What's the tradeoff between obedience and discipline there? How is education imposed (or not) where you live? Which careers might be well suited—and not—for youth who've matriculated through the Korean system?

Chapter 6

Misozi Mkandawire never stops strategizing ideas to add more kiosks to her mobile-banking business in Lusaka, Zambia, and designing new mobile-phone platforms to empower women and young people to launch new businesses. Where do you think she gets her energy and ambition? What aspects of her life in Zambia resonate with yours and which do not? Is it easy to obtain funding and guidance to launch new startups where you live? If so, what resources support entrepreneurs, and if not, what's needed to support a more robust ecosystem of invention and industry?

Chapter 7

Srey Pouv Kai describes her early childhood in the refugee camps on the border of Cambodia and Thailand, left fatherless at three months of age and emotionally motherless as well, severely lacking in both material and familial resources. Nevertheless, her first idea for a career was in nursing, and her two current jobs entail helping villagers attain microloans and providing rice seeds to farmers. She tries to help her extended family and community members to "stand up" as she did, from poverty into power and prosperity. Can you find any clues in her story as to how she wound up with such deep compassion when her own childhood was bereft of it? And in your own work, are there ways in which you pull others forward into greater financial or personal empowerment?

Chapter 8

Sena Ahiabor managed to combine his family's legacy of farming with his personal affinity for engineering ("designing equipment") in his agri-processing company in the Volta Region of Ghana, West Africa. What's your family's job legacy? List as many of your ancestors' occupations as you can recall. Enlist the help of family members if possible. Does your own current work connect back to any of their skills and contributions? If so, would you credit that solely to a sort of in-house apprenticeship learning, or do you believe you have inherited specific talents from them? Is there such a thing as "occupational DNA"?

Chapter 9

Mary Gibutaye receives a mobile phone from a nonprofit program in Mbale, Uganda, and learns to operate what she calls "the computer" to study weather patterns and market pricing, to resolve crop diseases and implement crop rotation. Thinking at first that she was too old to learn, Mary ends up delighted with her handheld database, and she now teaches other farmers what she's learned. Her informed innovations seem pretty radical in the rural area where her neighbors still farm with hoes and hands; and, lacking electricity, Mary has to use a solar cell just to recharge her phone. How do you react to new technologies in your field? Do you embrace or resist new applications and programs?

Chapter 10

Alberto Alaniz recalls an early experience of racial prejudice in Chicago, Illinois, in an encounter with police officers and joins the Latin Kings gang, simply because his mentor and friends are already in it. Later, inside prison, Alberto has a revelation when he sees opposing gang members helping each other out. He symbolizes his new vision of multicultural unity and strength by transposing a Mexican eagle over his gang tattoo, and once released, he teaches art to young black men emerging from jail and gangs. How did his prison experience prepare him for the career he now has? Can you track any adversities that led you to your current work? As a first-generation immigrant from Mexico, Alberto achieves the American dream of obtaining an education, career, family, and home ownership. Has your family faced hurdles due to your cultural background? Finally, despite the impactful work Alberto does with youth, he cites *fatherhood* as his most important role. Can you imagine an economic system in which caring for family members receives remuneration and benefits?

Chapter 11

Tania Wong teaches many modalities of dance at her studio in Toronto, Canada. She asserts that, with sufficient practice, anyone can learn the technical moves of choreography but that, when dancers allow the music to evoke emotion in them, their movement becomes art and has the power to heal both audience and dancer. She envisions a program of therapeutic dance, in which students could overcome low self-esteem, depression, grief, and family and psychological issues through self-confidence acquired through dancing. What are the ways you use your art and skills to nurture people with whom you work?

Chapter 12

Michele Peregrin works in Washington, D.C., the capital of the United States, at the über-bureaucratic State Department. She's one of 70,000 worker-bees who pass through high security every day with the intention of improving relationships around the world, yet she humanizes her work by describing transnational projects with visual artists, musicians, and museums and insisting that only through person-to-person cultural exchange can nations hope to succeed in governmental conflict resolution. Would you classify Michele as working top-down, from the most powerful government on Earth, or bottom-up, connecting grassroots artists with one another to create empathy across difference? Are there feasible ways to work as an activist within the "system"?

Chapter 13

Junior Walk chose the most controversial job in coal country, an activist striving to save the last mountaintop in West Virginia. His neighbors have slashed the tires on his pickup truck, hurled rocks through his apartment windows, and made threats to kill him. Does your job have physical or mental dangers inherent in it? Is Junior kidding himself to hope that locals can find work outside coalmining? How is the tragedy of deep poverty, ill health, and job scarcity in West Virginia reflective of other areas in the United States and elsewhere? When Junior states that he would support only industries—whether in coal, wind farms, or anything else—controlled by and paying full profits to locals—can you think of any examples from your own past and present work built on a model like that? Is there any cause that you believe in so strongly that you would work for it, even if some people disowned you, hated you, and threatened you?

Chapter 14

Greg Khalil says that his appearance as a Palestinian American allows him to "pass for so many things" in other countries. He calls it both a blessing and a curse, because "when people assume you're something you're not, they'll often open up in ways that reveal their biases and prejudices." Although the racism he experiences on the job as a Middle East peace diplomat sometimes feels like a knife in his gut, he utilizes the information to further understand how to help people get along. Have you ever experienced on-the-job racism, sexism, homophobia, or other biases based on your appearance? Can you discern any nugget in those experiences that could inform your work or relationships, or was it purely baleful abuse?

How does the way Greg interacts with people of opposing views contrast with the approach taken by the governments in Israel, Palestine, and the U.S.?

Chapter 15

Mickey Bergman works more jobs than we can count—teaching at Georgetown University, consulting for The Aspen Institute and the Clinton Global Initiative as well as a few nonprofits, and managing his own enterprise. He's made a conscious choice not to be "full-time in an office, working on Excel," but to serve as a contractor only to projects that advance his personal mission of "Fringe Diplomacy." However, in developing economies, according to the International Labour Organization, three of four workers endure "vulnerable employment," cobbling together multiple odd jobs with no benefits or security. What's privilege for one person is dire necessity for another. What factors contribute to the growth of the informal/gray/gig economy? How fast is this job-sector growing, and why? Have you worked in the gig economy or juggled multiple jobs? How, for better or worse, has that affected your sense of identity and wellbeing?

CHAPTER NOTES

Preface

1. To view the list of jobs, visit the Career Planner page: careerplanner.com/ListOfCareers.cfm.

2. Crabtree, Steve. "In U.S., Depression Rates Higher for Long-Term Unemployed: Mental health poorest among those jobless for six months or more." Gallup, (June 9, 2014). news.gallup.com/ poll/171044/depression-rates-higher-among-long-term -unemployed.aspx.

3. Linn, M.W., Sandifer, R., and Stein, S. "Effects of unemployment on mental and physical health." *Am J Public Health*, (May 1985). ncbi.nlm.nih.gov/pmc/articles/PMC1646287.

4. Robert Woodward Johnson Foundation. "How Does Employment, or Unemployment, Affect Health?" Robert Woodward Johnson Foundation, (March 12, 2013). rwjf.org/en/library/ research/2012/12/how-does-employment--or-unemployment --affect-health-.html.

5. Doyle, Alison. "How Often Do People Change Jobs?" The Balance Careers, (January 24, 2018). thebalancecareers.com/ how-often-do-people-change-jobs-2060467.

6. un.org/en/story/2018/04/1008562.

Chapter 1

1. Thanks to my clean-tech investor colleague back in San Francisco, Tom Ferguson of Imagine H2O (imagineh2o.org/team), who introduced me to Mike.

2. For more details and gambling statistics, visit the Gambling Commission: http://www.gamblingcommission.gov.uk/news-action-and-statistics/Statistics-and-research/Statistics/Gambling-key-facts.aspx.

3. Bevilacqua, L. and Goldman, D. "Genes and Addictions." *Clinical Pharmacology and Therapeutics*, 85, no.4 (2009). ncbi.nlm.nih.gov/pmc/articles/PMC2715956.

4. Chalabi, Mona. "UK's gambling habits: what's really happening?" *The Guardian,* (2014). theguardian.com/news/datablog/2014/jan/08/uks-gambling-habits-whats-really-happening.

Chapter 2

1. I traveled to Honduras with Karen and John Godt, a couple from Cleveland, Ohio, who launched Hope 4 Honduran Children after meeting Kevin and twenty-three other "abandoned, starving boys living in an old forgotten pig barn." They provide scholarships and holistic care to Honduran youth. See Karen's insightful article on mishaps in international development: skees.org/story/no-quick-fixes-in-humanitarian-work-firsthand-lessons-from-the-field.

2. Kevin is very proud of his lineage: Soule, Jean-Philippe. "Garifuna." Native Planet. nativeplanet.org/indigenous/garifuna.htm.

3. Crilly, Rob. "The majority of homicides are young people. It's so sad." *The Telegraph,* (2015). telegraph.co.uk/sponsored/lifestyle/honduras-gangs/11701324/honduras-murder-rate.html.

Chapter 3

1. Thanks to my friend Gary Tabasinske, founder of a leadership-training program, Association for Leadership in Guatemala, for nonprofit managers and social entrepreneurs. Gary allowed me to sit in on several classes and introduced me to some of his star graduates, like Sandra. For more info, visit liderazgoguatemala.org/en/about.

2. When Sandra uses this term, she's referring not to some funny, old-fashioned caveman antics: Violence against women in Guatemala is of national concern. The Guatemala Human Rights Commission documents and explains the prevalence of women murdered here. "For Women's Right to Live: FAQs." Guatemala Human Rights Commission/USA. ghrc-usa.org/Programs/ForWomensRighttoLive/FAQs.htm.

3. For more data about Guatemala, visit the Central Intelligence Agency's World Factbook (cia.gov/library/publications/the-world-factbook/geos/gt.html).

4. Asperger syndrome (AS) is a neurobiological disorder on the higher-functioning end of the autism spectrum. Learn more on the Autism Speaks website: https://www.autismspeaks.org/what-autism/asperger-syndrome.

5. Radoff, K.A., Lisa M. Thompson, KC Bly, Carolina Romero. "Practices related to postpartum uterine involution in the Western Highlands of Guatemala." *Midwifery*. 29, no.3 (2013). ncbi.nlm.nih.gov/pmc/articles/PMC3799972.

6. *Machista* or *machismo*: a strong or exaggerated sense of traditional masculinity, aggressiveness, physical courage, virility, and domination of women.

7. The end of the world, according to the Christian Bible book of *Revelation*.

8. WINGS (wingsguate.org) is a nonprofit dedicated to women's healthcare and reproductive rights.

Chapter 4

1. The Akilah Institute (akilahinstitute.org) is a two-year college for East African women with majors in the region's fastest growing sectors: information systems (IS), entrepreneurship, and hospitality management. Akilah graduates have a 90 percent average job placement and earn incomes 5X higher than the national average. See: skees.org/story/closing-the-gender-gap-in-east-africaaos -fastest-growing-sectors. Akilah is a grantee partner of the Skees Family Foundation.

2. Tourism in Rwanda is expected to reach 7.5 percent of gross domestic product (GDP) by 2025.

3. "All about Rwanda—the Land of a Thousand Hills." Kabiza Wilderness Safaris. (2017). kabiza.com/kabiza-wilderness -safaris/all-about-rwanda-the-land-of-a-thousand-hills.

4. See Nadine discuss the numbers and her experience, starting at 1:50: Barbra Klein, Karen Sherman, Nadine Niyitegeka. *23 Panel: Safe Passage for Young Women*, (2015; Futures Without Violence), YouTube. youtu.be/uf0Tnc_tdIk.

5. From April–July 1994, members of the Hutu ethnic majority in Rwanda murdered 800,000 people, mostly of the Tutsi minority. The genocide also created two million refugees (mainly Hutus) from Rwanda. For more information, see: "Rwandan Genocide." History. history.com/topics/rwandan-genocide.

6. This article tries to explain the world's—particularly the United State's—silence: "The Rwandan Genocide." Unite to End Genocide. endgenocide.org/learn/past-genocides/the-rwandan-genocide.

7. For more on the numbers killed, see: "Numbers." Human Rights Watch. hrw.org/reports/1999/rwanda/Geno1-3-04.htm. Also see: Verpoorten, Marijke. "The Death Toll of the Rwandan Genocide: A Detailed Analysis for Gikongoro Province." *Population* 60, (2005). cairn-int.info/article-E_POPU_504_0401 --the-death-toll-of-the-rwandan-genocide-a.htm.

8. For more on how Kigali has transformed itself in the decades since the Rwandan genocide, see: Buchan, Kit. "Rwanda reborn: Kigali's culture, heart and soul." *The Guardian*, (2014). theguardian.com/travel/2014/apr/11/rwanda-kigali-reborn -culture-heart-soul.

9. For information on TVET schools in Rwanda and their role in ending poverty, see: "Rwanda—Technical and Vocational Education and Training." vvob: education for development. vvob.be/vvob/en/programmes/rwanda-technical-and-vocational -education-and-training. Also see: "Technical and Vocational Education and Training." The World Bank. worldbank.org/ projects/P087347/technical-vocational-education -training?lang=en.

10. Akilah Institute initially supported Rwanda's brightest and neediest young women, but in order to scale across the country and East Africa, the college began accepting paying students in addition to scholarships based on need. To learn more about their plan, see: akilahinstitute.org/tuition.

11. Also known as "community score cards." Look at Rwanda's community score cards here: Organization for Social Science Research in Eastern and Southern Africa: Rwanda Chapter. "Rwanda Citizen Report and community Score Cards." World Bank. (2006). siteresources.worldbank.org/EXTSOCIALDEVELOPMENT/ Resources/244362-1193949504055/4348035-1298566783395/ 7755386-1298566794345/7755368-1298581402948/

63_Rwanda.pdf. You can also check out the Rwanda Governance Board's page about Ubudehe: http://www.rgb.rw/ home-grown-solutions/rwandas-hgs-good-practices/ubudehe/.

12. The United Human Rights Council gives a succinct summary of a complex atrocity here: "Genocide in Rwanda." United Human Rights Council. http://www.unitedhumanrights.org/genocide/ genocide_in_rwanda.

13. The BBC reports on the assassination of President Juvenal Habyarimana here: "1994: Rwanda presidents' plane 'shot down.'" BBC. bbc.co.uk/onthisday/hi/dates/stories/april/6/ newsid_2472000/2472195.stm.

14. Wikipedia; Wikipedia's "Assassination of Juvénal Habyarimana and Cyprien Ntaryamira" entry: Wikipedia's entry on the Assassination of Juvénal Habyarimana and Cyprien Ntaryamira. en.wikipedia.org/wiki/Assassination_of_Juv%C3%A9nal_ Habyarimana_and_Cyprien_Ntaryamira.

15. Weiner, Joann. "I've seen the Future of Rwanda, and her name is Nadine." *The Washington Post.* (2014). washingtonpost.com/ blogs/she-the-people/wp/2014/09/12/ive-seen-the-future-of -rwanda-and-her-name-is-nadine.

16. Anonymous. "How can one tell whether someone is Hutu or Tutsi?" Quora. (2013). quora.com/How-can-one-tell-whether -someone-is-Hutu-or-Tutsi.

17. Everyone Nadine's age and over grew up with Kinyarwanda as a first language and French second. Only in 2008 did the govern- ment declare Rwanda's official language as English.

18. For more information, visit the UN Women's page of regional and county offices here: unwomen.org/en/where-we-are/africa/ regional-and-country-offices.

Chapter 5

1. This blog talks about the downside of Western foreigners teaching English in Korea: Cale, Meg. "8 uncomfortable truths about teaching English on South Korea." Matador network. (2015). matadornetwork.com/notebook/8-uncomfortable-truths -teaching-english-south-korea.

2. See this list of top ten traits of Koreans that includes being addicted to technology and being nationalistic: Kim, Keith. "10 Personality Traits about Koreans You Should Know!" Seoulistic. (2014). seoulistic.com/korean-culture/personality-traits-about -koreans-you-should-know. And CNN's list of "10 Things South Korea Does Better Than Anywhere Else" includes gaming, cell phones, blind dates, and education: Cha, Frances. "10 things South Korea does better than anywhere else." CNN. (2017). cnn.com/2013/11/27/travel/10-things-south-korea-does-best.

3. Sociologists agree with her take: "To be a South Korean child," Yale academic See-Wong Koo tells *The New York Times*, "ultimately is not about freedom, personal choice or happiness; it is about production, performance and obedience," in an article on the price Korean kids pay for the country's top academic achievements. The Organisation for Economic Cooperation and Development claims that Koreans spend 20 percent of household income on after-school private academies called *hagwon* or "cram schools" and that 75 percent of all children attend this type of extracurricular study.

4. *Transformers Ride @ Universal Studios, Singapore,* by Patrick Love (2011; Patrick Love), YouTube. youtu.be/hbfChvEY1-4.

5. Read about this and other Korean wedding customs: Popovic, Mislav. "Strange wedding traditions." Traditionscustoms. traditionscustoms. com/wedding-traditions/strange-wedding-traditions.

6. According to *The Economist*, relations with both North Korea and China have deteriorated sharply in recent years: "South Korea and Its Neighbours: The Poor Relations." *The Economist.* (February 18, 2016). economist.com/news/asia/21693265 -souths-trustpolitik-towards-north-korea-has-unravelled -poor-relations.

7. The BBC says that Korea, formerly one of the most affluent countries in Asia, has slipped into "poverty and totalitarianism." See: "South Korea country profile." BBC. (2018). bbc.com/news/ world-asia-pacific-15289563.

Chapter 6

1. Watch an excellent video of Misozi describing Zambia and working through a typical day on the job: *Misozi—A Zoona Entrepreneur*, by Misozi Mkandawire (2015; Juiced Robot), YouTube. youtu.be/BMCSzVywoYU.

2. It's tradition in Zambia to name your child after social events occurring on her or his day of birth: "Zambian Names Are A Reflection of Significant Social Events." Zambia-Advisor. zambia-advisor.com/zambian-names.html.

3. I'm in Zambia with Elizebeth Tucker of Grameen Foundation (grameenfoundation.org), which has provided early-stage impact investment funding to Zoona. They've asked me to visit the pro- gram to interview clients and employees and to evaluate through stories how mobile banking is working here.

4. That sounds a lot better in context than out of it: $1 million Zambian kwacha = about $193USD that Misozi has been able to amass and save.

5. Update: See her LinkedIn profile (zm.linkedin.com/in/

misozi-mkandawire-03233b4a) and read on in this chapter to
learn about Fappis Solutions, named in honor of her dad.

6. Misozi also talked about how much she wished to travel far
   beyond Zambia and South Africa. Soon after our interview,
   she won a Young African Leaders Initiative (YALI) fellowship
   through the U.S. State Department that brought her to the U.S.
   (Washington, D.C. area) to study entrepreneurship for five weeks.
   She says it changed her perspective on everything.

Chapter 7

1. A shout-out to my friend Christopher Hest, who reconnected me
   with Karl after I lost track of our world-wandering friend. Christopher calls Karl "an amazing humanitarian," and he is: Check out
   Karl's work at karlgrobl.com. Thanks also to my friend Jill Cohen
   for sharing the visit and interview that led to this chapter.

2. *Microfinance*, which used to be called "microcredit," means extend-
   ing financial services such as loans, savings, insurance, and remittances to the poor, whose low incomes and lack of assets block
   them from accessing traditional banks. For a more detailed explanation of microfinance, visit: https://www.investopedia.com/
   terms/m/microfinance.asp.

3. Srey Pouv translates Cambodian currency into USD, unless
   otherwise noted, throughout this chapter.

4. Both in the U.S. and globally, the poor are unbanked and have
   few options when they need cash. When Nobel-peace-prize
   winner Muhammad Yunus first developed the concept of microcredit, he intended it to be a social-mission industry that would
   offer dignified and affordable financing to the poor to allow them
   to build micro-businesses. The model later became corrupted

and controversial (for more information, read the article cited in note 5 of this chapter). Today in Cambodia, Pouv charges slightly less interest than even the NGOs (nonprofits), whose rates run 22–40 percent APR. She's flexible if there is a particularly bad year in terms of crop yield (e.g., due to drought)—she allows customers to roll the payment into the next year.

5.   Toyama, Kentaro. "Lies, Hype, and Profit: The Truth About Microfinance." *The Atlantic*. (January 28, 2011). theatlantic.com/business/archive/2011/01/lies-hype-and-profit-the-truth-about-microfinance/70405.

6.   Moneylenders can be even more expensive, not to mention dangerous: They loan to about half of Cambodia's poor families and charge 120 percent interest: Renzenbrink, Anne. "Informal lending still thriving." *The Phnom Phen Post*. (2013). phnompenhpost.com/business/informal-lending-still-thriving.

Chapter 8

1.   You can view Sena's organic tomato products (TomaFresh) at the Ghana Trade website here: ghanatrade.gov.gh/Food-Beverage/tip-top-food-limited.html. Also, you can watch this video of Sena's home factory: *Tip Top Foods*, by Justine Levesque (2012; Lumana Village Ventures), YouTube. youtu.be/Jt9n5MbEDO0. And see how Sena and his family and neighboring farmers live by taking a video tour through Ghana, here: *What you need to know before going to Ghana!*, by Myriam (2013; MimiOnline), YouTube. youtu.be/biY3x-_4Bxk.

2.   On principle, I do not pay for interviews, but I did reimburse Sena for his expenses that day.

3.   Volta is in the easternmost border of the country and east of Lake

Volta (earth's largest human-made lake), right next to the Togo
border. This area, originally inhabited by Sena's ancestors from
the Ewe tribe, was occupied by the British, French, and Germans
until 1956, when the Europeans divided "Togoland" into Eastern
Ghana and Togo. Known for its natural beauty with rolling hills
and valleys, its main industry is fishing.

4. For videos that explain the way small-scale farmers get priced out
of the market, while Ghana imports tomatoes and sauces from
Europe, and how fair trade for Ghanaian tomatoes could end
entrenched poverty and create African union: Trading Injustice,
see: *The Ghana Tomato Story – PART 1 of 2*, David Marks (2007;
david7marks), YouTube. youtu.be/4bd4u-MJ1eo. Also see: *Trading Injustice: The Ghana Tomato Story – PART 2*, David Marks
(2007; david7marks), YouTube. youtu.be/MyNi79BELy4.

Chapter 9

1. Learn how Grameen reaches the poorest of the poor with
business support and mobile-phone technology in this video:
https://youtu.be/HBBkoUHsBUg, and read more about
Mary here: https://grameenfoundation.org/mary-lifting-her-
family-and-her-community-out-poverty.

2. Grameen's CKW program creates a network of peer advisors
who use their mobile phones to share farming, crop, and market
information with their neighbors to increase production and
profits. Read more at their Grameen Foundation page: Grameen
Foundation. "Agriculture." Grameen Foundation. https://
grameenfoundation.org/what-we-do/agriculture. You can
also watch: *CKWs Help Poor, Rual, Farmers Fight 'Information
Poverty,'* Sean Krepp, Michael Lin, Willy Okello, Samson Sabiti

Olet, and Benson Taiwo (2012: Grameen Foundation), YouTube. youtu.be/NOv4dqj_eSM.

Chapter 10

1. For an in-depth look into life on Chicago's South Side and the work of The Center, see my four-part series: Skees, Suzanne. "'G Laws Won't Impact Us Here' in the Line of Fire, Say Peace Workers: Part 1 of 4." *Huffington Post.* (2013). huffingtonpost. com/suzanne-skees/gun-laws-wont-impact-us-here_b _3659832.html.

2. Shifleet, Amber. "Is a back of the house job right for you?" Snag. (February 2014). snagajob.com/resources/is-a-back-of-house -job-right-for-you.

3. For more information on the Centre for Justice & Protection, visit their website, which gives an introduction to restorative justice, here: restorativejustice.org/restorative-justice/about -restorative-justice/tutorial-intro-to-restorative-justice/ #sthash.nI7AUBAh.dpbs.

4. Read this article from Precious Blood Ministry of Reconcili- ation to learn more about restorative art: pbmr.org/sermons/ restorative-art.

Chapter 11

1. Read about Phil's work at prideinpersonnel.com/company.htm.

2. Visit the Dance ConneXion website (thedanceconnexion.com).

3. View Tania's dance videos on YouTube: Wong, Tania. "Videos." YouTube. (2018). youtube.com/user/EnamorarseDance/videos.

4. Visit the Aventura website (www.aventuraworldwide.com).

5. See examples of Tania's wedding first dances here: *Dance ConneXion Toronto Wedding First Dance Choreography*, by Tatiana Wong (2015; Tania Wong), YouTube. youtube.com/watch?v=FcoKamcCwZg. For articles in both Chinese and English on Tania's media page, see: "TV & Newspapers." The Dance ConneXion. thedanceconnexion.com/media. Also, visit Tania Wong's profile on the Dance ConneXion website (thedanceconnexion.com/tania-wong). And visit Tania's Facebook profile (facebook.com/TaniaWongDancer).

6. Visit Renaud Ayotte's profile on the Dance ConneXion website (thedanceconnexion.com/renaud-ayotte).

7. *Renaud & Tania 1st place Kings of Bachata Competition 2014 - Choreography Round*, by Renaud Ayotte and Tania Wong (2014; Tania Wong), YouTube. youtu.be/8sI4ATqINXc.

Chapter 12

1. Michele wishes to clarify that any opinions or views that she shares in this book are solely hers and do not necessarily represent the U.S. Department of State.

2. Thanks to Michele's mom, Sharon Peregrin, my friend and connection to Michele.

3. *Anthropology* is the study of people throughout the world, their evolutionary history, how they behave and adapt to different environments, communicate and socialize with one another. For a more detailed definition of anthropology, visit Discover Anthropology's "What is Anthropology?" page here: discoveranthropology.org.uk/about-anthropology/what-is-anthropology.html.

4. *International education* is the study of world cultures to gain understanding of the historical, geographic, economic, political,

cultural, and environmental relationships among world regions
and peoples; examining cultural differences and national or
regional conflicts; and acting to influence public policy and
private behavior for international understanding, tolerance, and
empathy: McJimsey, Marianna, Becky Ross, and Sandra Young.
"Global and International Education in Social Studies." National
Council for the Social Studies, (2016). https://www.socialstudies
.org/positions/global_and_international_education.

5. Kosovo is a disputed territory in Southeastern Europe that
declared its independence from Serbia in 2008. For more details
about Kosovo, visit the Central Intelligence Agency's World
Factbook (cia.gov/library/publications/the-world-factbook/
geos/kv.html).

6. The Islamic Republic of Pakistan is a country in South Asia
created in 1947 as an independent nation for Muslims that shares
borders with India, China, Afghanistan, and Iran. For more
details about Pakistan, visit the Central Intelligence Agency's
World Factbook (cia.gov/library/publications/the-world
-factbook/geos/pk.html).

7. Indonesia, a Southeast Asian nation located north of Australia and made up of thousands of volcanic islands, is home to
hundreds of ethnic groups speaking many different languages.
For more details about Indonesia, visit the Central Intelligence Agency's World Factbook (cia.gov/library/publications/
the-world-factbook/geos/id.html).

8. Learn more about the University of North Carolina at Chapel
Hill's hip-hop exchange program here: http://nextlevel-usa.org/.

9. If you are interested in applying or want to see which artists are
currently stationed across the world, visit americanartsincubator
.org. ZERO1 is an initiative of the U.S. State Department.

10. If you are interested, you can look at the Creative Arts Exchange application form here: eca.state.gov/files/bureau/3_pogi_cae _community_engagement_through_the_arts.pdf.

11. Venezuela is a country on the north coast of South America known for its biodiversity, poverty, and corruption. For more details about Venezuela, visit the Central Intelligence Agency's World Factbook (cia.gov/library/publications/the-world -factbook/geos/ve.html).

12. Cuba is a communist nation in the Caribbean with which, after fifty years of sanctions, the U.S. began in 2015 to rebuild dip- lomatic and economic relations. For more details about Cuba, visit the Central Intelligence Agency's World Factbook (cia.gov/ library/publications/the-world-factbook/geos/cu.html).

13. Michele may be up to six figures by now, based on this tracking of her recent wages as a public servant. You can find more details from the Federal Pay website here: federalpay.org/employees/ department-of-state/peregrin-michele-s.

14. The Arab Spring was a 2010–2011 pro-democracy movement in the Middle East and North Africa in which protestors used demonstrations and social media to reach critical mass. Read more here: Tesch, Noah. "Arab Spring: Pro-Democracy Protests." Encyclopedia Britannica. (2012). britannica.com/event/ Arab-Spring.

Chapter 13

1. See Junior in a video talking about how he became an activ- ist: *Junior Walk, Outreach Coordinator, Coal River Mountain Watch,* Junior Walk (2017; Coal River Mountain Watch), YouTube. youtu.be/DvkdaxNukmI; and about using drones

to monitor environmental-law violations in his community:
Duhaime-Ross, Arielle. "This guy is using his drone to fight a
West Virginia coal mining company's toxic lake." Vice News,
(September 27, 2017). news.vice.com/en_us/article/d3xwpz/
meet-the-activist-who-uses-drones-to-monitor-coal-companies.

2. The head of a holler is the beginning of a valley between two
    mountains. See The Kentucky Network for a PBS series on life
    in Appalachia: *Head of the Holler*, produced by Berea College
    (2010; Berea: Kentucky Educational Television, 2010). ket.org/
    series/KHEHO/all.

3. For images of mountaintop removal, take a look at this Earth
    Justice slideshow: earthjustice.org/slideshow/images-of
    -mountaintop-removal-mining.

4. Ramps are an early-spring, floppy-green vegetable that taste like
    a cross between garlic and onion: Devenyns, Jessi. "Everything
    You Need to Know About the Elusive Ramps." Wide Open Eats.
    (May 4, 2018). wideopeneats.com/everything-you-need-to-know
    -about-ramps.

5. Ramp dinners, a communal feast tradition that dates back to early
    settlers in Appalachia, can be small affairs or turn into festivals
    hosting up to one thousand locals. Ramps can be fried in bacon
    grease, used in soups or sandwiches. Learn more about the tradi-
    tions of ramp dinners in this article by West Virginia Explorer:
    wvexplorer.com/recreation/agritourism/ramp-dinners-festivals.

6. Called "dry-land fish" because of their fishy taste, others find them
    nutty and rich. All about morels: May, Terri. "Molly Mooching!"
    Invironmental, (April 16, 2017). medium.com/invironment/
    molly-mooching-c13f17f3569f.

7. A coal prep plant is where coal is washed, crushed, and stockpiled

for transport to sell. See a coal prep plant in three dimensions in this video: *Coal Processing Plant – 3D Visualization*, Pixel Studios (2011; Pixel Studios), YouTube. youtube.com/watch?v=nsmigELzKiQ.

8. A dam built to hold back solid and liquid waste that results from the washing of coal. See the dam by Junior's elementary school, and learn more from this article by South Wings: southwings.org/our-work/coal-slurry-ash.

9. Coal camps were built across the Appalachian Mountains in the 1930s–'40s and were wholly owned by the coal companies. Read more about southern West Virginia coalfields on the Coal Camp USA website: coalcampusa.com/sowv/index.htm. Also, read Junior's article: Walk, Junior. "Five Things People with Power Don't Want You to Know About West Virginia." *Huffington Post*, (May 14, 2014). huffingtonpost.com/junior-walk/west-virginia_b_5320263.html. To learn more about the traditions of coal, visit the National Coal Heritage Area & Coal Heritage Trail website: coalheritage.wv.gov/visitors/Pages/Coal-Camp-Maps.aspx. And for photographs of past and present coal-camp homes in Raleigh County, WV, where Junior's family lives, visit this page on the Coal Camp USA website: coalcampusa.com/sowv/river/raleigh/raleigh.htm.

10. Cherokees, Daniel Boone, and many others throughout history have dug, used, and sold ginseng. More on the medicinal properties and earning potential of what West Virginians call "sang:" Taylor, David A. "Getting to the Root of Ginseng: questions about the herb's health benefits haven't cooled the red-hot market in wild American ginseng." *Smithsonian*, (July 2002). smithsonianmag.com/science-nature/getting-to-the-root-of-ginseng-65654374.

Chapter 14

1. This article from the Jewish Virtual Library traces the history of the Jewish diaspora since the sixth century BCE: "Ancient Jewish History: The Diaspora." Jewish Virtual Library: A Project of Aice. jewishvirtuallibrary.org/jsource/History/Diaspora.html.

2. See the website of the Yad Veshem Holocaust Memorial Museum in Jerusalem for history and eyewitness accounts: yadvashem.org/yv/en/holocaust/about.html

3. The Middle East conflict between Israelis and Palestinians over a ten-thousand-square-mile area of land that both call their historical and spiritual homeland did not begin in 1948. For a balanced view and succinct analysis of the complicated history by independent academics, read the Middle East Research and Information Project's article "Primer on Palestine, Israel and the Arab-Israeli Conflict." You can find the article here: merip.org/primer-palestine-israel-arab-israeli-conflict-new.

4. adc.org/greg-khalil-bio.

5. *What is Telos?*, (2016; Telos), Vimeo. vimeo.com/148895574. Also, visit the Telos website (telosgroup.org).

6. See more at Third Side (thirdside.org). Also see Professor William Ury's TED Talk: *The Walk From "No" To "Yes,"* by William Ury (2010; TEDxMidwest), TED. ted.com/talks/william_ury?language=en.

7. Our Fringe Diplomat narrator, Mickey Bergman (Chapter 15), was a soldier in the Israeli Defense Force that invaded South Lebanon to protect it, while Greg's family lived and worked in nearby Damascus, Syria. These two *My Job* narrators are now friends and coworkers striving toward Mideast peace.

8. *Focal dystonia* is the cramping of the hand due to overuse that can lead to loss of control. For more information on this, see the

Dystonia Medical Research Foundation's page on focal hand dys-tonia: https://www.dystonia-foundation.org/what-is-dystonia/ forms-of-dystonia/musicians-dystonias/focal-hand-dystonia.

9. This update includes excerpts from Greg's Facebook posts. See him playing the violin again with great joy and skill: *Greg Violin*, by Gregory Khalil (2017; Gregory Khalil), Vimeo. vimeo.com/ 197464871.

Chapter 15

1. For background information on the IDF, visit this Wikipedia page: en.wikipedia.org/wiki/Israel_Defense_Forces. Both the IDF's air force and ground troops have been ranked among the top armed forces in the world and the top for the Middle East region. For more information on this, see: Bender, Dave. "Studies: Israel Air Force World's Best; Army Top in Middle East." The Algemeiner. (2014). algemeiner.com/2014/10/28/studies-israel -air-force-worlds-best-army-top-in-middle-east-video. Also see: "2018 Israel Military Strength: Current military capacities and available firepower for the nation of Israel." Global Firepower: Strength in Numbers. (2018). https://www.globalfirepower.com/ country-military-strength-detail.asp?country_id=Israel.

2. Learn more about the Aspen Institute and see some of their featured experts at: aspeninstitute.org/people?expertise=266 and aspeninstitute.org/policy-work/global-alliances.

3. Mickey has written extensively about his work for several publications. See some of his writing on Huffington Post (huffingtonpost.com/mickey-bergman).

4. The Telos Group (telosgroup.org) aims to achieve "security, dignity, and freedom" by holding a triple-priority, "pro-Israeli,

pro-Palestinian, pro-American" value that to them equals *pro-peace*. Learn more from Telos co-founder Greg, in Chapter 14.

5. Al Jazeera. "Al Jazeera journalists freed from Egypt prison: Mohamed Fahmy and Baher Mohamed have been released from prison following Eid al-Adha pardon." *Al Jazeera*. (September 23, 2015). aljazeera.com/news/2015/09/al-jazeera-journalists -pardoned-egypt-150923112113189.html.

6. Rich, Tracey R. "The Land of Israel." Judaism 101. jewfaq.org/ israel.htm.

7. The New York Times. "Israel pauses to give diplomacy a chance— Africa & Middle East - International Herald Tribune." *The New York Times*. (August 10, 2006). nytimes.com/2006/08/10/ world/africa/10iht-web.0810lebanon.2435407.html.

8. The Elders (theelders.org) are a group of global leaders working for peace and human rights.

9. Read more at the Aspen Institute blog: Verstandig, Toni. "Partnerships for Peace." The Aspen Institute. (August 19, 2013). https://www.aspeninstitute.org/blog-posts/partnerships-peace/.

10. Check out Sadara Ventures at sadaravc.com.

INDEX

traveling for dance, 226–27
typical workday, 231
dancer
 choosing dance as career, 230
 dancing from the heart, 227–28
 dealing with drama and harassment,
  232–34
 healing potential of tango, 234
 personal dreams, 234–35
 psychology of dance, 235–36
 teaching dance, 228–30
 traveling for dance, 226–27
 typical workday, 231
Deatherage, Todd, 290, 303
Depo-Provera, 61
depression, 34
diplomacy. *See also* arts cultural-exchange
  officer, State Department;
  fringe diplomat; Mideast peace
  diplomat
 fringe, 319–20, 345
 people-to-people, 240, 247
divorce, 185
domestic violence
 in Guatemala, 56, 59–60
 in Honduras, 31–32
 in Rwanda, 88–89
drama among dance students, dealing
  with, 232–34
DuBois, Phil, 228, 229, 230
 competition in dance industry, 225
 friendship with Tania Wong, 224
 harassment, dealing with, 232–33
 helping others through dance,
  235–36
 work schedule, 231
Dulwich College Prep School, England, 9

E

education
 of Kelly Kang, 105, 107
 of Kevin Zazo, 35, 36–38, 39
 of Michael Bergman, 326–27
 of Michele Peregrin, 245–46
 of Mike Kenward, 8–9
 of Misozi Mkandawire, 121
 of Nadine Niyitegeka, 87–91, 94–95
 of Sandra López, 57–58

of Sena Ahiabor, 162
educational model, at Akilah Institute for
  Women, Rwanda, 91–92
Ehrman, Sara, 328
The Elders, 330, 376n8
Elvel School, Honduras, 36–37
empowerment of women, 97–98, 137
engagement, 340–41
English teacher
 class schedules, 108–9
 general discussion, 103–4
 in Honduras, 38–39, 41
 interactive learning environment, 106
 personal interest in students, 111–12
 student behavior, 109–11
 wages for, 116
environmental activism
 arrest for protesting, 280–81
 coal camps, 273–74
 Coal River Mountain Watch,
  275–77, 278–81
 coal slurry dams, 270–72
 coal slurry in water, 274
 deaths from black lung, 283–84
 fighting oppression, 285
 harassment, dealing with, 277
 land ownership in West Virginia, 267
 lobbying work, 279
 mountaintop removal, 268
 typical workday, 279
 underground coal mining, 268
 wages, 279–80
exercise, stress management through,
  23–24

F

family
 of Alberto Alaniz, 214–15, 218
 of Junior Walker, 281–83
 of Kelly Kang, 104–5, 113–14
 of Kevin Zazo, 31–32
 of Mary Gibutaye, 186
 of Michael Bergman, 326–27,
  342–43
 of Michele Peregrin, 259–60
 of Mike Kenward, 5–8, 26–27
 of Misozi Mkandawire, 123–24
 of Sandra López, 58, 59, 67–68

ABOUT THE AUTHOR

Suzanne Skees edits the *My Job* book series—collections of first-person narratives by artists, bankers, farmers, healthcare workers, teachers, and more, across the United States and around the world. All author proceeds from the series fund job-creation programs to end poverty. She also serves as founder and board chair of the Skees Family Foundation, which supports innovative self-help programs in the U.S. and developing countries in education and job creation. Skees studied English literature (Boston College) and world religions (Harvard Divinity School) and worked previously as a journalist and book editor. She hopes to continue interviewing fascinating people to create as many volumes of *My Job* as there are job stories to be shared. She lives at the Pacific Ocean's edge, south of San Francisco, California.